ASSESSMENT IN COUNSELING: A GUIDE TO THE USE OF PSYCHOLOGICAL ASSESSMENT PROCEDURES

Albert B. Hood, EdD
and
Richard W. Johnson, PhD

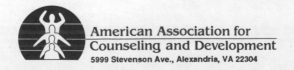
American Association for
Counseling and Development
5999 Stevenson Ave., Alexandria, VA 22304

American Association for Counseling and Development
5999 Stevenson Avenue
Alexandria, VA 22304

Cover design by Sarah Jane Valdez

Library of Congress Cataloging-in-Publication Data

Hood, Albert B. (Albert Bullard), 1929–
    Assessment in counseling : a guide to the use of psychological assessment
procedures / Albert B. Hood and Richard W. Johnson.
      p.   cm.
    Includes bibliographical references.
    ISBN 1-55620-074-9
    1. Psychological tests. 2. Counseling. I. Johnson, Richard Wilbur,
    1934–   . II. Title.
    [DNLM: 1. Counseling. 2. Psychological Tests. WM 145 H776a]
    BF176.H66   1991
    153.9'3—dc20
    DNLM/DLC
    for Library of Congress   90-769
                                                                     CIP

Printed in the United States of America

Contents

SECTION II: COGNITIVE ASSESSMENT

SECTION III: CAREER AND LIFE PLANNING ASSESSMENT

SECTION IV: PERSONALITY ASSESSMENT

SECTION V: PROFESSIONAL PRACTICES AND CONSIDERATIONS

SECTION VI: APPENDICES

Foreword

Psychological tests first became available in this country during the early part of the century, the 1910s and 1920s. Lewis Terman's Stanford Binet became public in 1916, a carefully standardized and individually administered intelligence test that initiated the famous $MA/CA = IQ$. This remained a basic test for the next 7 decades and beyond. In 1921 Arthur Otis, a former student of Terman's, published the first Group Intelligence Test, a paper-and-pencil test utilizing the extensive research performed on the Army Alpha and the Army Beta tests of World War I. E. K. Strong, Jr., opened another area when the Vocational Interest Blank was published in 1927. This test, with major revisions and additions, has become one of the most widely used tests of the century. (I found Table 1–1 fascinating.) Robert Woodworth's Rating Scale appeared early in the 1920s. Around 1930 *personality tests* began to make their appearance, with pioneering productions by Robert Bernreuter and Hugh Bell. All but one of these productions originated at Stanford University. They became part of my life because I did my graduate work at Stanford at about that time (1928–32) with Terman and Strong as my MA and PhD advisors. I did my bit in these early ventures by bringing out the first edition of the Study Habits Inventory in 1935.

Let me add to the personal note of these years by recalling that during my first year at Stanford I was given an appointment as what we would now call a student personnel assistant, Stanford's first. This involved counseling in the registrar's office and giving admissions tests for the university. Stanford had pioneered in those early days in giving what we would now call scholastic aptitude tests as part of the admissions process. I made trips each spring throughout the state giving the Thorndike Intelligence Test to prospective students at Stanford testing centers. Kathleen, my wife, accompanied me and scored the tests as we moved along—at 25¢ an hour!

After 8 years at Stanford, I accepted an appointment at the University of Minnesota (1936–64) and again moved into another center of intense test activity. Over these past 70 years I have seen an accelerating development of psychological tests and other types of assessment, tests for many purposes. During World War II, tests were used in *selecting* millions of war workers, in *assigning* other millions in the Armed Forces, and in *diagnosing* the mental and social health problems of men and women under stress. Today also tests are used to make decisions *for* or *against* a client. This is not a counselor's use of tests; a counselor uses tests or other assessment measures to help clients understand themselves. The authors of this book state this very clearly in words that should appear in large black type: *"In the counseling setting . . . psychological tests are used to help the clients understand themselves . . . .* [They are] *used primarily to assist individuals in developing their potentialities to the fullest and to their own satisfaction"* (italics mine) from "Final Statement," chapter 18, p. 237.

This is a significant book in my experience, a book written by two professionals whose scholarship, depth of experience with assessment in counseling, and sheer desire to be helpful to the reader are apparent on every page. It is a pragmatic book, focusing on what has been useful to others and using a simple problem-solving model. The authors clearly indicate how tests are used differently in different counseling settings: schools, university counseling centers, hospitals and mental health centers, banks, business, government, and private practice.

The first four chapters introduce the reader to basic concepts in psychological assessment and to the statistical understandings necessary in the selection and interpretation of tests, not in their construction. The last four chapters deal with special populations, communications, and ethics in the use of tests.

Chapters 5–15 treat with care and skill the use of 109 tests, inventories, and other assessment measures in each of 11 categories. Seven tables, 13 figures, three appendices, and reference citations provide a great deal of information in compact bundles. The treatment of the literature is admirable—no long quotations in varying styles of writing, but interpretations and applications all in the same simple, consistent wording of the two authors.

By this time the reader may begin to suspect that I like this book. I do indeed! I commend it to counselors and psychologists without reservation. I wish that it would have been available to me during my lifetime of service. I would have been a better counselor.

—*C. Gilbert Wrenn*

Preface

The purpose of this book is to provide information about the various psychological assessment procedures that are specifically relevant for practicing counselors and human development professionals. The book deals with the use of such tests in the counseling process and includes illustrative case studies. It emphasizes the selection, interpretation, and communication of psychological test results. It also emphasizes the importance of integrating test results with other information about the client.

The book is not designed to be a textbook or desk manual on the various tests themselves. There are a number of excellent books that describe psychological tests and other assessment procedures (e.g., Anastasi, 1988; Walsh & Betz, 1990). It is expected that counselors will make use of such texts, along with other sources (such as the *Mental Measurements Yearbooks* and Kapes & Mastie, 1988) and the test manuals themselves, which deal with the construction, reliability, and validity of the various assessment instruments.

In a book such as this, many arbitrary decisions must be made regarding which instruments to include and which to leave out. From among the many hundreds of psychological tests that exist, we have selected those most often used by counselors and human development professionals in their daily practice. No attempt has been made to include instruments not regularly used by counselors.

Although a few basic statistical concepts are provided in chapter 3, only those specifically related to test interpretation are discussed. The statistics techniques used in test construction and the various statistical formulas used in computing test-related statistics are not included. It is expected that any counselor or human development professional using psychological tests will have had a basic course in relevant statistical procedures. The material in chapter 3 may provide a brief refresher for a few of the commonly used descriptive statistical concepts but is not intended as a substitute for at least a basic knowledge of psychological statistics.

The volume has been organized into five sections. Section 1 presents basic concepts of psychological assessment. It includes an introduction to the nature and use of psychological assessment procedures in counseling, briefly describes certain important measurement concepts, and discusses initial assessment procedures. The second section covers cognitive assessment and the various tests that assess intelligence, academic aptitude, and academic achievement. The third section deals with procedures used by counselors to assist clients in making decisions regarding their careers and life plans. In section 4, personality assessment is considered, including several personality inventories and other personality measures. It also includes instruments used for assessment of interpersonal relationships, of various aspects of mental health, and of certain mental disorders. The final section deals with professional practices and considerations. It includes assessment of ethnic and special populations; guidelines for the communication of test results, both in interviews and case reports; and a discussion of the significant ethical and social issues that arise when psychological assessment procedures are used in counseling.

Excerpts from documents outlining ethical and test standards particularly appropriate to counselors and human development professionals in their use of assessment procedures are reproduced in the Appendix. The final section of the Appendix lists the names and addresses of publishers of tests commonly used by counselors, along with the instruments that may be ordered from those publishers.

In graduate courses that cover the use of tests and other appraisal procedures in counseling, information about the various instruments is typically covered, but actual use in the counseling process and the interpretation of results in the counseling interview must be learned by the beginning counselor primarily through trial and error. It is the purpose of this volume to remedy this situation by providing information to assist the counselor in choosing, administering, and interpreting psychological test results.

Acknowledgments

Albert B. Hood wishes to acknowledge the contributions of many colleagues at various institutions who, at formal presentations as well as informal conversations at lunch and at social gatherings, have helped him stay abreast over the years of developments in the psychological testing field. He also expresses his thanks to Ginny Travis and Reta Litton for the word processing of numerous manuscript drafts as rough notes were transformed into finished chapters.

Richard W. Johnson would like to acknowledge the influence of his mentors at the University of Minnesota who first taught him to appreciate the importance of assessment in counseling. He is thankful to the following people for their assistance and support in the preparation of this book: the staff members and trainees at the University Counseling Service, University of Wisconsin-Madison; Kent Burnett, director of the Assessment Laboratory for the Department of Counseling Psychology and Counselor Education at the University of Wisconsin-Madison; Bernard Cesnik of the Dane County Mental Health Center in Madison; and Earl Nolting and Dennis Keierleber of the Department of Counseling for Continuing Education and Extension at the University of Minnesota.

Both authors are grateful to their wives—Jean and Adelle—for their patience with the reduced social activities and deferred home maintenance schedules during the time that this volume was being written.

—*Albert B. Hood*
Iowa City, Iowa

—*Richard W. Johnson*
Madison, Wisconsin

January 1991

About the Authors

Albert B. Hood is professor of education and chair of the Division of Counselor Education at The University of Iowa. He received his BA degree (1951) from the University of New Hampshire in psychology and his EdD degree (1957) from Cornell University in counseling and student personnel administration.

He has been the assistant director of the Student Counseling Service at Princeton University and a counseling psychologist in the Student Counseling Bureau at the University of Minnesota. In addition to using psychological tests regularly in his counseling practice, he worked with several colleagues at the Educational Testing Service in Princeton and with several test authors as he conducted research studies on academic aptitude (Ralph Berdie, MSAT, MCI), interest inventories (David Campbell, SVIB), and personality measures (Starke Hathaway, MMPI). Now at The University of Iowa, he has coauthored several student development inventories and has consulted with staff members of the American College Testing Program. He held a research fellowship in Kyoto, Japan, and has been a visiting faculty member at the University of Utah and at San Francisco State University.

Author of more than 90 books, monographs, and professional articles, Dr. Hood received the Contribution to Knowledge Award of the American College Personnel Association (ACPA) in 1985. He was the editor of ACPA's *Journal of College Student Personnel* from 1970 to 1976 and is a fellow in the American Psychological Association's Division 17 (Counseling). Hood's scholarly work has dealt primarily with research on the psychological, educational, and vocational development of college students, and a large proportion of the over 50 PhD dissertations he has directed have dealt with psychological assessment.

Richard W. Johnson is associate director of the University Counseling Service and adjunct professor of counseling psychology and counselor education at the University of Wisconsin-Madison. He obtained his PhD degree in counseling psychology at the University of Minnesota in 1961, after graduating with honors in psychology from Princeton University in 1956. Prior to joining the Counseling Service at the University of Wisconsin-

Madison in 1968, he taught and counseled at the University of Massachusetts-Amherst and the University of North Dakota.

Dr. Johnson has served on the board of editors for three journals of the American Association for Counseling and Development: the *Journal of College Student Development*, *Measurement and Evaluation in Counseling and Development*, and *The Career Development Quarterly*. He has also been a frequent contributor to the *Journal of Counseling Psychology*, *Journal of Vocational Behavior*, *Journal of Applied Psychology*, and the *Mental Measurements Yearbooks*. His professional interests include psychological assessment, career development, cognitive-behavioral counseling, and individual differences.

Section I

Basic Concepts of Psychological Assessment

CHAPTER 1

Use of Assessment Procedures in Counseling

Assessment has always played an important part in counseling and developmental guidance. During the early days, counseling and testing were virtually synonymous. Many of the counseling centers established during the 1930s and 1940s were called Counseling and Testing Centers. At that time, counseling typically involved helping students to make educational or vocational plans on the basis of test results.

In recent years, the role of counseling has broadened to include many issues beyond academic and career planning. Counselors and human development professionals help clients resolve a variety of problems related to such issues as self-esteem, shyness, personal growth, family and couple relationships, sexual identity, sexual abuse, cross-cultural communication, substance abuse, eating disorders, depression, anxiety, and suicidal ideation. Many counselors now work in community mental health settings, private practices, hospitals, and businesses, as well as in educational institutions. During the same period, the nature of psychological assessment has expanded to assist counselors and clients in all of these areas.

Assessment aids in counseling by providing information for both counselors and clients. Counselors and human development professionals need information gained in assessment to understand and to respond to their clients' concerns. They also rely on assessment for program planning and evaluation. Clients use information obtained by assessment to understand themselves better and to make plans for the future. The assessment process can be therapeutic in itself by helping clients to clarify goals and to gain a sense of perspective (Paritzky & Magoon, 1982; Smith, 1976).

For most purposes, counseling can be conceptualized in terms of problem solving (Maloney & Ward, 1976; Walsh & Betz, 1990). This chapter begins with a discussion of the purpose of psychological assessment within the framework of a problem-solving model. The definition of psychological assessment is then considered, followed by a discussion of counselor and client attitudes toward psychological assessment. Finally, results of surveys of psychological test usage by counselors are presented.

PURPOSE OF PSYCHOLOGICAL ASSESSMENT

The problem-solving model provides a convenient means for summarizing the purposes of psychological assessment procedures in counseling. These purposes can be described by means of the five basic steps in the problem-solving model presented by D'Zurilla and Goldfried (1971). Each step in the problem-solving model entails the need for information that can be gained through psychological assessment.

Problem Orientation

The first step requires that the client recognize and accept the problem. If the client denies the problem, it cannot be dealt with in an adequate manner. Almost any assessment procedure can be used to increase sensitivity to potential problems. Instruments that promote self-awareness and self-exploration can stimulate clients to cope with developmental issues before they become actual problems.

Surveys of groups or classes can help counselors to identify common problems or concerns that can be taken into account in planning programs for clients. A number of needs assessment instruments (e.g., alcohol screening inventories and sexual behavior questionnaires) have been developed for this purpose.

Both client and counselor need to recognize the problem. As soon as a problematic situation is recognized, they can begin to approach it in a systematic fashion as indicated by the problem-solving model. The problem-solving model helps to "normalize" a client's concerns. It implies an acceptance of problems as a normal part of life. The counselor provides support and perspective for the client as the client begins to address the problem. Recognition of the problem, together with a means of addressing it, helps the counselor to establish rapport with the client.

Problem Identification

In this step, the counselor and the client attempt to identify the problem in as much detail as possible. Assessment procedures can help clarify the nature of the client's problem. For example, problem or symptom checklists can be used to assess the type and the extent of a client's concerns. Personal diaries or logs can also be used to identify situations in which the problem occurs. Personality inventories can help counselors and clients to understand personality dynamics underlying problematic situations. Information gained during the course of identifying client problems can be used to specify counseling goals.

Problem identification improves communication with clients. Clients are more likely to continue in counseling if the counselor and client agree on the nature of the problem (Epperson, Bushway, & Warman, 1983; Pekarik, 1988). Identification of the problem also aids in communication with others, such as referral sources.

Generation of Alternatives

In the third step, the counselor and client generate alternatives to address the problem. Assessment procedures enable counselors and clients to identify alternative solutions for client problems. For example, an interest inventory can suggest alternative career choices for clients. An assessment interview can be used to determine what techniques have worked for the client in the past when faced with a similar problem. Checklists, such as a study skills inventory, or free association tests, such as an incomplete sentences blank, yield data that can be used to generate alternatives.

Test results can help clients to view problems from different angles. For example, the use of instruments that measure personality styles provides clients with alternative ways of looking at their behavior or the behavior of others. Assessment exercises can identify positive self-statements of clients, which can also open up alternatives for clients (Parks & Hollon, 1988). Counselors use assessment procedures to assist clients in discovering strengths upon which they can build to overcome difficulties or enhance development (Duckworth, 1990).

Decision Making

In deciding on a solution to a problem, clients need to anticipate the consequences of the various alternatives. According to classical decision theory, choice is a function of the probability of success and the desirability of the outcome (Horan, 1979). This equation underlines the importance of assessing both the likelihood of the success of various alternatives and the attractiveness of those alternatives for the client. Clients will usually want to consider those alternatives that maximize the likelihood of a favorable outcome.

Counselors use assessment materials to help clients weigh the attractiveness of each alternative and the likelihood of achieving each alternative. For example, values clarification exercises can assist clients in evaluating the attractiveness of various alternatives. Experience tables that show the success rate for people with different types of test scores or characteristics can help clients to estimate their chances of success in different courses of action (Goldman, 1971). Balance sheets or decision-making grids enable clients to compare the desirability and feasibility of various alternatives (Cochran, 1983).

Although assessment data help clients to make an informed decision, clients should not expect to obtain certainty or to avoid subjectivity in their choices (Gelatt, 1989). Knowledge is limited and the future is uncertain. For these reasons, clients should be encouraged to be flexible and imaginative in their decision making. Counselors should help clients to expand their sources of information and the manner in which the information is processed.

People vary in their decision-making styles (Harren, 1979; Heppner & Krauskopf, 1987). Rational types emphasize logic in systematically collecting and weighing data to arrive at a decision. Intuitive types place greater importance on feelings in deciding among alternatives; they may collect data to confirm a choice they have already made. Both approaches possess merit. To ensure a broad perspective, clients should be taught to use both decision-making styles in obtaining data and resolving problems.

Verification

Counselors need to evaluate the effectiveness of their counseling. They need to verify that the client's problem has been resolved or reduced. The counselor should discuss with the client how the client will know when the problem has been solved. This step requires that goals be clearly specified, that they be translated into specific behavioral objectives, and that the possibility for progress in accomplishing these goals be realistically viewed. Assessment procedures for this purpose may include goal attainment scaling (Kiresuk & Sherman, 1968; Paritzky & Magoon, 1982), self-monitoring techniques, and the readministration of tests that the client completed earlier in counseling.

Besides serving as a guide for the counseling process, verification efforts also provide a means of accountability for the counseling agency. Positive feedback from clients can be used to gain support for the agency. Negative feedback can be used to help revise programs to make them more attractive to clients.

DEFINITION OF PSYCHOLOGICAL ASSESSMENT

According to *Standards for Educational and Psychological Tests*, an authoritative source for all test users (Wagner, 1987), the term *assessment procedure* refers to "any method used to measure characteristics of people, programs, or objects" (American Educational Research Association, American Psychological Association, & National Council on Measurement in Education, 1985, p. 89). This is a broad definition that can be analyzed in terms of three parts as indicated below.

For the sake of simplicity, the terms *assessment* and *testing* are often used interchangeably in this book. Strictly speaking, a test refers to a task upon which people are asked to try their best, such as an aptitude or achievement test (AERA, APA, & NCME, 1985). Tests measure *maximum* performance, in contrast with questionnaires and inventories, which evaluate *typical* performance (Cronbach, 1984). Questionnaires and inventories, such as personality and interest inventories, elicit self-reports of opinions, preferences, and typical reactions to everyday situations.

Standardized Versus Nonstandardized Assessment

In the first part of the definition for an assessment procedure, "any method" includes both standardized and nonstandardized assessment procedures. Standardized procedures must meet certain criteria of test construction, administration, and interpretation (Anastasi, 1988). Many assessment procedures used in counseling fail to meet these criteria. Nonstandardized assessment procedures include rating scales, projective techniques, behavioral observations, and biographical measures. Because counselors frequently rely upon such nonstandardized procedures, they need to be familiar with their use.

Nonstandardized techniques produce results that are less dependable (that is, less reliable and valid) than do standardized techniques; however, they allow counselors to consider aspects of behavior or the environment not covered by traditional psychological tests. Counselors must be concerned not only about the *dependability* of test results, but also the *exhaustiveness* of the results (Cronbach & Gleser, 1965). Tests that provide highly dependable information often describe only a small part of the information that a counselor needs. Assessment procedures such as interviews, projective techniques, or essays, which provide less dependable information, can nonetheless aid counselors in obtaining information on topics that would be missed by formal testing procedures. Exhaustive procedures should be used when counselors need to obtain a large amount of information pertaining to a variety of decisions (e.g., which problems to address or which treatments to consider). Information obtained in this manner can be verified in subsequent assessment with more dependable measures.

Nomothetic Versus Idiographic Assessment

The phrase "any method" in the definition of a psychological assessment procedure also encompasses both nomothetic and idiographic assessment techniques (Allport, 1937). *Nomos* is the Greek word for "law"; the Greek term *idios* means "personal." In nomothetic assessment, emphasis in placed on those variables that show lawful or meaningful distinctions among people. The group provides a frame of reference for determining which variables to assess and how to interpret the results. In idiographic assessment, on the other hand, emphasis is placed on those variables that can be most helpful in describing the individual. The individual serves as the reference point both to identify relevant variables and to interpret data.

Most psychological tests, such as interest and personality inventories, use the nomothetic approach. These tests use the same scales to describe all clients. Scores are interpreted in regard to a set of norms. In contrast, many of the informal assessment procedures, such as the interview, case study, or card sorts, employ an idiographic approach. A different set of variables is used to describe each client depending on the client. Nomothetic techniques can be more readily interpreted, but they may not be as relevant or as penetrating as idiographic methods, which have been designed to measure variations in individuality (Neimeyer, 1989).

Quantitative Versus Qualitative Assessment

The second part of the definition of a psychological assessment procedure, "to measure characteristics," pertains to both quantitative and qualitative assessment. It includes both refined scaling procedures (e.g., scores on individual intelligence tests) and simple classifications (e.g., "outgoing" versus "reserved" personality type).

Quantitative procedures, which include most psychological tests, yield a specific score on a continuous scale. Qualitative procedures, such as an interview or autobiography, produce a verbal description of a person's behavior or of a situation that can be placed into one of several categories. Although more research has been conducted on techniques that produce some type of continuous score, procedures that employ descriptive categories are often used in counseling. Such categories (e.g., developmental stages or personality types) can provide a means for conceptualizing a case or considering treatment strategies.

By their very nature, quantitative assessment methods have been more thoroughly studied in terms of reliability and validity. Qualitative assessment methods, on the other hand, possess a number of advantages. Compared with quantitative methods, they provide a more holistic and integrated view of clients, they encourage greater activity on the part of clients, they more often form part of the treatment in addition to assessment, and they can more easily be adapted for clients from different types of backgrounds (Goldman, 1990).

Individual Versus Environmental Assessment

The last part of the definition of psychological assessment indicates that psychological assessment refers to *people, programs, and objects.* Counselors have usually devoted more attention to assessment of people, but assessment of the environment (that is, programs and objects) is also necessary. In recent years, counselors have placed greater attention on the influence of the environment in determining behavior than in previous years (Walsh & Betz, 1990). The client's behavior depends both on individual and situational characteristics (Barrios, 1988). Counseling can be most effective when psychological assessment includes both the individual and the environment.

Counselors need to be familiar with all of the different aspects of psychological assessment included in its definition. All of these aspects are reviewed in this book.

ATTITUDES TOWARD PSYCHOLOGICAL TESTS

Psychological testing, which was very popular during and after both World War I and II, lost some of its appeal during the time of social upheaval in the 1960s and 1970s (Haney, 1981). People became concerned about the lack of predictive validity of tests, the use of test scores to label or judge others, and test bias in regard to minority groups. In an influential article, Goldman (1972) lamented the shortcomings of standardized tests, particularly ability tests, and the counselor's lack of preparation and skill in the use of such tests.

Most of the criticisms of tests have their basis in unrealistic expectations for tests or in their misuse. Tests do not provide a magic answer; instead, they should be looked upon as one additional source of information that may be helpful in problem solving. Tests can be especially helpful in counseling if they are designed to stimulate self-exploration and self-development, if they are accompanied by extensive interpretive materials, and if counselors are well schooled in their use (Prediger, 1972).

To offset criticisms of tests, counselors need to become aware of both the strengths and limitations of the various tests used in counseling. They need to learn effective and appropriate procedures for selecting, administering, and interpreting tests in counseling. They need to be able to integrate the use of psychological assessment procedures with other aspects of counseling to help clients with self-understanding and self-determination. Principles and procedures to aid counselors in these endeavors are presented throughout this book.

SURVEYS OF TEST USAGE

Despite adverse criticism, psychological tests continue to play an important part in counseling. Recent surveys of test usage in different counseling settings are described below. Although preferences for particular tests have changed somewhat over the years, counselors continue to make extensive use of tests for a variety of purposes.

Counseling Agencies

Zytowski and Warman (1982) studied changes in the usage of psychological tests by counseling agencies over a 25-year period. They asked counseling agencies approved by the International Association of Counseling Services to indicate which tests they used and how frequently they used them. Of the 239 agencies asked to respond, 198 provided usable returns. Respondents included 99 college and university counseling centers, 15 community college counseling services, and 84 private counseling agencies.

The tests used most frequently at the time of their study are shown in Table 1–1. The tests are ranked in terms of their weighted sum, which reflects the frequency with which the tests were used across all agencies. The Strong-Campbell Interest Inventory (now referred to as the Strong Interest Inventory) was used three times as much as the next most popular measure. Some tests were used frequently, but by a few agencies (e.g., American College Testing Assessment). Others were used infrequently, but by a large number of agencies (e.g., Allport-Vernon-Lindzey Study of Values). Zytowski and Warman noted that counseling agencies use tests of typical behavior (interest and personality inventories) more frequently at the present time than they did formerly. They also use tests of maximum performance (intelligence and achievement tests) much less frequently now than they did 25 years ago.

Secondary Schools

In contrast with the adult counseling services studied by Zytowski and Warman (1982), Engen, Lamb, and Prediger (1982) found that secondary schools were more likely to use achievement or aptitude tests than interest

TABLE 1–1
Usage of Psychological Tests in Counseling Agencies

Rank of Psychological Test	Weighted Sum	Percent of Agencies That Use Test
1 Strong-Campbell Interest Inventory	3328	92%
2 Kuder Occupational Interest Survey	1213	68
3 Edwards Personal Preference Schedule	963	80
4 Nelson-Denny Reading Test	909	50
5 16 Personality Factor Questionnaire	896	68
6 Self-Directed Search	895	65
7 Wechsler Adult Intelligence Scale	716	81
8 American College Testing Assessment	681	24
9 Survey of Study Habits and Attitudes	656	55
10 Minnesota Multiphasic Personality Inventory	654	72
11 College Board Scholastic Aptitude Test	653	30
12 Miller Analogies Test	548	33
13 Myers-Briggs Type Indicator	547	47
14 Kuder Preference Record (Forms C & E)	539	51
15 Career Assessment Inventory	483	44
16 Wechsler Intelligence Scale for Children	456	53
17 Differential Aptitude Test	452	65
18 Bender Gestalt	427	67
19 Allport-Vernon Study of Values	372	70
20 Draw-a-Person	326	58

Note. From "The Changing Use of Tests in Counseling," by D. Zytowski and R. E. Warman, 1982, *Measurement and Evaluation in Guidance, 15*, p. 149. Copyright 1982 by the American Association for Counseling and Development. Adapted by permission.

or personality inventories. They obtained survey responses on test usage from 547 schools (grades 7 through 12) from a target sample of 882 schools.

Over 90% of the schools used career guidance tests, primarily the Armed Services Vocational Aptitude Battery (ASVAB). ASVAB was used twice as often as the next most popular test. The next most frequently used career guidance tests were also aptitude measures: the Differential Aptitude Tests and General Aptitude Test Battery. Following the aptitude measures, various forms of the Kuder and Strong interest inventories were used most frequently. Personality inventories were rarely used by any of the schools. The respondents indicated that they would use more tests if they could afford to do so, but they were constrained by their budgets. The ASVAB enjoys wide usage at least in part because it is administered and interpreted by the Armed Services without cost to the school system.

Counseling Psychologists

Two thirds of a random sample of counseling psychologists reported that they were involved in objective testing (Watkins, Campbell, & McGregor,

1988). Usage of tests varied considerably depending upon the setting in which the counseling took place. Interest inventories (e.g., Strong Interest Inventory) and objective personality inventories (e.g., Edwards Personal Preference Schedule) were more likely to be used in university counseling centers, whereas neuropsychological tests (e.g., Bender Visual Motor Gestalt Test) and intelligence or ability tests (e.g., Wechsler Intelligence Scale for Children-Revised and Wechsler Memory Scale) were more likely to be used in mental health clinics, private practices, or hospitals. The Minnesota Multiphasic Personality Inventory, Wechsler Adult Intelligence Scale-Revised, and sentence completion blanks were widely used across all settings.

Most of the tests identified by means of the test usage surveys will be discussed in this book. Counselors need to become familiar with the most popular tests so that they can use them effectively in their own practices and so that they can interpret scores from these tests for clients referred to them by other counselors.

SUMMARY

1. Psychological assessment is an integral part of counseling. Assessment provides information that can be used in each step of the problem-solving model. The assessment process can be therapeutic in and of itself.

2. Assessment serves the following functions: (a) to stimulate counselors and clients to consider various issues, (b) to clarify the nature of the problem or issue, (c) to suggest alternative solutions for problems, (d) to provide a method of comparing various alternatives so that a decision can be made or confirmed, and (e) to enable counselors and clients to evaluate the effectiveness of a particular solution.

3. Psychological assessment refers to all methods used to measure the characteristics of people, programs, or objects. This is a broad definition that encompasses measures that are nonstandardized, idiographic, and qualitative, as well as those that are standardized, nomothetic, and quantitative. It pertains to environmental as well as individual assessment.

4. Negative attitudes toward psychological tests can be traced to unrealistic expectations regarding tests and to the misuse of tests. Psychological assessment needs to be seen in perspective, and counselors must be trained in the proper use of tests.

5. Surveys of test usage show that counselors use a wide variety of assessment procedures. Public school counselors more often use aptitude and achievement tests (measures of maximal performance), whereas college and university counselors more often employ personality and interest inventories (measures of typical performance).

CHAPTER 2

Nature of Psychological Assessment in Counseling

Counselors and human development professionals need to be informed about the basic characteristics of psychological assessment procedures. They must be able to compare and evaluate different assessment procedures. Information presented in this chapter should aid counselors in these endeavors.

In this chapter, we review the different criteria that have been used to distinguish among psychological assessment procedures. We then refer to these criteria in describing six common assessment procedures. These procedures include standardized tests, rating scales, projective techniques, behavioral observations, biographical measures, and physiological measures. We next identify standards that have been established for evaluating tests and test usage. The chapter concludes with a list of sources of information about assessment procedures.

DISTINCTIONS AMONG PSYCHOLOGICAL ASSESSMENT PROCEDURES

Psychological assessment procedures differ from each other in a variety of ways. As indicated below, these differences can be categorized by six basic questions regarding the nature of the assessment procedure itself.

Who Is Making the Assessment?

Is the person making a self-assessment or is another person making the assessment? Block (1961) differentiated between "S-data" based on self-reports and "O-data" based on the reports of others. Both types of data are needed to obtain a full appraisal of the individual. O-data can be used to validate self-reports; S-data can provide valuable insights regarding self-perception not available in the reports of others.

What Is Being Assessed?

"What" here refers to the subject of the assessment procedure. Is the individual or the environment the subject of the assessment? As noted in chapter 1, counselors have usually been interested in individual assessment; however, instruments that evaluate the environment, (e.g., classroom atmosphere or residence hall settings) can also provide important information in understanding or treating a problem.

If the individual is being appraised, does the content of the assessment deal primarily with *affective* (feeling), *cognitive* (thinking), or *behavioral* (doing) aspects of the individual? These three aspects of the individual may be further subdivided as discussed below.

Affective characteristics may be subdivided into *temperamental* and *motivational* factors (Guilford, 1959). Temperamental factors include the characteristics assessed by most personality inventories, for example, self-sufficiency, stability, and impulsiveness. Motivational factors, on the other hand, refer to interests or values. According to Guilford, temperament governs the *manner* in which an individual performs, whereas motivation determines *what activity* the individual will choose to pursue.

Cognitive variables may be based on learning that takes place in a specific course, (*course-related*), or learning that is relatively independent of specific coursework (*non-course-related*) (Anastasi, 1988). This distinction describes a basic difference between achievement and aptitude tests. Achievement tests evaluate past or present performance; aptitude tests predict future performance. Achievement tests measure learning that has taken place in a particular course or series of courses. Aptitude tests assess capacity to learn based on items that are relatively independent of the classroom or of any type of formal educational experience.

Behavioral measures include responses that are either *voluntary* or *involuntary* in nature. Voluntary responses may be assessed either by self-monitoring or by other-monitoring techniques. A systematic record is kept of measurable items such as calories consumed or hours spent in watching television. In the case of involuntary responses (e.g., blood pressure or heart rate), various types of physiological measures are used to assess individual reactivity. Biofeedback devices, often used to teach relaxation methods, are a good example of the latter type of assessment measure.

Where Is the Assessment Taking Place?

The location in which the assessment takes place is important in the sense that it helps to differentiate between test results obtained in *laboratory* settings from those obtained in *natural* settings. Many psychological tests must be administered under standardized conditions so that the test results can be interpreted properly. For these tests, a testing room or laboratory is usually used. If the circumstances of test administration differ from person to person, differences in the testing conditions can influence test results. Some measures such as employee ratings are obtained in natural settings under conditions that may vary considerably for different individuals. Variations in job circumstances can greatly affect the ratings. Interpretations of the results must take into account the settings in which they were obtained.

When Is the Assessment Occurring?

The question of when an assessment takes place is of value in distinguishing between assessments planned in advance (*prospective*) as opposed to those based on recall (*retrospective*). Self-monitoring techniques are usually planned in advance. For example, students may be asked to keep track of the number of hours that they studied or the number of pages that they read during a study period. In contrast, biographical measures such as life history forms are recorded to the best of the individual's recollection after the event has occurred.

Why Is the Assessment Being Undertaken?

The question of why pertains to the reason for administering the test rather than to the nature of the test itself. The same test can be used for a variety of purposes, such as counseling, selection, placement, description, and evaluation. When tests are used in counseling, all data obtained must be regarded as confidential. Such *private data* may be contrasted with *public data*—data originally obtained for another purpose such as selection or placement. Examples of public data include academic grades, educational level, or occupational status. Counselors use public as well as private data in helping clients to address certain issues, because the public data can provide a great deal of information about the client's past performance under various circumstances.

How Is the Assessment Conducted?

"How" here refers both to the manner in which the test material is presented and to how the score for the assessment procedure is obtained. First, is the type of behavior that is being assessed *disguised* or *undisguised*? Projective techniques (described in chapter 12) are designed so that the respondent is typically unaware of the true nature of the test or of any "preferred" answer. Because the intent of the test is disguised, it is more difficult for respondents to fake their answers to produce a particular type of impression.

Are the scores arrived at *objectively*, that is, independently of individual judgment, or *subjectively* depending on the scorer's best judgment? Any response that can be counted is considered to be an objective measure. Tests that can be scored by means of a scoring stencil are objective. That is, different persons using the same scoring stencil with an answer sheet should obtain the same score if they are careful in counting the number of correct answers. In contrast, rating scales are subjective—the score assigned a ratee will often vary depending on the individual rater.

TYPES OF PSYCHOLOGICAL ASSESSMENT METHODS

The various assessment methods used in counseling may be conveniently classified by using different combinations of the criteria discussed in the previous section. Six popular types of psychological assessment methods are described below with the use of these criteria.

Standardized Tests

Standardized tests are discussed at length throughout the book; they will therefore be mentioned only briefly here. The term *standardized tests* refers to tests that must be administered and scored according to specified procedures. The testing conditions must be uniform for all clients. All scoring must be objective. Standardized test scores are usually interpreted by means of normative data obtained from a representative sample of people. Most standardized tests have been studied in terms of their reliability and validity.

Standardized tests include the following types of tests, each of which are discussed in this book: achievement tests, aptitude (or ability) tests, personality inventories, interest inventories, value inventories, and environmental inventories. Some standardized tests designed for specialized purposes such as neuropsychological assessment (e.g., Halstead-Reitan Neuropsychological Test Battery) and the evaluation of learning disabilities (e.g., Woodcock-Johnson Psycho-Educational Battery) are not reviewed in this book.

Rating Scales

Rating scales, which provide estimates of various behaviors or characteristics based on the rater's observations, are a common method of assessment. In contrast with standardized tests, rating scales are derived from subjective rather than objective data. Rating scales include self-ratings, ratings of others, and ratings of the environment. Interview data are often summarized by means of rating scales.

Because of their subjectivity, rating scales suffer from a number of disadvantages. Three common errors associated with rating scales include (a) halo effect, (b) error of central tendency, and (c) leniency error. In the case of the halo effect, raters show a tendency to generalize from one aspect of the subject to all other aspects. For example, if a person is friendly, that person may also be rated highly in unrelated areas such as intelligence, creativity, leadership, and motivation. The error of central tendency describes the tendency to rate all people as "average," or near the middle of the rating scale. The leniency error refers to the tendency to rate the characteristics of people more favorably than they should be rated.

To control for such errors, raters are sometimes asked to rank people on each rating scale. As an alternative, raters may be forced to distribute their ratings across the entire rating scale according to the normal curve or a similar system. When these techniques are applied to a large number of people, they prevent ratings from bunching up in the middle of the distribution or at the top end of the distribution. Kenrick & Funder (1988) offered the following suggestions for improving the validity of ratings: (a) use raters who are thoroughly familiar with the person being rated, (b) require multiple behavioral observations, (c) obtain ratings from more than one observer, (d) employ dimensions that are publicly observable, and (e) identify behaviors for observation that are relevant to the dimension in question. These suggestions can help counteract limitations posed by the various sources of invalidity.

Examples of rating techniques include the semantic differential and situational tests. The semantic differential technique requires raters to rate concepts (e.g., "my job") by means of a series of 7-step, bipolar scales (e.g., competitive versus cooperative). This technique can be readily adapted to a variety of situations. A list of bipolar scales that can be used to represent different dimensions appears in Osgood, Suci, and Tannenbaum (1957).

Situational tests require the person to perform a task in a situation similar to that for which the person is being evaluated. For example, the "in-basket technique" requires candidates for an administrative position to respond to the daily tasks of an administrator by means of an "in-basket" (work assignment basket) that simulates the actual work assignments of administrators. Situational tests can often meet the conditions suggested by Kenrick and Funder (1988) noted above. For this reason, they often prove to be beneficial in predicting performance in a situation similar to that of the test. Situational tests are frequently used to assess leadership or management skills.

Projective Techniques

Projective tests employ vague or ambiguous stimuli to which people must respond. Because the stimuli (e.g., inkblots, ambiguous pictures, or incomplete sentences) are vague, people tend to make interpretations of the stimuli that reveal more about themselves than they do about the stimuli. They "project" their own personality onto the stimuli. Responses are usually scored subjectively. Common projective techniques include the Rorschach Inkblot Test, Thematic Apperception Test, and Rotter Incomplete Sentences Blank. For many years projective tests dominated the field of personality testing, but during the past few decades objective (standardized) tests have become more popular. The use of projective techniques in counseling is discussed further in chapter 12.

Behavioral Observations

Behavioral observations refer to behaviors that can be observed and counted. The observations are planned in advance or based on recent events. The behaviors, which usually occur in a natural setting, are monitored by the client, by an observer, such as spouse or parent, or both. The observer usually records the frequency of a discrete behavior, for example the number of "I" statements made in an interview or the number of conversations initiated. Frequently the duration of the response and the intensity of the behavior (as rated by the observer) are also recorded.

Behavioral observations have the advantage of pertaining directly to a behavior that a client is concerned about. The behavior can usually be included as part of a goal. The measure is directly related to the client's treatment.

Biographical Measures

Biographical measures refer to accomplishments or experiences as reported by the subject or as reflected in historical records. For example, an employment resume or college application form usually provides an extensive amount of biographical information. Biographical measures differ from behavioral measures in that the observations are not planned in advance. They differ from rating scales in that the information is usually a matter of fact rather than a matter of judgment. Biographical data (biodata) include information maintained in cumulative records by schools or in personnel records by businesses, such as academic grades, extracurricular achievements, job promotions, hobbies, and volunteer work experiences.

The value of biographical measures in assessment is expressed in the well-established psychological maxim: "The best predictor of future performance is past performance." As a rule, the best single predictor of college grades for an individual is usually that person's high school grades. A person who has functioned well in a particular job in the past will probably perform well in related types of activities in the future.

Biographical data are usually collected by means of a written form or during the course of an initial interview with a client. Although this information is most often used subjectively, it can also be quantified for assessment purposes (Owens, 1983).

Biographical measures are both economical and efficient. They can provide information for areas such as leadership experiences or creative accomplishments that may be difficult to assess by other means. On the other hand, they may be inappropriate or difficult to interpret if the person's experiences have been unusual or severely limited. Biographical measures yield a broad range of information, but the meaning of the information requires additional interaction with the client or others familiar with the situation.

The Quick Job-Hunting Map (QJHM) by Richard Bolles (1979) represents an example of a biographical measure. The QJHM asks clients to review their accomplishments in terms of the transferable skills that are involved. It provides a systematic means of analyzing one's history in regard to career opportunities.

Physiological Measures

Physiological measures promise to become increasingly important in understanding and monitoring client behavior (Sturgis & Gramling, 1988). Such measures refer to bodily states or bodily functions that are primarily involuntary in nature, including skin temperature, muscle contractions, and blood pressure. Recent advances in instrumentation (biofeedback devices) make it relatively easy to include such variables in the assessment process.

STANDARDS FOR EVALUATING TESTS AND TEST USAGE

Several sets of standards have been published by professional organizations concerning the development and use of psychological assessment procedures. Counselors should be familiar with each set of standards or guidelines for test usage presented in this section.

Responsibilities of Test Users

The American Association for Counseling and Development (AACD) and the Association for Measurement and Evaluation in Counseling and Development (AMECD), one of the subdivisions of AACD, have published a policy statement that lists responsibilities of test users in seven categories: test decisions, qualifications of test users, test selection, test administration, test scoring, test interpretation, and communicating test results (AACD & AMECD, 1989). Counselors should be familiar with the recommendations made in this policy statement. These recommendations will be considered at different points in this book where they are relevant to the issues being considered. The most significant recommendations for counselors are reproduced in appendix A.

Standards for Educational and Psychological Testing

The *Standards* provide criteria for evaluating both tests themselves and use of the tests. The criteria were prepared by a joint committee of the American Educational Research Association, the American Psychological Association, and the National Council on Measurement in Education (AERA, APA, & NCME, 1985). The current version of the *Standards* represents the fifth in a series of documents on this issue beginning in 1954. Whereas previous editions of the *Standards* emphasized the responsibilities of the test developer, the present edition devotes more attention to the responsibilities of the test user. Increased emphasis on the appropriate use of tests should help to reduce criticism caused by the misuse of tests (Wagner, 1987). Excerpts from the *Standards* that pertain to the use of tests in counseling are presented in appendix B in this book.

The *Standards* also address, at least in part, the problem of potential bias in tests by stating a series of guidelines to be followed in testing linguistic minorities or people with handicapping conditions. These issues will be discussed further in chapter 16.

Test User Qualifications

Test users from several professional organizations have recently joined together to establish model test user qualifications. The Test User Qualifications Working Group (TUQWoG) of the Joint Committee on Testing Practices, an interdisciplinary committee including members from the American Association for Counseling and Development, the American Psychologial Association, the American Educational Research Association, the National Council on Measurement in Education, and the American Speech-Language-Hearing Association, has published guidelines that can be used to evaluate the qualifications of people interested in using various tests (Eyde, Moreland, Robertson, Primoff, & Most, 1988).

TUQWoG identified a total of 86 skills required for the proper use of different instruments. Factor analytic research indicates that the 86 skills can be reduced to seven broad factors. These include comprehensive assessment, proper test use, psychometric knowledge, integrity of test results, scoring accuracy, appropriate use of norms, and interpretive feedback. Counselors must be educated to perform ethically and effectively in each of these areas. TUQWoG has stressed educational efforts, not restriction of access, as a means of ensuring qualified test users.

TUQWoG has worked with test publishers to prepare qualification forms for potential customers. These forms ask test purchasers to indicate the purpose for which they will use the test, their level of training, the specific training that they have received in the use of tests, their professional memberships, and the manner in which they will use the test.

Code of Fair Testing Practices in Education

The *Code of Fair Testing Practices in Education* (1988), which was prepared by the Joint Committee on Testing Practices, lists standards for educational test users and developers in four areas: developing/selecting tests, interpreting scores, striving for fairness, and informing test takers. The code lists 22 standards that specify the responsibilities of counselors and other test users in each of these areas. Most of the responsibilities described by the code are discussed in appropriate sections of this book in succeeding chapters.

Test Publisher Requirements

Requirements for test usage vary depending upon the complexity of the test. Some test publishers distinguish between level *a* tests (no restrictions), level *b* (purchasers must have completed a college course in tests and measurements), and level *c* (purchaser must have completed an advanced degree in an appropriate profession, belong to an appropriate professional organization, or be licensed or certified in an appropriate profession). Study skills checklists are often classified as level *a* tests, career interest inventories are usually categorized as level *b* tests, and personality inventories are frequently listed as level *c* tests. Counselors need to be aware of the level of training required for the specific tests they wish to use. *Counselors should not attempt to use tests for which they lack adequate preparation*. Most test publishers require the people who purchase their tests to verify their qualifications to use them.

SOURCES OF INFORMATION ABOUT ASSESSMENT PROCEDURES

Although there are vast numbers of tests available in the United States, and there is a constant stream of new tests and revisions of old tests on the market, most of the tests are published by a few large publishers such as the Consulting Psychologists Press, the Psychological Corporation, and

Psychological Assessment Resources. These publishers distribute test catalogs from which manuals, scoring keys, and the tests themselves may be ordered. A list of addresses for the largest test publishers and some of the tests they publish appears in appendix C.

The best general source of information about tests is the *Mental Measurements Yearbook* series. First published in 1938 by Oscar K. Buros at Rutgers University, the series is now published at the Buros Institute of Mental Measurements at the University of Nebraska at Lincoln. The Yearbooks provide descriptive information about the tests, including publishers, prices, and persons for whom the test is appropriate, along with critical reviews by one or more test experts. A complete list of published references pertaining to each test is included and updated with each new volume of the Yearbook. Beginning with the 10th edition, published in 1989, the *Mental Measurements Yearbook* will be published biennially. In alternating years, the Institute will publish a softbound *Supplement*. More than 350 tests are reviewed in the 10th edition (Conoley & Kramer, 1989).

Critical reviews are not published for each test in each Yearbook, as each new volume is designed to add to, rather than replace, information found in prior volumes. A listing of all tests published in English-speaking countries is provided in another volume, also initiated by Buros, entitled *Tests in Print*. The most recent version is *Tests in Print III* published in 1983. Recent test entries for these volumes can now be obtained by means of an online computer service at the Buros Institute at the University of Nebraska.

In addition to the Buros Institute, counselors can consult the publications of the Test Corporation of America. This organization publishes *Tests* and *Test Critiques*. *Tests*, now in its third edition, provides updated information on over 3,200 assessment instruments (Sweetland & Keyser, 1990). The information includes a description of the test, its cost, scoring procedures, and publisher information. The eight volumes of *Test Critiques* offer in-depth reviews of psychological assessment instruments (Keyser & Sweetland, 1984–1990). The reviews, which average eight pages in length, provide a discussion of the practical applications of each test as well as its technical aspects.

Most of the information required for administering and scoring any particular test is found in its test manual. Although many manuals do not provide complete information, they should contain information regarding the construction of the test together with directions for administering, scoring, and interpreting the test. Norms should be reported, including a description of the norm group and the sampling techniques used to obtain the norms. Information regarding the reliability and validity of the test scores should also be presented in the manual. The manual should contain enough information so that prospective test users can evaluate the instrument before determining when and how they will use it. Most test publishers offer a specimen set of a test that includes the test itself, answer sheets, scoring keys, and a test manual at a nominal cost.

Professional journals and textbooks also provide extensive information about tests. *A Counselor's Guide to Career Assessment Instruments* offers reviews of popular assessment procedures used in career counseling together with a list of sources of information about assessment procedures in general (Jordan & Jepsen, 1988; Kapes & Mastie, 1988). Counselors are most likely to find test information pertinent to their work in the following journals: *Measurement and Evaluation in Counseling and Development, Journal of Counseling and Development*, and *Journal of Counseling Psychology*.

Information may be difficult to obtain for some proprietary tests that are exclusively owned and used within an organization such as a psychological consulting firm. Counselors should be cautious in relying upon the results of a test that has not been submitted for professional review.

SUMMARY

1. Psychological assessment procedures can be distinguished from each other in terms of *who* is making the assessment, *what* is being assessed, *where* the assessment takes place, *when* the assessment occurs, *why* the assessment is undertaken, and *how* the assessment is conducted. These distinctions can be used to classify tests into six broad categories: standardized tests, rating scales, projective tests, behavioral observations, biographical measures, and physiological measures.

2. Standardized tests have been the most thoroughly studied of all psychological assessment procedures in terms of reliability and validity; however, they cover a limited domain of behavior or situations. Counselors need to employ a broad range of assessment procedures to obtain information on relevant matters not included in standardized tests.

3. Counselors should be familiar with professional recommendations for evaluating tests and test usage. The two most important sets of guidelines are *Standards for Educational and Psychological Testing* and *The Responsibilities of Test Users* (the RUST statement revised).

4. The most important sources of information about psychological tests are the *Mental Measurements Yearbooks*, *Test Critiques*, test manuals, and professional journals.

CHAPTER 3

Measurement Concepts and Test Interpretation

To adequately understand and make use of tests, counselors and human development professionals must understand certain elementary statistical concepts that are used in conjunction with the development and interpretation of tests and test scores. In this chapter only a few descriptive statistical concepts involved in understanding and interpreting tests are presented. Neither the underlying concepts of statistics nor their calculation, elements commonly found in a basic statistics course, is included. This chapter describes (a) some of the measures used to organize and describe test information, (b) the concepts of test reliability and test validity, and (c) the interpretation of reliability and validity information.

A simple raw score on a psychological test, without any type of comparative information, is a meaningless number. If a graduate student obtains a raw score of 58 on a midsemester examination in a course "Theories of Counseling," the student's next question will be about the meaning of that score. A student whose score falls in the top 5% of the class—at the 96th percentile—will obviously react very differently from one whose score falls in the bottom 5%, at the 4th percentile.

Some type of interpretive or comparative information is necessary before any information is conveyed by a score as such. To say that a client obtained a raw score of 37 on an anxiety measure conveys no useful information, nor does the fact that this raw score of 37 is out of a possible total score of 60, nor the fact that this score of 37 meant that the client answered 62% of the anxiety items. To know that the same client obtained a raw score of 48 on a 60-item measure of tolerance does not indicate that he or she is more tolerant than anxious, nor does it yield any other useful information. Some frame of reference, usually stated in terms of the performance of some standardization group, is necessary to give a test result meaning and this is usually stated in terms of norms for that standardization group (Anastasi, 1988).

NORMS

Norms are established by administering the instrument to a standardization group and then referencing an individual's score to the distribution of scores obtained in the standardization sample. The individual's raw score is converted into some type of derived score, which indicates the individual's relative standing to the normative sample. This then provides a comparative measure of the individual's performance on whatever characteristic that instrument is assumed to measure.

Rank

A person's rank or standing within a group is the simplest norm-referenced statistic, with its interpretation based upon the size and composition of the group. It is used extensively for grades—for example a student's high school grade point average ranks him or her 12th in a graduating class of 140—but it is seldom used in describing psychological test results.

Percentile Rank

Percentile rank is much more often used because it is not dependent on the size of the comparison group. Percentile scores are expressed in terms of the percentage of persons in the comparison group who fall below them when the scores are placed in rank order. A percentile rank of 65 indicates a score or rank that is as high or higher than those made by 65% of those in the comparison group. A percentile can be interpreted as a rank out of 100 persons in the comparison group (see Figure 3–1). Higher scores yield higher percentile ranks and the lower the percentile, the lower the person's standing. The 50th percentile corresponds to the middle-most score or the median. The 25th percentile is the first quartile point marking the bottom quarter of the distribution and the 75th percentile is the third quartile point above which is found the top one quarter of the scores. The advantage of using percentiles is that they are easily calculated and easily understood by most people (provided it is made clear that a percentile indicates ranking in the comparison group rather than the percentage of correct responses).

The principal disadvantage to percentile ranking is that the distribution of most scores resembles the familiar bell-shaped curve, whereas the distribution of percentiles is always rectangular in shape. Ten percent of the cases fall between the 40th and 50th percentiles in the same way that 10% fall between the 80th and 90th percentiles. Because of the pile-up of scores near the center of a distribution, a small difference in middle raw scores can yield a large difference in percentile ranks, as can be seen in Figure 3–1. At the extreme high and low ends of the distribution, on the other hand, large raw score differences may yield only small differences in percentile ranks. Percentile ranks are generally intended as a means of conveying information concerning a person's relative rank in a group, but because of the nature of percentiles, they are generally not used in additional statistical computations.

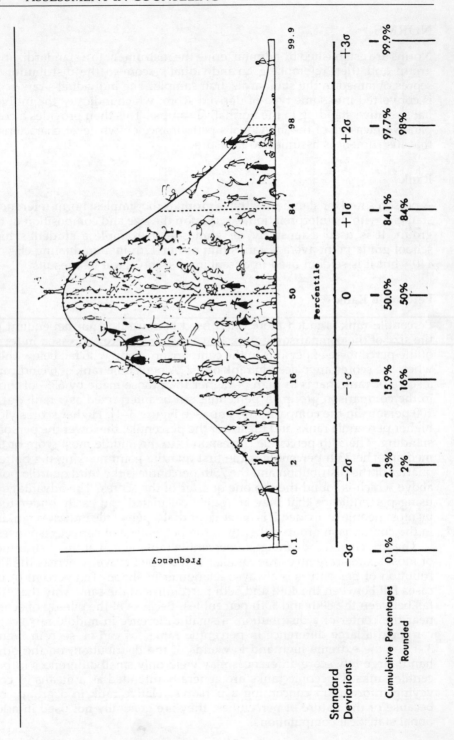

Standard Deviations	−3σ	−2σ	−1σ	0	+1σ	+2σ	+3σ
Cumulative Percentages	0.1%	2.3%	15.9%	50.0%	84.1%	97.7%	99.9%
Rounded		2%	16%	50%	84%	98%	

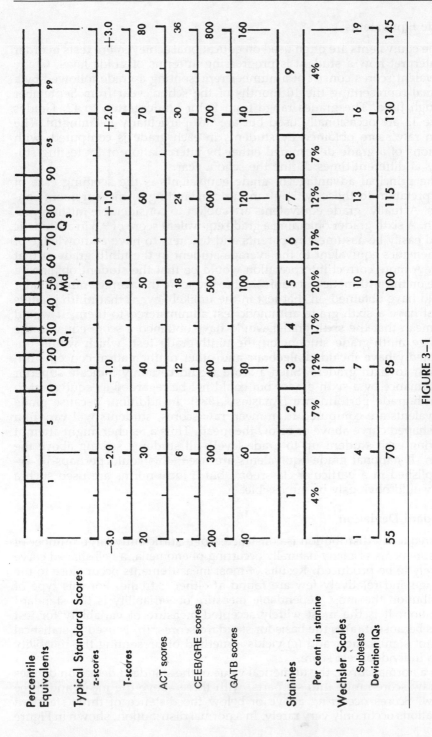

FIGURE 3–1

Relationship Among Different Types of Standard Scores and Percentiles in a Normal Population

Grade Equivalents

Grade equivalents are often used on educational achievement tests in order to interpret how a student is progressing in terms of grade level. Grade equivalent scores consist of a number representing a grade followed by a decimal representing the 10 months of the school year from September through June. The grades range from K for kindergarten to 12. Grades above 12 are occasionally used but are not particularly meaningful. The mean raw score obtained by students in each grade is computed, with fractions of a grade determined either by interpolation or by testing students at different times during the school year.

The principal advantage of grade equivalents is the seeming ease of interpretation to those without any understanding of measurement concepts. Actually, grade equivalents are subject to considerable misinterpretation. A sixth grader obtaining a grade equivalent score of 9.3 in arithmetic could easily be assumed by parents and teachers to have a knowledge of mathematics equivalent to the average student in the ninth grade at that time. A more correct interpretation would be that the student obtained a score on the arithmetic test equivalent to the score the average ninth grader would have obtained on that test in the unlikely event that ninth graders might have a sixth-grade arithmetic test administered to them. It would not mean that the sixth grader would have obtained a score equal to the average ninth-grade student on the ninth-grade test, which would undoubtedly have included algebraic and other mathematical concepts unfamiliar to sixth graders. Such a score would certainly indicate superior performance by a sixth grader but could not be regarded as equivalent to a ninth-grade performance (Anastasi, 1988). In addition, because grade equivalents are computed from mean raw scores, students will vary in a bell-shaped curve above or below the mean. Thus a teacher might attempt to bring each student up to grade level—all students scoring above the mean. If national grade equivalents are used, this could perhaps be accomplished in a particular classroom, but if local norms are used such a feat would obviously be impossible.

Standard Deviation

If a frequency distribution is constructed of a sufficiently large number of measurements of many naturally occurring phenomena, a bell-shaped curve is likely to be produced. Results of most measurements occur close to the average and relatively few are found at either extreme. For this type of distribution the most dependable measure of variability is the standard deviation. It is the most widely accepted measure of variability for test users because it (a) is the basis for standard scores, (b) is used in statistical tests of significance, and (c) yields a method of presenting the reliability of an individual test score.

In a normal curve, the numerical value of the standard deviation divides the raw score range into six parts, with three above the mean and three below. Scores occurring above or below the distance of three standard deviations occur only very rarely. In a normal distribution, shown in Figure

3–1, approximately 34% of the sample lies between the median and one standard deviation above it and another 34% in the standard deviation below it. Thus the distance of one standard deviation in each direction encompasses approximately 68% of the sample. An additional 14% or so of the sample is found within the second standard deviation above the mean and 14% below the mean, and approximately 2% is found in each of the measurements occurring in the third standard deviation above the mean and below the mean.

A person scoring two standard deviations below the mean, therefore, falls at the second percentile, and at one standard deviation below, at the 16th percentile. A person scoring at the median or mean is at the 50th percentile; a person scoring one standard deviation above the mean is at the 84th percentile, and a person scoring two standard deviations above the mean is at the 98th percentile. These percentages and points along the normal curve are shown in Figure 3–1. Because the standard deviation is the basis of standard scores, which are utilized in reporting the results of most psychological tests used by counselors and human development professionals, these percentages and points along the normal curve should be thoroughly understood and memorized by anyone who makes any substantial use of psychological test results.

Standard Scores

Because there are several problems related to using percentiles and other measures of variability, many tests make use of standard scores as the most satisfactory method of reporting test results. Standard scores are based on standard deviations and means. A standard score is defined as a score expressed as a distance, in standard deviation units, between a raw score and the mean. The basic standard score is the *z-score*. A z-score of −1.5 on this scale indicates that the raw score falls one and a half standard deviations below the mean of the reference group. A z-score of 0 means the raw score falls exactly at the mean, and a raw score falling two standard deviations above the mean would yield a z-score of +2.0. Because z-scores produce both decimals and negative values, they cause difficulties in computations and interpretation, so other types of standard scores have been developed based on a linear transformation of the z-score.

The most common standard score is the *T-score*, which is used on a number of the most widely used personality tests and interest inventories. By definition, the *T*-score has an arbitrary mean of 50 and an arbitrary standard deviation of 10. The *T*-score is rounded to the nearest whole number, and because most raw scores do not exceed plus or minus three standard deviations from the mean, *T*-score distributions usually range from 20 to 80.

Other test publishers have selected different scales using different means and standard deviations, which can be interpreted the same way as z-scores or *T*-scores. The College Entrance Examination Board and the Graduate Record Examination scores are reported in standard scores that utilize a mean of 500 and a standard deviation of 100. Thus a raw score falling one standard deviation above the mean, which would yield a z-score of +1, produces a standard score of 600. All scores are reported in increments of 10. This produces a scale that is recognizable for these instruments, although the scores may be thought of simply as T-scores with an additional zero added. This type of scale can cause a minor problem in that small differences in raw scores may seem to be much larger, because of the large scaled score differences that range through 600 points (200 to 800).

There is some additional confusion concerning the Scholastic Aptitude Test portions of the College Entrance Examination Board (which is discussed further in chapter 6). The mean of 500 that was established many years ago when a much smaller proportion of college-bound students took college board tests is no longer the mean for college-bound students, as many people still believe.

The American College Testing Program (ACT) uses standard scores similar to those developed for the Iowa Tests of Educational Development (ITED). The ACT and the revised Enhanced ACT have been standardized to have a mean of 18 and a standard deviation of 6, yielding a range of standard scores from 1 to 36.

Standard scores developed for the General Aptitude Test Battery (GATB) used by the U.S. Employment Service yield a mean of 100 and a standard deviation of 20.

When the first intelligence tests were developed, a ratio of mental age to chronological age was developed and this ratio multiplied by 100. This ratio was later called the Intelligence Quotient or IQ. This ratio IQ had a number of problems, and the ratio became invalid beginning in the adolescent years. Deviation IQ standard scores have since been developed to replace ratio IQs. Current results still report the mean at 100, as was the case with ratio IQs, but they report a standard score based on standard deviation units. Therefore, tests such as the Wechsler scales and the Stanford-Binet established a mean of 100 and a standard deviation of 15 or 16 depending upon the test. The positions at which these standard scores fall along the normal curve are shown in Figure 3–1. Again it is important in interpreting test results using any of these types of standard scores to have firmly in mind the points along the normal curve where these scores fall and the proportions of the population on which the standard scores are based that fall at various points on the normal curve.

Another type of standard score is the *stanine*, based on the term *standard nine*. Stanines have a range of 1 to 9 and a mean of 5. The stanine of 1 and 9 at the ends of the distribution contain 4% of the cases, and these increase as in the normal curve so that the center stanine of 5 includes 20% of the cases. Test scores can be converted to stanines by referring to the normal curve percentages in Figure 3–1. Stanines are infrequently used because of the difficulty in explaining their meaning. Their chief advantage lies in the single digit numbers, which do not imply greater accuracy than most tests can deliver. On the other hand, single digits can sometimes suggest a significant difference between two individuals where none exists.

RELIABILITY

Reliability and validity are two technical subjects that may not be of great interest to most people-oriented counselors and human development professionals, but they are extremely important for those who use psychological tests. They are concepts that need to be well understood when administering and interpreting psychological tests.

Inherent in the concept of reliability of psychological tests is the recognition that none of these instruments measures perfectly. Educators and behavioral scientists are interested in measuring much more complicated human characteristics than people's physical aspects. Anxiety, intelligence, depression, or potential to become a substance abuser are complex qualities that are difficult both to define precisely and to measure.

Reliability refers to how consistently a test measures, and the extent to which it eliminates chance and other extraneous factors in its results. Synonyms for reliability include dependability, reproducibility, stability, and consistency. A score that a person receives on a test is made up of two elements: the person's true score and an error score that may add to or subtract from the true score. A test with perfect reliability would be one on which everyone's scores remained in the same relative position on each administration (although they would not necessarily receive the exact same scores each time). In computing a correlation coefficient for a group of people on two sets of scores, the perfect relationship would yield a correlation of 1.00. If the test scores were completely unreliable, the relationship between the two would be a chance relationship and the correlation would be approximately 0.

Reliability is concerned both with the natural variation in human performance and with the technical aspects of psychological measurement. The stability of the trait or variable being measured obviously influences the amount of variation expected or considered normal when measured at different times. It would be expected that ability variables would have less variation than psychological states, but changes in ability measures can still occur as a result of growth and development. On the other hand, measures of personality variables, such as a state of depression, a state of anxiety, or a state of stress, could be expected to vary considerably at different times and under different circumstances.

Factors that are irrelevant to the purpose for which the test is designed represent error variance. Attempting to maintain uniform test conditions by controlling the instructions, time limits, and the testing environment are designed to reduce error variance and make test scores more reliable. No test is perfectly reliable, and because psychological measurement is often imprecise, it is important to check the accuracy and consistency of the instrument constantly to ensure that the unreliability of the instrument is kept within reasonable limits.

Reliability coefficients usually run within the range of .80 to .95, but what is considered to be minimal reliability varies substantially. For national testing programs such as the Graduate Record Examination or the Iowa Tests of Educational Development, reliability coefficients are expected to be above .90. For certain other types of psychological tests, reliability is substantially lower. A score on the Depression scale of the MMPI, for example, is an indication of the person's mood at the time the inventory was administered. Because peoples' moods change, a very high test-retest reliability would be neither expected nor desired. Thus, for personality measures, interest measures, and attitudinal measures, reliability coefficients will often fall below .90, although if they fall below .70, the consistency of the instrument becomes suspect.

Types of Reliability

Reliability can be measured in several different ways so there is not a single reliability for a test but different coefficients depending on how they are determined. There are four basic methods of estimating the reliability of an instrument.

Test-Retest

Test-retest reliability is a common method of estimating traits that are expected to be relatively stable over time. The correlation coefficient in this case indicates the relationship between scores obtained by the same persons on two administrations of the test. Test-retest correlations tend to decrease as the interval between the test administrations lengthens. If the interval is brief, there are potential problems of practice and memory, which tend to make the reliability estimation spuriously high. If the time interval is too long, variation can be influenced by events that occur to subjects between the two test administrations, and spuriously low estimates of reliability may be obtained.

For tests that yield a profile of scores on a number of different scales, the concept of profile reliability may be more appropriate than a mean reliability coefficient from a number of different scales of varying reliability. Profile reliability is obtained by computing the overall similarity of two profiles obtained for the same person at two different times. If the profile reliability is greater than .75, there is little difference in the interpretation given to the profile by counselors (Hoyt, 1960).

Alternate Form

A second method is that of alternate form or parallel form reliability. This form of reliability is computed by comparing the scores of the same individual on two alternate but equivalent forms of the same test. Because the test items are different, the effect of memory and other carryover effects are eliminated. The crucial question remains of whether in fact the two alternate forms of the test are actually equivalent.

Two tests that measure the same content, or variables, and that are equivalent in difficulty level, can be administered on the same day or very close to each other without concern about the practice effect. They can be alternated so that test A is given to one group first and test B to the other group first, and the practice effect can thus be controlled.

The problem with this type of test reliability is that it is often difficult enough to come up with one good form of a test—much less two good forms. Therefore, unless there is a national testing program with a staff working on developing test forms, as is the case with some of the national testing programs such as the Medical College Admissions Test or the ACT tests, hope for this form of reliability is unrealistic.

In national testing programs, the problem of developing equivalent forms is met by administering experimental items with each test administration. The persons taking the test respond both to items that count and to those that are being tried out. The latter do not count in scoring the subjects for that administration but provide data for the construction of future forms of the test. The experimental items do not have to be the same for all those taking the test on a particular date, as item information can be collected from random subsamples. This is how national testing programs are able to produce equivalent forms year after year.

Split Half

Split-half reliability is a popular form of establishing reliability because it can be obtained from a single administration by dividing the tests into two comparable halves and comparing the resulting two scores for each individual. It is administered all at once, so no time-to-time fluctuation occurs. In most tests, the first half and the second half would not be comparable because of differences in the difficulty of the items, as well as effects of practice and fatigue that are likely to vary from the beginning to the end of the test. Therefore, most tests are split into odd and even items, except where several items deal with a specific problem, in which case the entire group is assigned to one or the other half. An important weakness in the split-half approach lies in the general principle of sampling—that is, usually the greater the number of items, the more stable will be the concept being measured. All things being equal, the longer the test, the more reliable it will be. The split-half procedure cuts the test length in half, thus decreasing the reliability estimate. To correct the computed reliability, an estimate is made utilizing the Spearman-Brown Prophecy Formula to correct for the shorter length and to yield an estimate of what the reliability would be if it were obtained on the test's full length.

Interitem Consistency

Another index of reliability that has the advantage of requiring only a single administration of a single form is based on the consistency of responses to all of the items in the test. This estimate of test reliability is obtained from the average intercorrelations among the items on a test. Depending upon the type of response called for on the instrument, formulas known as the Kuder-Richardson Formula 20 for two-response answers (e.g., true or false, yes or no), or Cronbach's Alpha reliability coefficients for more than two alternatives are computed. These reliability coefficients are influenced by the consistency with which the items sample the trait being measured.

This is a measure of internal consistency that assesses the extent to which the items on the test are related to the total score on the test and consequently are related to other items on the test. Because the individual items for each person are taken into consideration in this method, it is useful to place all of the test items for the entire sample in a computer file. A computer can analyze these indices very easily and is particularly useful when the answers can be read into the computer using mark sensing or optically scannable answer sheets. This measure of reliability is not typically used when results must be computed by hand.

Considerations in Reliability

There is no easy answer to the question of which method of reliability testing is the best. The appropriateness of a particular method depends on the nature of the trait being measured, particularly in terms of the stability or consistency of the trait. If one is interested in a measure of internal consistency and accuracy of a test, then the split-half or interitem consistency technique would be recommended; if the concern is with dependability for predictive purposes, then the test-retest or parallel forms with an increased time interval would be more appropriate.

Again, the most important consideration is the nature of the trait being measured. A paper-and-pencil IQ test with a reliability coefficient of .75 would not be acceptable, whereas the same coefficient for a measure of anxiety would be fairly acceptable for use. Reliabilities of tests can be compared with those of other similar instruments, remembering that the lower the reliability, the less confidence is possible in using and interpreting the resulting test data.

Reliability estimates are also influenced by the nature of the group on which the reliability measure was computed. In a group that is heterogeneous on the characteristic being measured, there will be a greater range and greater variability and hence a higher reliability coefficient. An introductory course at the undergraduate level is likely to have a relatively heterogeneous group of students, with the result that a relatively poorly constructed final examination may yield a considerably higher reliability coefficient than a carefully constructed final examination in a graduate level course, which will likely contain a much more homogeneous group of students. Thus, in examining the reliability of a particular instrument, it is necessary to look at the type of sample on which the reliability coefficient was obtained as well as the type of reliability that was obtained. Information on reliability in a test manual should include the means and standard deviations, as well as the demographic characteristics of the sample on which the reliability coefficients were computed.

An important point to remember regarding reliability is that longer tests are usually more reliable than shorter tests. It is also true that speed measured tests can yield correlations that show high reliability, but the reliability is really based on how many items the person completed and not how well the test is measuring what it is supposed to be measuring. On highly speed measured tests such as those assessing clerical aptitude or manual dexterity, individuals are likely to complete approximately the same number of odd and even items and do not receive credit for items at the end of the test because they did not get that far. This results in a similarity of performance between the two halves and therefore yields a spuriously high split-half reliability coefficient.

Reliabilities of scored essay tests have always been quite poor, a problem when national testing organizations have attempted to use writing samples as criteria for college admissions. Even well-trained raters often vary substantially in the ratings they give to writing samples required by some institutions.

Standard Error of Measurement

The standard error of measurement (*SEM*) yields the same type of information as does the reliability coefficient, but is specifically applicable to the interpretation of individual scores. Its most common use is to construct bands of confidence around an individual's obtained score. It represents the theoretical distribution that would be obtained if an individual were repeatedly tested with a large number of exactly equivalent forms of the same test. Such a cluster of repeated scores would form a curve, with a mean and standard deviation of the distribution, and that standard deviation is called the standard error of measurement. An individual's single score on a test is assumed to be the mean of repeated scores, and the standard error of measurement can be interpreted in terms of normal curve frequencies. Thus if a student's true raw score was 40 on a particular test and the standard error of measurement was 3, then if we repeated the test many times, 68% of the individual's scores would fall between 37 and 43 and we could be 95% confident that the individual's true score would be between 34 and 46—two standard error of measurement units above or below the obtained score.

The *SEM* is easily computed when the standard deviation and the reliability coefficient of the test are known by using the following formula: The *SEM* equals the standard deviation of the test (*SD*) × the square root of 1 minus the reliability of the test.

$$SEM = SD \times \sqrt{1 - reliability}$$

As an example, the Standard Aptitude Test (SAT) scores of the College Entrance Examination Board have a standard score mean of 500, a standard deviation of 100, and a reliability of approximately .90. The standard error of measurement is approximately 30, which allows one to compute the odds of a person's true score falling, for example, within 30 points above or below the obtained score. Similar estimates can be made of the true scores for individuals on the ACT test which, with a mean of 18, a standard deviation of approximately 6, and reliability coefficients of about .90, have a standard error of measurement in the vicinity of 2. In the case of the Wechsler Intelligence Scales with full scale score standard deviations of 15 (mean of 100) and reliability coefficients in the vicinity of .96, the *SEM* equals 3.

VALIDITY

Whereas reliability is concerned with whether or not the instrument is a consistent measure, validity asks the question of whether it measures what it is supposed to measure. Does a test that is supposed to measure arithmetic skills really measure arithmetic skills, or is it composed of word problems of such reading difficulty that it is actually measuring reading ability instead? It is possible for a test to have high reliability without validity (but in order to have good validity, high reliability is necessary).

The question must always be asked, "validity for what?" The Strong Interest Inventory, for example, has considerable reliability with regard to many of the different scales found on it, particularly the occupational scales—including test-retest reliability—even when the second test is taken many years later. The typical person's interest patterns do not change much between, for example, age 25 and age 50. Thus, that instrument can be considered a reliable measure of interest.

When it comes to validity, though, the problem becomes much more complicated. Because of the large number of scales and the different types of scales, specific definitions must be developed before they can be applied to a criterion to obtain validity. As will be seen later, when it comes to predicting the occupation that a person is likely to enter in the future, the Strong does have some validity. On the other hand, it is not particularly valid for predicting success in an occupation. Persons who enter an occupation for which they get a low score on the Strong may very well not stay in that occupation. People who score high are much more likely to stay in the occupation, but the low scorers who stay in that field are just as likely to be successful as those who score high. Therefore, a score on a Strong scale may have some validity for predicting whether people will enter an occupation, and if so, how long they will stay in it, but it will have little validity when it comes to predicting success in that occupation.

The range of validity coefficients runs much lower than that of reliability. Whereas coefficients of .80 to .90 are sought for reliability, validity coefficients seldom run above .60 and are more typically in the range of .30 to .50. Validity coefficients as low as .10 and .20 can still be useful in predicting future behavior (Rosenthal, 1990; Rosnow & Rosenthal, 1988). In predicting grades in college from test scores, coefficients are practically never obtained above .60. Even when other measures of high school achievement, personality, and some type of achievement motivation are all combined, validity coefficients for college grades that run above .60 are seldom achieved.

Content Validity

There are several types of validity, one of which is content validity. This is the type of validity in which the items on a test are examined carefully to determine whether the items measure what the test is supposed to be measuring. If the test is designed to measure achievement in high school physics, a number of high school physics teachers, and perhaps some college physics teachers, examine the items on the test to determine whether these items are in fact measuring knowledge of what is typically taught in high school physics. Content validity involves judgment by persons competent in that field.

Content validity is not face validity, which is not really validity at all, but merely deals with the question of whether the items seem to be relevant to the person taking the test.

Criterion-Related Validity

One type of criterion-related validity is *concurrent validity*. This is a type of *empirical* validity, in which the validity of the instrument is measured against a criterion. For example, in developing a test of mechanical aptitude, it might be given to a group of working machinists, and then the ratings that they receive by their supervisors might be examined to determine whether the mechanical aptitude scores were related to their current work as machinists. Usually measures of concurrent validity are obtained because the test is going to be used in the future to estimate some type of behavior—such as the ability to do the work of a machinist.

A second type of criterion-related validity is *predictive validity*. For a scholastic aptitude test designed to predict college grades, the grades that the students earn in college are examined to determine whether the scholastic aptitude test has predictive validity. Does it predict what it is supposed to be predicting—in this case college grades?

One of the problems in measuring either concurrent or predictive validity is that of a restricted range if any type of measure, which is in any way related to the instrument being examined for criterion-related validity, has been used previously to select persons in the group being studied. Because scholastic aptitude test scores are often used to select students for a particular institution, and many students with low scores are eliminated, the group being studied to measure the test's predictive validity will have a narrower range, with a resulting lower validity coefficient. One way of avoiding this is to administer the instrument before any selection has taken place and to have the selection take place without regard to the criterion being assessed. For example in one of the validation studies for the General Aptitude Test Battery of the U.S. Employment Service, the entire battery was given to all applicants for jobs in an industrial plant that was being built in a particular town. Workers were then selected without regard to their GATB results. Performance ratings for the workers were obtained at a later date and these were then related to the previously obtained GATB results.

Spuriously high validity coefficients can also be obtained from a form of criterion contamination if, for example, the persons doing the rating know the test results. They may be influenced by this knowledge, which could result in a higher relationship between test results and later ratings or assessments.

An important concept related to the validity of a test concerns the base rates of the characteristic that is being measured in the population. Base rates are important because they have a marked influence on how useful or valid tests are in making predictions. If the base rates are either very low or very high, the predictions made from the tests are not likely to be useful. If almost every student admitted to medical school graduates, then scores on the Medical College Admission Test are unlikely to differentiate between those who will graduate and those who will not. The best prediction to be obtained would be not to use the test scores but merely to predict that every student admitted will graduate. Suicide rates are examples of low base rates. Although persons who obtain high scores on a scale that measures depression are more likely to commit suicide than those with lower scores, most people who obtain high scores on a measure of depression do not commit suicide. Because suicide is relatively rare, the base rate is so low that even with a high score on a depression scale, the best prediction to be made would still be that any individual is not likely to commit suicide.

The purpose of tests is, of course, to provide more information than could be obtained by chance or other unreliable means. Validity of tests is evaluated in terms of how much they contribute beyond what could be predicted without them. When a test is used to make a dichotomous, either/or decision (acceptable or unacceptable, successful or unsuccessful, positive diagnosis or negative diagnosis) cut-off scores are usually used. Many times a test does not need to have a very good correct prediction rate because the rate of predicting success is high without the test (the base rate)—for example, most of the students attending medical school eventually graduate. The overall proportion graduating is called the base rate, and the real value of the Medical College Admission Test (MCAT) comes if the correct prediction rate can be increased beyond that available without the use of the test. On the other hand, if the base rate is very low the correct prediction rate can be low but still above that of the base rate, so that the test results could still be valuable.

Questions concerning base rates and hit rates (proportion of successful predictions) often deal with relative cost. In some cases a miss can be very costly; for example, concluding that someone is not suicidal because he or she is below a cut-off score on a suicide potential scale when in fact the person is suicidal. The cost of this type of miss could be that a suicide takes place that might have been preventable. This type of case is called a "false negative." The person fell below the cutting score and was therefore predicted *not* to be suicidal when in fact he or she was suicidal. A "false positive" occurs when a person obtains a score above the cutting score and, for example, is predicted to be successful on the job but in fact fails and is discharged. Again, the time and money invested in training the person are likely to influence where the cutting score is placed and therefore to influence the proportion of false positives.

The amount of variability in a criterion that a correlation coefficient is considered to account for is the square of the correlation. Thus a correlation coefficient of .30 means that the predictor accounts for 9% of the variance. In using a correlation coefficient for prediction, however, Rosnow and Rosenthal (1988) showed that the correlation coefficient can be taken to indicate the improvement in success of prediction over chance or over the base rate by the percentage indicated by that correlation. Thus a correlation of .30 means that utilizing that variable in prediction improves the prediction by approximately 30%. When considered in this way, a moderate correlation can be seen to have considerable usefulness in counseling over that which would have been obtained had that test not been taken into consideration.

Construct Validity

A third type of validity is called construct validity and is a more complex concept. This type of validity asks the question—Do the test results make psychological sense? Are the test results related to things that they ought to be related to and not related to things that they ought not be related to? For example, do results on the test change according to what we know about developmental changes? Do older students do better on the test than younger students, for example sixth graders doing better on arithmetic tests than third graders? Is the test picking up the kinds of changes known to occur as people develop? Two aspects of construct validity are those of *convergent validity* and *discriminant validity*. Tests should be expected to show a substantial correlation with other tests and assessments that measure similar characteristics. Measures of mathematical aptitude ought to be related to grades in mathematics. Most validation studies report convergent validity. Another aspect of construct validity is that tests should not show a substantial correlation with other tests from which they are supposed to differ—discriminant validity. A test of mathematical ability probably should not show a strong correlation with a test of clerical speed and accuracy. A measure of sociability should be negatively related to the score on a schizophrenic scale and positively related to a scale of extroversion.

If an instrument is related to a particular psychological theory, then the results should fit that theory. Factor analysis is used to determine whether the test items fall together in different factors the way that the theory suggests they should. If a test is constructed along the lines of Jungian theory, such as the Myers-Briggs Type Indicator, the resulting factors from a factor analysis should be related to such Jungian concepts as introversion versus extroversion, sensing versus intuition, and thinking versus feeling.

An additional type of construct validity is *internal consistency*. This is the same type of index that is used as a measure of reliability, and shows the extent to which the items in the test are related to the total score on the test. If the items in the test are highly related to each other, and therefore to the total score, the instrument has some internal consistency reliability and therefore a certain amount of construct validity. When test scales are internally consistent, they are easier for the counselor to interpret because a single construct is being measured.

There is yet another type of validity that may be considered by counselors and clinicians. It has been termed *treatment validity*: "Do the results obtained from the test make a difference in the treatment?" (Holland, 1985b; Barrios, 1988). If the test results are useful, if they make a difference in the counseling process, then the test could be said to have treatment validity.

The question, then, is not simply "Is the test valid?" but "What types of validity does the test possess and are they relevant to the purpose for which the test is being used?" Criterion-related validity is important, for example, if the test is to be used for selection, whereas content validity is important if it is to be used as a measure of achievement. In the overall construction and development of a test various validation procedures are applied throughout the developmental stages. All the types of validity can also be conceived as contributing to the construct validity. Measures of internal consistency are built into the early stages of development, and criterion-related validation, typically, in some of the latter stages. Validation continues long after the test has been published and distributed for use.

SUMMARY

In this chapter some of the basic statistical concepts necessary to understand and interpret tests were presented. These concepts include:

1. Norms and certain descriptive statistics necessary to relate an individual's score to that of the norm group, including percentiles, grade equivalents, and standard scores.

2. Reliability, including its definition, expected ranges, and its four different types: test-retest, alternate form, split-half, and interitem consistency.

3. The interpretion of reliability coefficients, standard errors of measurement, and error bands.

4. Validity, including its definition and four types: content, concurrent, predictive, and construct.

5. The understanding and interpretion of validity data.

CHAPTER 4

Initial Assessment in Counseling

What assessment procedures should counselors and human development professionals pursue at the beginning of counseling? What steps should be taken to ensure that assessment procedures are appropriately selected and administered? This chapter addresses these questions.

First, the counselor needs to determine the client's orientation toward problem solving. Next, the counselor needs to assess the nature and severity of the client's problems. Assessment procedures that can aid in these endeavors are described in the first parts of this chapter. The chapter concludes with a consideration of the principles of test selection, administration, and scoring.

CLIENT ORIENTATION TOWARD PROBLEM SOLVING

Clients differ in their expectations of counseling and their problem-solving styles. Counselors can be more effective with clients if they take these differences into account. Different models or conceptualizations of counseling held by clients are presented below, followed by a discussion of different problem-solving styles.

Models of Helping and Coping

Clients' expectations for counseling will vary depending on their view of the problematic situation. Clients differ in the extent to which they accept responsibility for the problem or its solution. This distinction is important because it makes it possible to separate *blame* for the problem from *control* of its solution. Brickman et al. (1982) identified four different orientations toward counseling based on the client's views. As indicated below, clients may subscribe to any one of four models:

Moral Model

People are responsible for their problems and solutions. Clients who fit this model look upon counselors as consultants who can help direct them to resources, such as self-help books and personal growth groups, that they can implement on their own. They perceive themselves as lazy people who must work harder. Clients seek stimulation from counselors to do what they know they must do.

Compensatory Model

People are not responsible for their problems, but are responsible for solutions. Clients with this point of view perceive counselors as advocates who can help them to overcome a problem that they did not cause (e.g., poor education, which can be helped by tutorial programs). They think of themselves as deprived individuals who must assert themselves. Clients look to the counselors for empowerment to help them to correct situations causing problems.

Enlightenment Model

People are responsible for their problems, but not for solutions to the problems. Clients who endorse this model look upon counselors as saviors who can provide long-term care for them by means of ongoing support groups or other methods. They see themselves as guilty persons who must submit to a higher authority. Clients expect counselors to help provide them with discipline that they lack themselves.

Medical Model

People are not responsible for problems or solutions. Clients who fit this model view counselors as experts who will be able to remedy their problems by external means (e.g., by prescibing a treatment program that will cure their ailments). They regard themselves as ill people who must accept advice or treatment from the proper authority. Clients expect counselors to prescribe the solution, which the client will then follow.

The problem-solving process can be aided by taking into account the orientation of the client and that of the counselor. If the counselor assumes a different viewpoint from the client in terms of responsibility for the problem or the solution, the two might be working at cross-purposes. For example, clients with active coping styles (moral or compensatory models) make more progress in treatments that stress self-control rather than counselor control (Dance & Neufeld, 1988).

Counselors can usually determine their client's orientation by means of the interview. They can ask clients who (or what) is to blame for their problem, and who (or what) is in control of solving the problem. They can use the distinctions among the models indicated in the preceding paragraphs to help frame questions for clients. Internal versus external locus of control scales may also be helpful in this regard (Corcoran & Fisher, 1987). Clients who believe that they are in control of their destiny (internal locus of control) fit the moral or compensatory models; clients who believe that they are the victims of chance or their environment (external locus of control) conform to the enlightenment or medical models.

The compensatory model produces the best results for counselors in many situations (Brickman et al., 1982). It has the advantage of absolving clients of blame for the problem, thus justifying their request for assistance, at the same time that it places them in control of removing or reducing the problem. As indicated in a number of studies reviewed by Brickman et al., changes that occur as a result of counseling are most likely to persist when clients feel that they were responsible for the change. If change is attributed to the counselor's efforts, the change in client behavior is less likely to endure. Counselors can help clients to reattribute solutions for their problems to factors that they can control (Dorn, 1988).

Problem-Solving Style

Individuals differ in how they define the problem, how they solve the problem, and which part of the problem-solving process they tend to emphasize (defining the problem or solving the problem). The Myers-Briggs Type Indicator (MBTI) provides a convenient means of describing one's problem-solving style. As indicated in chapter 11, the MBTI includes four bipolar dimensions. Each of these dimensions can be used to describe an important aspect of the client's problem-solving style.

First, the Extroverted versus Introverted dimension indicates the extent to which the person chooses to solve problems either as part of a group or individually. Second, the Sensing versus Intuition dimension offers insight into the manner in which the client defines a problem. Does the client give predominant consideration to facts (Sensing type) or possibilities (Intuitive type)? Third, the Thinking versus Feeling dimension indicates the extent to which the person solves the problem by logic (Thinking type) or values (Feeling type). Finally, the Judging versus Perceiving dimension shows which function (problem definition or problem solving) the client will emphasize. Judging types place greater importance on solving the problem, whereas Perceiving types give primary consideration to defining the problem.

Counselors can use the MBTI to help clients to identify their problem-solving style. They can help clients to recognize both strengths and weaknesses in their preferred styles. Counselors can teach clients to "stretch" their styles when necessary to include some of the advantages of the other personality styles.

DEFINING THE PROBLEM

What is the nature of the client's problem? How severe is it? How does it affect the client's life? Answers to these questions can help counselors to plan and to evaluate treatment for their clients. In this section, a number of systematic procedures for addressing these questions will be considered.

Counselors can gather significant information from clients in a short period of time by means of an initial contact (or intake) questionnaire, a problem checklist, and an interview. The initial contact counselor uses this information in arranging counseling for the client or in making a referral.

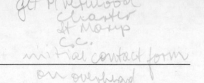

Initial Contact Form

An Initial Contact (IC) form contains questions about client status and presenting issues that can help guide the first counseling session. Common questions include name, address, sex, age, ethnicity, educational and work history, presenting problem(s), previous counseling, and urgency of request for counseling. Initial Contact forms vary somewhat from agency to agency depending on the particular type of services offered by the agency.

Information obtained from the IC form orients the counselor toward the client's problem, serves as a checklist to make sure that important points are covered, and provides a record for future counseling contacts. This information can also be compiled and used to describe the nature of the clientele served by a counseling center during a given time period. These data can be helpful in budget and program planning.

Use of the IC Form in Counseling

Specific recommendations for using the IC form in counseling are listed below:

1. Include a checklist of common problems presented at the agency on the IC form. Use the checklist to identify issues that need to be discussed with the client. Most clients mark more than one issue. Counselors can refer to the checklist to make certain that no issues are overlooked in the initial interview.

2. Use the IC form to learn about the client's status. The college student counselor, for example, can take into account aspects of the client's status such as new student, returning adult student, or student with disability in preparing for and conducting the interview.

3. Note the client's sense of urgency regarding the need for counseling. Be sure to assess the nature of the emergency if the client answers "Yes" to this question on the IC form.

4. Note whether the client is receiving counseling elsewhere. Does the client's current request for counseling conflict with the counseling received elsewhere? Consider referring the client back to the other counseling agency or have the client sign a release of information form so that it may be possible to consult with that agency.

5. Keep the IC form short so that it does not become an imposition in counseling. Consider the possibility of supplementing the IC form with additional questionnaires designed for particular issues, such as career planning, study skills, or relationships, as counseling progresses.

6. Maintain the IC form for clients in an agency file. Changes in status (including type of problems) for clients who return for counseling can be easily noted by referring to such files.

7. Ask clients who have been referred by a particular person for more information about the referral. What type of response does the referral party expect? Can significant information be gained by contacting the person who made the referral? Ask the client to sign a release of information form if necessary so that the referral source may be contacted.

8. Use the IC form as a means of communicating to clientele the nature

of the problems addressed by the agency and of informing clients about the agency's policies.

9. Notice the manner in which the client completed the IC form. Were all items answered? Ask about omissions. Was the client too distressed to finish the form? Be sure to note comments that the client has added to the form. Such comments can help clarify a client's status or concerns.

10. Establish a database for client statistics that can be used to describe the types of clients and problems served by the agency. This information can be used to establish agency needs and to communicate these needs to others.

Problem Checklists

Problem checklists or screening instruments are used by many counselors in conjunction with an IC form to obtain a quick, comprehensive, and systematic evaluation of a client's concerns. These instruments usually ask clients to check which ones of a variety of problems or symptoms may have been troubling them during the past week or two. Several checklists that have been widely used or that seem to be particularly valuable for use in counseling are described below. In addition to the instruments discussed below, other popular or promising checklists or screening inventories include the College Adjustment Scale (Baker & Siryk, 1984), the Psychological Distress Inventory (Lustman, Sowa, & O'Hara, 1984), the Porteus Problem Checklist (Porteus, 1985), the Personal Problems Checklist-Adult (Schinka, 1984), the Personal Problems Checklist-Adolescent (Schinka, 1985), and the Psychological Screening Inventory (Lanyon, 1978).

Inventory of Common Problems (ICP)

The ICP was developed by Jeffrey Hoffman and Bahr Weiss (1986) for use as a screening instrument in college counseling centers. It lists 24 specific problems that college students may confront (see Figure 4-1). These items represent six major types of problems as follows:

- Depression—Items 1–4
- Anxiety—Items 5–8
- Academic Problems—Items 9–12
- Interpersonal Problems—Items 13–16
- Physical Health Problems—Items 17–20
- Substance-use Problems—Items 21–24

Clients must indicate to what extent each of the 24 problems has distressed, worried, or bothered them in the past few weeks. Answers range from "1" (*Not at all*) through "5" (*Very much*). Scores for each scale can vary from 4 to 20; total scores can vary from 24 to 120.

Normative data for a random sample of college students collected by the authors showed no significant sex differences. The same set of norms may be used with both men and women. The highest mean score (11 points) was obtained on the Academic Problems scale whereas the lowest mean score (5 points) was recorded for the Substance-use scale. The mean total

Instructions: The following items represent common problems of college students. How much has each problem distressed, worried, or bothered you in the past few weeks? Please circle the answer that is most nearly correct for you.

Not at all	A little bit	Moderately	Quite a bit	Very much
1	2	3	4	5

1. Feeling depressed, sad, dejected?   1 2 3 4 5
2. Blaming, criticizing, or condemning myself?   1 2 3 4 5
3. Feeling discouraged or like a failure?   1 2 3 4 5
4. Suicidal thoughts or concerns?   1 2 3 4 5
5. Feeling irritable, tense, or nervous?   1 2 3 4 5
6. Feeling fearful?   1 2 3 4 5
7. Spells of terror or panic?   1 2 3 4 5
8. Feel like I'm "going to pieces?"   1 2 3 4 5
9. Academic problems?   1 2 3 4 5
10. Difficulty caring about or concentrating on studies?   1 2 3 4 5
11. Indecision or concern about choice of career or major?   1 2 3 4 5
12. Feeling like I'm not doing as well in school as I should?   1 2 3 4 5
13. Problems with romantic or sexual relationships?   1 2 3 4 5
14. Family problems?   1 2 3 4 5
15. Difficulty getting along with others?   1 2 3 4 5
16. Feeling lonely or isolated?   1 2 3 4 5
17. Physical health problems?   1 2 3 4 5
18. Headaches, faintness, or dizziness?   1 2 3 4 5
19. Trouble sleeping?   1 2 3 4 5
20. Eating, appetite, or weight problems?   1 2 3 4 5
21. My use of alcohol?   1 2 3 4 5
22. My use of marijuana?   1 2 3 4 5
23. How many psychoactive drugs I use?   1 2 3 4 5
24. How many prescribed drugs I use?   1 2 3 4 5
    If so, what? _____

Note. From "A New System for Conceptualizing College Students' Problems: Types of Crises and the Inventory of Common Problems" by J.A. Hoffman and B. Weiss, 1986, *Journal of American College Health, 34*, p. 262. Reprinted with permission of the Helen Dwigh Reid Educational Foundation. Published by Heldref Publications, 4000 Albemarle St., N.W., Washington, DC 20016. © 1986.

FIGURE 4–1
Inventory of Common Problems

score for college students was approximately 45 points with a standard deviation of about 10 (Hoffman & Weiss, 1986).

The ICP possesses sufficient reliability and validity for its use as a screening instrument but it should not be looked upon as a diagnostic instrument (Hoffman & Weiss, 1986). The results should be used primarily to suggest topics for further exploration in counseling. It can also be readministered to clients to obtain a rough measure of progress during the course of counseling.

From a practical point of view, the ICP offers several advantages for the counselor. It can be completed by most clients within 5 to 10 minutes, it represents most of the problems that clients are likely to encounter, and it can be reproduced for little cost if the original source of the instrument is acknowledged (J. A. Hoffman, personal communication, April 18, 1988).

Case Example

Linda came to the university counseling center as a senior because of dissatisfaction with her major. She felt particularly uneasy because most of her peers were participating in job interviews for the next year. She was majoring in banking, but was not happy with it. She did not like the competitiveness of the students in her field. According to the initial contact form that she completed at the same time as the ICP, she wanted help in "Choosing a major" and "Career planning." She marked all of the items except one in the first three categories (Depression, Anxiety, and Academic Problems) of the ICP as "4" or "5." She was feeling very distressed by her career indecision.

The initial contact counselor attributed Linda's problems to developmental issues, not preexisting psychopathology. Based on the counselor's judgment, short-term counseling was arranged. Linda needed help in dealing with developmental tasks, especially in resolving her career choice, not in making fundamental changes in her personality.

Linda met with a counselor for six sessions for help in acquiring decision-making and assertiveness skills and for assistance in working through conflicted feelings about her career choice. She decided to add personnel management as a second major to that of banking. This combination was supported by the tests (including Strong Interest Inventory) that she had taken and by the information that she had gained in her career exploration.

The ICP was readministered at the conclusion of counseling. Linda marked no "4" or "5" responses the second time she completed the inventory. Her total score, which dropped from 66 to 34, and all of her subscores were well within the normal range compared with other college students upon retesting. The ICP was helpful with Linda both in determining the nature and the severity of her initial complaints and in evaluating the progress she showed in counseling. Linda's rapid progress in counseling supported the perception of the initial contact conselor that her problems were developmental, not psychopathological, in nature.

Symptom Check List-90-Revised (SCL-90-R)

The SCL-90-R and its forerunners, the SCL-90 (Derogatis, Lipman, & Covi, 1973) and the Hopkins Symptom Checklist-58 (HSCL-58) (Derogatis, Lipman, Rickels, Uhlenhuth, & Covi, 1974), have been widely used for research and clinical purposes in a variety of medical and mental health settings (Derogatis, 1983; Tennen, Affleck, & Herzberger, 1985). As indicated by its name, the SCL-90-R contains a list of 90 symptoms such as "Headaches," "Feeling critical of others," and "Feeling tense or keyed up." Clients respond to items in terms of how much they were distressed by that symptom during the past week. Each item is answered on a 5-step scale ranging from 0 (*Not at all*) through 4 (*Extremely*). Most clients complete the SCL-90-R in 15 minutes. With practice it can be easily hand-scored.

The SCL-90-R provides scores for the following nine scales: Somatization, Obsessive-Compulsive, Interpersonal Sensitivity, Depression, Anxiety, Hostility, Phobic Anxiety, Paranoid Ideation, and Psychoticism. Scores for each scale show the mean response for the items in that scale. It also yields three total scores—Global Severity Index (GSI), Positive Symptom Total (PST), and Positive Symptom Distress Index (PSDI). GSI, the best single index of psychological disturbance, shows the mean response to all 90 items. PST indicates the number of symptoms reported (all items marked "1" or higher). PSDI, which shows the mean response to all items included in PST, reflects the severity of the client's symptoms.

Scores on the SCL-90-R vary depending upon age and sex. Adolescent nonpatients report more symptomatology than do adult nonpatients. Women acknowledge more symptoms than do men. The SCL-90-R manual provides separate-sex norms for adolescent nonpatients, adult nonpatients, adult psychiatric inpatients, and adult psychiatric outpatients.

The SCL-90-R scales possess adequate internal consistency and test-retest reliability over short time periods. It seems to be most valid as a broad measure of psychological disturbance. Factor analytic research indicates that the SCL-90-R primarily measures one large factor, which can best be thought of as depression or general psychological distress (Cyr, McKenna-Foley, & Peacock, 1985).

The SCL-90-R is particularly valuable as a screening instrument to detect cases that need additional assessment. As a general rule, Derogatis (1983, p. 28) suggested that counselors should refer clients for psychiatric evaluation if their scores on GSI or any two of the individual scales equal or exceed the 90th percentile compared with adult nonpatients.

At least two abbreviated versions of the SCL-90-R have been developed. The Brief Symptom Inventory (BSI) contains 53 of the 90 items on the SCL-90-R (Derogatis & Melisaratos, 1983). Administration time for the BSI is approximately 10 minutes, compared with 15 minutes for the SCL-90-R. Intercorrelations between the two sets of scales range from .92 to .99. According to its authors, the BSI has become a more popular instrument for research and clinical use than the SCL-90-R.

The Symptom Check List-10 (SCL-10) contains 10 items that have contributed most to the primary factors in the SCL-90-R based on factor analysis (Nguyen, Attkisson, & Stegner, 1983). It includes 6 items from the Depression scale, 2 from the Phobic Anxiety scale, and 2 from the Somatization scale. The SCL-10 total score correlates highly with scores on other measures of psychological distress (Nguyen et al.; Sabourin, Laferriere, Sicuro, Coallier, Cournoyer, & Gendreau, 1989).

Mooney Problem Check List (MPCL)

The MPCL can be used to identify client problems in different content areas such as health, economic security, self-improvement, personality, home and family, courtship, sex, religion, and occupation (Mooney & Gordon, 1950). Separate forms exist for junior high school students, high school students, college students, and adults. The various forms aid counselors in identifying and discussing different types of problems that may be affecting clients. No scale scores are provided. The forms have been widely used in counseling settings, but now need updating after 40 years of use. Counselors who use the MPCL may want to add some items of their own that fit their particular setting.

Use of Problem Checklists in Counseling

Suggestions for using problem checklists in the first counseling interview are given below.

1. Identify critical items on problem checklist (e.g., items that refer to thoughts of suicide or violent behavior) that can be used to help detemine if the client is in a state of crisis. Be sure to make a suicide risk assessment (see chapter 14) if the client shows signs of suicidal thinking.

2. Examine the general level of responses. If a client marks a large number of extreme responses, consider the need for immediate counseling and possible psychiatric referral. Ask clients to discuss each of these responses, especially ones that they perceive to be most crucial.

3. Note the client's responses for substance abuse and health. These problems may be overlooked in the counseling interview if the counselor does not bring them up with the client.

4. Readminister the problem checklist at the conclusion of counseling or after a significant time period has elapsed to evaluate changes that have taken place during the course of counseling. Clients who have shown little improvement may need to be referred.

5. Use problem checklist scores to consult with supervisor or colleagues regarding treatment of the case. Problem checklist scores can be used to communicate the nature and severity of the client's issues within a few minutes.

6. Add items to a standard problem checklist to assess matters of importance to an agency. For example, one agency added the item "Urge to injure or harm someone" to the Inventory of Common Problems to identify potentially homicidal or abusive clients.

7. Administer problem checklists or screening inventories for specific topics (e.g., Michigan Alcohol Screening Test, My Vocational Situation, or Eating Attitudes Test) when these seem to be appropriate. Ask clients to identify any issues that they might be experiencing that are not represented on the problem checklist.

8. Consider the possibility that clients could be minimizing or exaggerating their problems. Use both the number and intensity of symptoms to help gauge possible distortion. If clients mark very few items at a low level of intensity, they could be minimizing their problems. Similarly, if they mark a large number of problems at a high level of intensity, they could be exaggerating their concerns.

9. Keep in mind that problem checkists primarily measure general psy-

chological disturbance. Do not place too much emphasis on individual scales or items. Use individual scales and items primarily as a means of identifying significant subject matter for discussion.

10. Use problem checklists to monitor the caseload in the agency. What types of clients are receiving treatment at the agency? How many of the clients express suicidal ideation? How many of the clients indicate problems with substance abuse? Use these data to develop local norms to help interpret problem checklist responses.

Initial Contact Interview

The purpose of the initial contact (IC) interview is to assess the nature and severity of the client's problems and to determine possible treatment programs. Initial interviews usually progress on a continuum from minimal structure to more structure. As the interview proceeds, the client may need help or direction in continuing to respond. Questions that probe or clarify can be used to obtain a clearer understanding of what the client feels or means. Questions like "Can you tell me more about . . ." or "Tell me more about how you felt when. . ." or "I don't think I understand what you mean by . . ." provide relevant information from the client's point of view and help to maintain rapport. Rephrasing questions can sometimes help to clarify client responses if other techniques have not been effective.

Most IC interviews cover the following topics: (a) general appearance and behavior, (b) presenting problem, (c) history of current problem and related problems, (d) present level of functioning in work, relationships, and leisure activities, (e) use of alcohol or other drugs including medications, (f) family history of mental illness, (g) history of physical, sexual, or emotional abuse, (h) previous counseling, and (i) attitude of client toward counselor. At the conclusion of the IC interview, the counselor must help the client to decide what steps to take next. These steps include additional counseling with the IC counselor or another counselor at the agency, referral to a counselor or helping professional outside the agency, or termination of counseling at the end of the IC interview.

Use of the IC Interview in Counseling

Suggestions for conducting an IC interview are listed below:

1. Study the IC form before seeing the client. Note any items that require further discussion.

2. Show interest in the client's problems and welfare. Help the client to feel comfortable and relaxed in the interview.

3. Find out why the client is seeking help at this particular time. Ask clients which issue they are most concerned about. Provide immediate crisis intervention if needed.

4. Evaluate the client's orientation toward reality if his or her thinking seems to be confused. Does the client experience any auditory or visual hallucinations? Is the client delusional, agitated, or euphoric?

5. Consult with a supervisor or other staff member regarding clients with issues or situations that are difficult to assess or treat. Refer clients

who may need medication, hospitalization, or long-term treatment for psychiatric evaluation.

6. Consider the possibility that the client's psychological symptoms may be caused by physical illness, particularly if the client has not responded well to counseling or psychotherapy, if the symptoms have not occurred previously, if the client reports physical as well as psychological symptoms, or if the client is disoriented (Diamond, 1989). If the client is on medications, check for possible side-effects of these medications in the current edition of the *Physicians' Desk Reference*.

7. Introduce crucial topics that clients might not discuss without prompting by the counselor. These topics include severe depression and suicidal ideation, alcohol or other drug abuse, and traumatic incidents such as sexual assault. Refer clients with these issues for further assessment and treatment as necessary. Ask clients if there are any additional points not covered in the interview that they would like to discuss.

8. Inquire about previous counseling including attitude toward counseling and its perceived helpfulness. This information can be helpful in assessing the client's readiness for counseling and in suggesting possible treatments.

TEST SELECTION, ADMINISTRATION, AND SCORING

Test Selection

Testing should be seen as a part of the counseling process and not as an interruption of it (Goldman, 1971). People often approach tests with some anxiety. This is particularly true of aptitude and achievement tests because of fear of failure. Anxiety regarding testing can influence the entire counseling process. Even interest and personality tests can reveal aspects of a person's character that may indicate weaknesses or undesirable features. To reduce the threatening aspects of testing, the counselor should make clear that the purpose of testing is to provide self-understanding, not evaluation of the client by the counselor. The counselor needs to convey to clients the feeling that they will be accepted whatever the test results happen to be.

If at all possible, clients should actively participate in the selection of tests that will be used in counseling (Duckworth, 1990; Healy, 1990). By learning about the purpose and nature of particular tests, clients can profit more from the test results. If convinced of the usefulness of the tests, clients will be more motivated to do their best on ability tests and to be accurate and truthful in responding to items on interest and personality inventories. By having participated in the decisions to use the tests, clients are also likely to accept the results and their interpretations with less defensiveness. They can be more objective in their perception of the test results.

In the case of academic or career counseling, clients often feel dependent on tests. They perceive the counselor as an expert who will select tests that will tell them what to do. Active participation by clients in test selection helps to counteract these tendencies.

Generally the client does not select specific tests. That is a technical matter that counselors must decide based on their knowledge of tests. Instead, the client helps to decide the types of tests that can provide the information most useful for whatever actions or decisions are going to be made. Clients are not nearly as interested in specific characteristics of tests as they are in the implications the results will have for them. The types of tests are therefore described in a general fashion. For example, a counselor should describe the Strong Interest Inventory to a client simply as "an interest inventory that enables you to compare your likes and dislikes with those of people in different occupations." The counselor should not overwhelm the client with a lengthy technical presentation of the instrument itself.

A client's statement of need for tests should not necessarily be taken at face value. An initial request for a personality test should result in an effort to explore the meaning of the request, not simply acceptance of it. The client may be experiencing a significant problem such as anxiety or depression that should be explored before tests are assigned. The client may be asking for help regarding a particular problem but having difficulty revealing the problem or asking for help directly. The request for tests serves as an avenue to get at the major problem.

Another important principle to be used in test selection is that other sources of data should also be explored. In a college counseling center little is gained by selecting aptitude tests when a record of college entrance tests, high school grades, and college grades are readily available. Other counseling agencies, of course, often start with no previous information. Nevertheless, counselors can first attempt to explore with the client previous experiences that may provide relevant information and self-descriptions. Recall of previous experiences can provide a great deal of information either to supplement test results or to eliminate the need for particular tests.

The time it takes to administer a test is sometimes a factor in determining whether or not the test will be used. Sometimes a short test can give an approximation adequate for a decision, whereas in other cases a longer and more reliable test may be needed for important decisions. The cost of testing is also important for many institutions and agencies with limited budgets. Whether test booklets are reusable, how tests must be scored, the time needed to score and interpret tests, and the cost of computer scoring, if available, are all factors that need to be taken into consideration.

Test Administration

The basic purpose of a test is to obtain a sample of behavior from which behavior in other situations can be inferred or predicted. In the case of standardized tests, the sample of behavior must be obtained in a specified manner under standardized conditions with standardized instructions. The person who administers the test must be familiar with the instructions and other aspects of the administration. The knowledge necessary for administering the test differs greatly depending upon the test. Standardized scholastic aptitude tests can be administered with relatively little training. On the other hand, the knowledge and skill needed to administer individual intelligence tests requires extensive coursework and practicum experience.

Most test manuals provide detailed instructions for the administration of a particular test, which should be followed exactly. It is the standardization of instructions that makes it possible to compare one person's scores with those of another or with different groups.

In administering tests, it is important that the examiner elicit the interest and cooperation of the test taker. In obtaining rapport, the examiner should attempt to convince the test takers that the results will be useful and that they are not wasting their time in a task that will be of little consequence or value to them. Usually clients are cooperative if they have voluntarily sought counseling. If they are being tested against their will, perhaps because of a court order or because they feel that the test information is not important, good rapport may be difficult to establish.

Inexperienced test administrators often do not fully appreciate the importance of the test administrator's role. On performance or aptitude tests, the test administrator must encourage examinees to follow intructions carefully and to perform as well as they can. With small children, tests may be presented as a game. For interest or personality inventories, examinees should be encouraged to answer honestly and frankly to preclude invalid results.

The administrator should be familiar with the test being administered so that subjects do not doubt the administrator's competence. Self-confidence should be exhibited together with a warm and friendly manner.

The testing environment should be suitable for test administration, with adequate seating, lighting, ventilation, and temperature. It should be free from noise, interruptions, and other distractions. Time limits should be followed exactly and measures taken to prevent cheating. Factors, even minor ones, that can alter test performance should be recognized and minimized. These factors contribute to the error variance in test scores. Any problems in administering the test should be noted and taken into account when interpreting the test results.

Individual Versus Group Tests

Some tests are designed to be administered to one individual at a time by a trained examiner; others can be administered to a group of people. Group tests allow information to be obtained from many people within a short period of time at relatively little cost. Individual tests, on the other hand, allow the examiner to adapt the test administration to the needs of the clients. Individual tests must be used with certain populations such as very small children and those with particular handicaps. Individual tests permit observational data to be obtained in addition to the test scores.

Speed Versus Power Tests

Speed tests place a heavy emphasis on rapidity of response. These tests often include a large number of easy items that a person must complete quickly. Both finger and manual dexterity tests and clerical aptitude tests represent tests of this nature.

In contrast, power tests contain items of varying difficulty, most of which the person is expected to complete within the time limits. If 90% of the people for whom the test is designed can complete the test within the time limits, the test can be described as a power test. Although speed can still be a factor for some students on power tests, speed would not have much influence on the total score for most students. Most intelligence tests, scholastic aptitude tests, and achievement tests are basically power tests.

Computer-Based Test Administration

Test administration by means of computers has become widespread in recent years with the availability of low-cost microcomputers. Computer-based testing offers a number of advantages compared with traditional pencil-and-paper methods. These advantages include the following: (a) reduced amount of time required for test administration, (b) immediate feedback concerning client performance, (c) improved standardization of test administration procedures, (d) use of new types of items that employ movement or sequential presentations, and (e) use of adaptive (or tailored) testing procedures that take into account the client's previous responses (Wise & Plake, 1990). The Adaptive Version of the Differential Aptitude Tests represents an example of computer-based testing.

In the use of computer-based tests, counselors should make certain that clients are familiar and comfortable with the computer equipment. The computer equipment should be checked routinely to make sure that it is functioning properly. Additional recommendations for the administration of computer-based tests can be found in the APA *Guidelines for Computer-Based Tests and Interpretations* (American Psychological Association, 1986).

Test Scoring

Tests can be scored by hand or by computer. Tests that are scored by hand usually involve the use of a scoring template that can be placed over the answer sheet to identify incorrect responses. In some cases, clients score their own tests by the use of "self-scorable" answer sheets that reveal the correct answers behind a seal on the reverse side of the answer sheet. Examples of measures that use self-scorable answer sheets include the Myers-Briggs Type Indicator and the Kuder General Interest Survey. If more than a few tests or scales are involved, hand scoring can become time consuming and subject to error. If at all possible, tests that are scored by hand should also be scored by another person to ensure accuracy of results (Goldman, 1971).

Compared with hand scoring, computer scoring is more rapid, more accurate, and more thorough (Wise & Plake, 1990). The computer makes it possible to undertake elaborate test scoring programs such as those required for the Strong Interest Inventory or Kuder Occupational Interest Survey that would be virtually impossible to do by hand. In addition to specific scores, computers can also generate test interpretations by means of scoring rules, or algorithms, stored in the computer's memory.

Computer-based test interpretations (CBTIs), such as those that have been developed for the Minnesota Multiphasic Personality Inventory (MMPI), provide a "second opinion" that counselors can use both to create and to test hypotheses about clients (Sampson, 1990). They should not be relied upon as the sole source of information regarding a client. Despite their popularity, the validities of CBTIs have not been well studied (Moreland, 1985). The scoring rules upon which the interpretations are based are often a "trade secret" so that it is difficult to evaluate how adequately they have been developed. Counselors should examine CBTIs in light of other information that they have been able to collect about the client. They should use their professional judgment to take into account any individual or situational factors that could alter the CBTI for a particular client (American Psychological Association, 1986).

SUMMARY

1. Counselors can use the "models of helping and coping" by Brickman et al. (1982) and the Myers-Briggs Type Indicator to help clients identify their orientation toward problem solving. Clients should be helped to recognize the advantages and disadvantages of their particular problem-solving style.

2. The nature and severity of a client's problems can best be determined by means of an initial contact form, a problem checklist or screening inventory, and an initial contact interview used in combination. The Inventory of Common Problems and the Symptom Checklist-90-Revised both contain comprehensive lists of client problems or symptoms that can be used systematically to clarify a client's concerns.

3. The client should be integrally involved in all aspects of test selection. A variety of assessment procedures should be considered for this purpose.

4. The counselor should be careful to establish rapport with the client and to follow the prescribed procedures for test administration.

5. Computer-based test interpretations, which have become increasingly popular, require thorough knowledge and understanding of the test itself, the testing circumstances, and characteristics of the client to ensure proper use. Computer-based test interpretations do not replace the need for counselor training and experience in psychological assessment.

Section II

Cognitive Assessment

CHAPTER 5

Assessment of Intelligence

Counselors and human development professionals who work in certain settings such as schools, or who are involved in employment or vocational counseling, make considerable use of the results of intelligence tests. Others, working in colleges and secondary schools, constantly make use of a particular type of intelligence measure—the scholastic aptitude test, whereas marriage counselors and those working with substance abusers, for example, seldom use these instruments. Some general knowledge of intelligence assessment is important, and test results influence many decisions clients make. All counselors are expected to have some knowledge of intelligence assessment and the ability to make use of test results in assisting clients in making decisions. In this chapter some of the most often used instruments are described along with considerations regarding their use. Scholastic aptitude measures are discussed in the next chapter. Assessment instruments designed for special populations are described in chapter 16.

Intelligence has been one of the most thoroughly studied fields throughout the history of psychology. It was Alfred Binet in France who, in the early 1900s, conceptualized intelligence as a general ability to judge, to comprehend, and to reason well. With this definition he then went about developing a series of measures by which he could identify children for whom it was necessary to provide special educational programs. The measures he used showed that mental processes increase as a child grows older. Three-year-olds could be expected to be able to point to their nose, eyes, and mouth and repeat two digits. The typical 7-year-old could distinguish right from left and name various colors and the 12-year-old could define various abstract words and make sense of a disarranged sentence.

In 1916, Lewis Terman, at Stanford University, revised and standardized Binet's test for use in the United States. It became known as the Stanford-Binet Intelligence Scale. Making use of the concept of mental age developed by Binet, the concept of the now-outdated intelligence quotient (IQ) was devised. This IQ score is a ratio calculated with the mental age and the chronological age. A child's mental age is divided by the child's chronological age and multiplied by 100. A child exactly 10 years of age with a mental age of 12 will obtain an IQ score of 120. This type of an IQ score has a number of problems connected with it. In the first place, answering all of the items correctly on the original Stanford-Binet yielded a maximum mental age of less then 20. Thus anyone 20 or older automatically received an IQ score of less than 100. The usefulness of the ratio score therefore disappears during the teen years. In addition, the concept of a person's IQ has been erroneously viewed by the public as a fixed measure similar to the color of a person's eyes, rather than as a particular score on a particular test at a particular time. The ratio IQ has therefore been replaced by the derived IQ standard score in order to circumvent some of these problems.

POPULAR INDIVIDUAL INTELLIGENCE TESTS

The Stanford-Binet

The Stanford-Binet became the best known intelligence test in the world and was used as a standard against which all other intelligence tests being developed were validated. The 1916 Stanford-Binet Intelligence Test had a number of weaknesses and was therefore revised to produce the 1937 scale, which also provided two parallel forms (L and M). The ratio IQ score was eliminated and standard scores were calculated to provide each age with a mean of 100 and a standard deviation of 16. A 1960 revision was developed and was restandardized in 1972 to provide more adequate norms, intended to be representative of the entire U.S. population.

The 1986 revision (Thorndike, Hagen, & Sattler, 1986a, 1986b), is the fourth edition of the Stanford-Binet Intelligence Scale. The authors attempted to provide a continuity with the previous editions by retaining the advantages of the early editions as an individually administered intelligence test and still take advantage of the more recent theoretical developments and new research in cognitive psychology. A wider variety of tests, particularly those of a nonverbal nature, are included.

The fourth edition includes 15 separate tests that cover four different content areas: (1) verbal reasoning, (2) abstract/visual reasoning, (3) quantitative reasoning, and (4) short-term memory. Whereas certain of the 15 subtests are administered to subjects of all ages, others have more restricted age ranges.

In the administration of the 1986 revision, as in the case of the previous editions, individuals are administered a range of tasks suited to their abilities. A level is established at which it is expected that they would have answered all of the previous lower level items correctly and testing continues to a point at a ceiling level. Answers on the vocabulary test along with the individual's chronological age provide a method by which the entry level is determined to begin testing on the remaining tests. Testing then proceeds on each test until at least three out of four items are missed, which determines a ceiling level on that test where further items can be expected to be answered incorrectly.

On most of the tests each item has only one correct answer and the raw score on each test is converted into a standard age score with a mean of 50 and standard deviation of 8. Standard scores are also provided for each of the four cognitive areas along with a total composite score that reflects general mental ability. Each has a mean of 100 and a standard deviation of 16. The total testing time for the fourth edition takes approximately an hour and 15 minutes. No individual is administered all 15 tests—a complete battery includes 8 to 13 tests depending on the individual's entry level.

The fourth edition was standardized on over 5,000 individuals from throughout the United States and included representative samples based on gender, age, ethnic group, and community size. Internal consistency reliabilities tend to be very high for the composite (above .95) and for each of the cognitive areas (above .93). In general, test-retest reliabilities on both the individual tests and the composites are higher for older rather than younger age levels. The authors have provided validity data on the fourth edition by using (a) constructs based on current research in the field of cognitive intelligence, (b) internal consistency and factor analytic methods, and (c) correlations with other intelligence tests.

The Wechsler Scales

The Stanford-Binet was originally developed for children, with some more difficult items added for adults. David Wechsler, working at Bellevue Hospital in New York, believed that there was a need for an intelligence test more suitable for adults and therefore developed the Wechsler Bellevue Intelligence Scale in 1939. In addition, believing that the Stanford-Binet placed too much emphasis on language and verbal skills, he developed a totally different performance scale measuring nonverbal intelligence.

The Wechsler Adult Intelligence Scale (WAIS)

The 1939 scale was revised in 1955 to correct a number of deficiencies that had been found in the earlier form and became the Wechsler Adult Intelligence Scale (WAIS) (Wechsler, 1981). The WAIS was revised in 1981 to produce the WAIS-R. It was standardized on a sample selected to match the proportions of the U.S. population in regard to race, occupational level, education, and residence as of the 1970 census and distributed over age levels from 16 to 74.

The Wechsler tests yield a profile of scores (such as that of the case example displayed in Figure 5–1 for the WAIS-R) showing the raw score and scale score for each of the 11 subtests along with verbal IQ, performance IQ, and the full-scale IQ scores. The mean and standard deviation for each of the 11 subtests are 10 and 3, respectively. For the performance, verbal, and full-scale IQ scores, the mean is 100 with a standard deviation of 15 (as compared with 16 for the Stanford-Binet). Standard error of measurement for the three IQ scores is reported to be approximately 2.5 for the full-scale IQ, 2.7 for the verbal IQ, and 4.1 for the performance IQ. A client's true full-scale score could thus be assumed at a 95% level of confidence to fall within five points in one direction or the other from the client's obtained full-scale IQ score.

Case Example

Peter, 24 years old and single, had the WAIS-R (see Figure 5–1) administered to him while undergoing treatment for alcoholism in a residential

WAIS-R RECORD FORM

WECHSLER ADULT
INTELLIGENCE SCALE—
REVISED

NAME **Peter**

ADDRESS

SEX **M**   AGE **24**   RACE **Anglo**   MARITAL STATUS **S**

OCCUPATION **Unemployed**   EDUCATION **10th grade**

PLACE OF TESTING   TESTED BY

TABLE OF SCALED SCORE EQUIVALENTS*

Scaled Score	Information	Digit Span	Vocabulary	Arithmetic	Comprehension	Similarities	Picture Completion	Picture Arrangement	Block Design	Object Assembly	Digit Symbol	Scaled Score
	VERBAL TESTS						**PERFORMANCE TESTS**					
19	—	28	70	—	32	—	—	—	51	—	93	19
18	29	27	69	—	31	28	—	—	—	41	91-92	18
17	—	26	68	19	—	—	20	20	50	—	89-90	17
16	28	25	66-67	—	30	27	—	—	49	40	84-88	16
15	27	24	65	18	29	26	—	19	47-48	39	79-83	15
14	26	22-23	63-64	17	27-28	25	19	—	44-46	38	75-78	14
13	25	20-21	60-62	16	26	24	—	18	42-43	37	70-74	13
12	23-24	18-19	55-59	(15)	25	23	18	17	38-41	35-36	66-69	12
11	22	17	52-54	13-14	23-24	22	17	15-16	35-37	34	62-65	11
10	19-21	(15)16	47-51	12	21(22)	(20)21	16	14	31-34	32-33	57-61	10
9	17-18	14	43-46	11	19-20	18-19	15	13	27-30	30-31	53-56	9
8	15-16	12-13	37-42	10	17-18	16-17	(14)	11-12	23-26	28-29	48-52	8
7	13-14	11	29(36)	8-9	14-16	14-15	13	(8)-10	20(22)	24-27	44-47	7
6	9(12)	9-10	20-28	6-7	11-13	11-13	11-12	5-7	14-19	21-23	37-43	6
5	6-8	8	14-19	5	8-10	7-10	8-10	3-4	8-13	16-20	30(36)	5
4	5	7	11-13	4	6-7	5-6	5-7	2	3-7	13-15	23-29	4
3	4	6	9-10	3	4-5	2-4	3-4	—	2	9-12	16-22	3
2	3	3-5	6-8	1-2	2-3	1	2	1	1	6-8	8-15	2
1	0-2	0-2	0-5	0	0-1	0	0-1	0	0	0-5	0-7	1

*Clinicians who wish to draw a profile may do so by locating the subject's raw scores on the table above and drawing a line to connect them. See Chapter 4 in the Manual for a discussion of the significance of differences between scores on the tests.

THE PSYCHOLOGICAL CORPORATION
HARCOURT BRACE JOVANOVICH, INC.

	Year	Month	Day
Date Tested			
Date of Birth			
Age			

SUMMARY

	Raw Score	Scaled Score
VERBAL TESTS		
Information	**12**	**6**
Digit Span	**15**	**10**
Vocabulary	**34**	**7**
Arithmetic	**15**	**12**
Comprehension	**22**	**10**
Similarities	**22**	**10**
Verbal Score		**55**
PERFORMANCE TESTS		
Picture Completion	**14**	**8**
Picture Arrangement	**9**	**7**
Block Design	**22**	**7**
Object Assembly	**25**	**7**
Digit Symbol	**35**	**5**
Performance Score		**33**

	Sum of Scaled Scores	IQ
VERBAL	**55**	**95**
PERFORMANCE	**33**	**76**
FULL SCALE	**88**	**85**

FIGURE 5–1
WAIS–R Summary Test Scores for Peter

alcohol detoxification center. He had been treated twice before for alcoholism, but, being single, without family or other support systems, found it easy to drift back into alcoholism upon discharge. He suffered from mild depression and antisocial tendencies and had been in trouble with the law in addition to his problems with alcohol. In the center, however, he was a model client and fully cooperated with the treatment and testing he received. His verbal score on the WAIS-R fell in the normal range although he scored substantially lower on the performance subtest, giving him a total score that would place him in the dull-normal range. The large difference between the verbal and performance portions of the WAIS-R may very likely have been caused by the effects of continued alcohol abuse.

Wechsler Intelligence Scale for Children (WISC-R)

The Wechsler Intelligence Scale for Children (WISC) was originally developed as a downward extension of the Wechsler Bellevue Intelligence Scale for use with children aged 6 to 16. It was revised in 1974 (WISC-R) to contain more child-oriented items, to include more Black and female figures, and to provide a normative sample more representative of children in the U.S. population (Wechsler, 1974).

The WISC-R contains 12 subtests, two of which are supplementary, to be used if needed. The subtests generally parallel those in the WAIS-R and provide verbal, performance, and full-scale IQ scores similar to the WAIS-R. The two supplementary tests provided are the digit span test, which may be substituted for a verbal test, and a maze subtest, which may be substituted for the coding test in the performance battery, if the examiner meets with difficulty in administering one of the regular subtests to a particular child. As with the WAIS-R, the subtests are administered by alternating the verbal and performance subtests.

The subtests, the two partial IQ scores, and the full-scale IQ scores have means and standard deviations similar to those of the WAIS-R. Scores are provided for each 4-month age group between 6 and 16.

Both split-half and test-retest reliabilities for all three IQ scores fall within the range of .90 to .96. The standard error of measurement for the full-scale IQ test is approximately three points. Thus a child's true WISC-R IQ score would be estimated to be no more than six points above or below the obtained score at a 95% level of confidence.

The Wechsler Preschool and Primary Scale of Intelligence (WPPSI)

In 1967, a downward extension of the WISC was developed for use with children 4 to 6½ years of age called the Wechsler Preschool and Primary Scale of Intelligence (WPPSI) and revised in 1989 to become the WPPSI-R (Wechsler, 1989). It includes 11 subtests of which 10 are used in obtaining the IQ scores. Eight of the subtests represent downward extensions of those from the WISC, and three unique subtests were added. Normalized standard scores for subtests and IQs are similar to those on the other Wechsler tests.

Advantages of Individual Intelligence Tests

Each of these four intelligence tests is individually administered and requires a highly trained examiner. Considerable training and practice in administering each test are necessary for a competent administration that produces reliable results. An experienced examiner has the opportunity to observe and judge a variety of behaviors and aspects of the individual's personality. Thus for the competent examiner these tests provide aspects of a clinical interview as well as a standardized test.

Because these individual intelligence tests provide several different types of IQ scores, the counselor has the opportunity to pay particular attention to those clients in whom the difference between the scores is substantial. In such cases, an exploration is warranted to attempt to discern factors that might account for the differences. The different subtest scores also provide an opportunity to examine the pattern of scores that appear as a profile on the report form, such as that shown for the WAIS-R of the case example of Peter in Figure 5–1.

There have been a number of hypotheses advanced regarding emotional, neurological, and pathological problems that yield differential subtest scores. Considerable research has shown differential diagnoses resulting from patterns on such profiles to be questionable. Because the different subtests vary in reliability, difference scores obtained among the subtests can be particularly unreliable. Nevertheless, most sophisticated users of the Stanford-Binet and the Wechsler tests regard differential patterns as suggesting certain types of dysfunctioning. For example, higher scores on various verbal scales and lower ones on certain of the performance scales are suggestive of such problems as brain damage, drug abuse (as in the case example), or in an older person, Alzheimer's Dementia. Verbal subtest scores falling well below performance scores may suggest poor reading ability or lack of motivation for academic achievement.

Many counselors do not obtain the coursework and practice to administer these instruments in their graduate training. Instead they refer clients to competent examiners and receive the results from them. Counselors should encourage such examiners to report their observations and any other information that can assist counselors in interpreting the results, particularly in regard to information that can help to explain any discrepancies.

GROUP INTELLIGENCE TESTS

Group intelligence tests are considerably more cost-efficient than individual tests in the time required for administration and scoring. They require simpler materials; typically only a printed booklet, a multiple-choice answer sheet, a pencil, and a scoring key are needed. They also usually offer more normative information as this type of data is easier to collect for group tests.

The development of group tests was stimulated by the need to classify almost 2 million U.S. Army recruits during World War I. The Army Alpha and the nonreading companion test, the Army Beta, were developed for military use. Group intelligence tests designed for educational and personnel uses were developed shortly thereafter, with these two tests as models. Such group-administered tests are now used at every educational level from kindergarten through graduate school. They are also used extensively by industry, by the military, and in research studies. In order to avoid the term *intelligence test*, because the term *intelligence* is so often misunderstood and misinterpreted, these tests, particularly those designed for school use, tend to be described as mental maturity, cognitive ability, school ability, or mental ability tests.

Six Group Intelligence Tests for School Use

Because these tests are administered across a number of grades throughout entire school systems, they are administered in the hundreds of thousands each year. The market for these tests is therefore a profitable one, and a large number are available for use. A half dozen of the most popular and most psychometrically sound instruments are briefly described here.

Henmon-Nelson Tests

The Henmon-Nelson Tests of Mental Ability (Lambe, Nelson, & French, 1973) contain four levels of tests designed to cover the grades kindergarten through the 12th grade, with each level covering three or four grades. The tests contain verbal and numerical types of items, and the resulting raw scores are converted into both deviation IQs and percentiles.

Cognitive Abilities Test

The Cognitive Abilities Test (Thorndike & Hagen, 1978) is the modern version of the Lorge-Thorndike Intelligence Tests. The test contains three different batteries, one for kindergarten and first grade, one for second and third grades, and a multilevel battery for use in grades 3 through 12. The Cognitive Abilities Test contains three separate sections providing three separate scores: verbal, quantitative, and nonverbal. The nonverbal section uses neither language nor numbers but geometric figures for tasks that require classification, analogies, or figure synthesis. In this portion, the effects of formal schooling, poor reading ability, or non-native-English speaking are minimized. Raw scores on each section can be converted into stanine and percentile scores for both age and grade levels so that the three scores can be compared both to norm groups and within each individual. In addition, the scores can be converted to standard scores that have a mean of 100 and a standard deviation of 16 to produce a deviation IQ score. The Cognitive Abilities Tests were standardized along with the Iowa Tests of Basic Skills for grades kindergarten through 9 and the Tests of Achievement and Proficiency for grades 9 through 12.

Kuhlmann-Anderson Test

The Kuhlmann-Anderson Test (Scholastic Testing Service, 1982) is made up of eight separate levels for all grades—kindergarten through 12th grade—each level containing several tests. It is the contemporary version of one of the earliest and most popular intelligence tests used in the schools. It is less dependent on language than most similar tests and yields verbal, quantitative, and total scores. Scores are presented as percentile bands (confidence intervals) as well as deviation IQ scores.

Test of Cognitive Skills

The Test of Cognitive Skills (CTB/McGraw-Hill, 1981) is the contemporary version of the long-used California Test of Mental Maturity-Short Form. In its original form the instrument was designed to be the group test equivalent of the Stanford-Binet, and to yield scores similar to those that would be obtained by individually administering the Stanford-Binet. This instrument is composed of four subtests with five batteries designed for grade levels 2 through 12. Age and grade stanines, percentiles, and standard score norms are available for each subtest and a Combined Cognitive Skills Index provides a deviation IQ score.

Otis-Lennon School Ability Test

The Otis-Lennon School Ability Test (Otis & Lennon, 1989) has five levels ranging from grade 1 to grade 12, and the test is published in two forms (R and S). The test represents a contemporary revision of a series of former Otis tests. The Otis-Lennon School Ability Test was jointly normed with the Metropolitan Achievement Tests and the Stanford Achievement Tests.

School and College Ability Tests

The School and College Ability Tests (SCAT) (Bogatz & Greb, 1980) contain three levels and are designed for grades 3 through 12. Two forms (X and Y) are available for all grade levels. The School and College Ability Tests (SCAT) contain a verbal test of verbal analogies and a quantitative test containing numerical comparison items. The tests yield three scores, verbal, quantitative, and a total score, and standard scores, stanines, and percentiles are provided for each grade level. The SCAT were normed concurrently with the Sequential Tests of Educational Progress (STEP) achievement battery. Because the SCAT were developed by the Educational Testing Service, which also administers the College Entrance Examination Board's Scholastic Aptitude Test (SAT), scores on the verbal and quantitative portions of the SCAT can be used to predict scores that a student is likely to obtain on the Scholastic Aptitude Test's verbal and quantitative scales.

Other Group Intelligence Tests

Wonderlic Personnel Test

The Wonderlic Personnel Test (Wonderlic, 1983) is a brief 12-minute test of mental ability for adults. Five forms of this paper-and-pencil intelligence test are available, along with extensive norms. It is widely used in business and industry for the selection and placement of employees. Validity data in regard to job success are undoubtedly available locally in many companies but typically are not found in the research literature. The test's validity has been questioned in regard to selection for certain positions when minorities obtaining lower scores on the instrument are screened out of various entry-level positions. This has resulted in the Wonderlic Personnel Test becoming the subject of various court cases in which test bias or lack of validity has been suggested in hiring procedures.

Multi-Dimensional Aptitude Battery

The Multi-Dimensional Aptitude Battery was developed by Douglas Jackson in 1984 as a group-administered paper-and-pencil test to yield the same types of results and scores as the Wechsler Adult Intelligence Scale. This test battery contains five tests on the verbal scale and five tests on the performance scale that involve very similar tasks to the subtests on the WAIS but in a paper-and-pencil format. Scores on the various subtests have a mean of 50 and standard deviation of 10, and total scores on the verbal, performance, and full-scale scores have a mean of 100 and a standard deviation of 15.

In the design of the Multi-Dimensional Aptitude Battery, Jackson made use of the capabilities of modern computers in the development of items and scales through item analysis and factor analysis techniques. The advantages of the battery are in its ease of administration and scoring; the highly trained examiner necessary to administer the WAIS or the Stanford-Binet is not required. As a group-administered battery, however, it does not provide the examiner with the observational data obtained in using individual instruments.

INTERPRETING INTELLIGENCE TEST RESULTS

The typical intelligence test administered in the United States assumes a relatively common cultural background found in contemporary society and English as the native language. For tests above the lower elementary levels, reading ability in English is also necessary to obtain valid results on most of the group-administered tests. To provide valid assessment devices useful in other cultures or for use with subcultures or minority cultures in this country, attempts have been made to develop culture-fair tests that function independently of a specific culture, primarily by eliminating, or at least greatly reducing, language and cultural content. These will be discussed in chapter 16.

Perhaps the most important point to remember in the interpretation of intelligence test results is that the IQ score obtained does not represent a fixed characteristic of the individual. Instead, it should be interpreted as a particular score obtained on a particular test at a particular time. As has been mentioned, this is especially important for younger clients, for whom test-retest reliabilities are lower, indicating that considerable change and development take place over time. In interpreting the result to a client rather than say that he or she has an IQ of 112, a better interpretation would be to say that the client scored in the top quarter of his or her peers on a test that measures an ability useful in learning academic subjects.

SUMMARY

This chapter dealt with the assessment of intelligence using both individual and group assessment instruments.

1. The concept of intelligence is widely studied in psychology, but IQ scores are widely misunderstood by the general public.

2. Binet designed the first intelligence test in France in the early 1900s; it was revised in 1916 at Stanford for use in the United States. The 1986 revision of the Stanford-Binet intelligence tests contains 15 subtests, only parts of which are administered to any individual, depending on the chronological age and answers on certain of the subtests.

3. Three different Wechsler scales represent individually administered intelligence tests designed specifically for three different age ranges.

4. Large numbers of group intelligence tests are administered each year in the schools in this country, and six of these tests were briefly described in this chapter.

CHAPTER 6

Academic Aptitude and Achievement

The assessment of various aptitudes has played an important role in the field of psychological testing. An aptitude is generally thought of as an ability to acquire a specific type of skill or knowledge. In the field of aptitude testing, the assessment of scholastic aptitude is particularly important, because academic or scholastic aptitude is significantly related to achievement in various educational programs in high schools, colleges, and professional schools. Because of the importance of higher education as a prerequisite for entering the majority of higher status occupations and professions in today's society, achieving acceptable scores on scholastic aptitude measures is becoming increasingly crucial for those aspiring to such occupations.

Even counselors in elementary schools or mental health agencies, who seldom see scholastic aptitude test scores in their work, are expected to be knowledgeable about these tests. They will probably at least be consulted by their relatives, friends, and colleagues whose children are beginning to apply to undergraduate or professional colleges and universities. In this chapter information about the two major national college testing programs is presented, along with considerations and data useful in the interpretation of test scores. Academic aptitude tests used for admission to several of the different types of professional colleges are briefly described, followed by a few points regarding the administration and interpretation of academic aptitude tests. Examples of academic achievement test batteries commonly used in the schools are briefly described along with a discussion of the use and misuse of such test batteries. Finally, the relatively new cognitive development theories and assessment instruments are mentioned because of the expectation that they will be of increasing interest to counselors and human development professionals.

TESTS FOR HIGHER EDUCATION

Scholastic aptitude tests are used as sources of information for the selection and admission of students to institutions of higher education at the undergraduate and graduate or professional levels. They are also used in awarding financial aid and student placement in courses, as well as for academic and vocational counseling and advising. The two most commonly required college-level aptitude tests are the College Entrance Examination Board's Scholastic Aptitude Test (SAT) and that administered by the American College Testing Program (ACT).

The Scholastic Aptitude Test

The SAT has been administered since 1926 and is the admissions test most often taken by college-bound high school students (Donlon, 1984). Its design, administration, and reporting is carried out by the Educational Testing Service (ETS) in Princeton, New Jersey. The SAT is a 3-hour multiple-choice test with two major sections: verbal (V) and mathematical (M), along with a test of written English and an experimental section that does not count in scoring but is used to test new items for future forms of the instrument. The SAT attempts to measure developed abilities or intellectual skills and is not meant to be an achievement test tied to particular high school courses or curricula. Reliabilities of the SAT-V and SAT-M generally have been found to be in the vicinity of .90.

The SAT has undergone a number of changes over its history. In 1941, the mean on each section for students taking the test was set at 500, with a standard deviation of 100, and scores since then are linked to that 1941 standardization group. Scores therefore range on a scale from 200 to 800. With these standard scores, many people believe that 500 represents the mean for college-bound students, which is no longer the case. Since 1941, the college-bound cohort completing the tests each year has changed drastically, and 500 no longer approximates the college-bound mean. Recently the mean for students taking this test has been in the vicinity of 425 to 430 for the SAT-V and 465 to 470 for the SAT-M.

The SAT-M is more dependent on curriculum-based learning than is the SAT-V, and the further the student progresses in mathematics courses in high school, the better the student will be prepared for the SAT-M. Students who have not taken mathematics courses for several years should be encouraged to review some of their basic algebra and geometry before sitting for the SAT.

PSAT/NMSQT

The Preliminary Scholastic Aptitude Test/National Merit Scholarship Qualifying Test (PSAT) (NMSQT) (College Entrance Examination Board, 1988) is typically taken in the 11th grade. It is considered by some students to be a practice or trial run for the SAT to be taken in the following year. It is also used to help students choose which colleges to consider in their college decision-making plans. It also plays an important role as the initial step in qualifying for National Merit Scholarships.

Scores on the PSAT/NMSQT, which range from 20 to 80, are designed to be comparable—with an additional 0 added—to the SAT scores that students would be expected to obtain when they take that test in the senior year. Like the SAT, it yields both verbal and math scores (from two 50-minute sections). Thus a student who receives a 45 on the PSAT verbal and a 55 on the PSAT math would be expected to receive scores somewhere in the vicinity of 450 on the SAT-V and 550 on the SAT-M. Such a student who had been planning to enter a very highly selective institution where the majority of those admitted score above 600 on both portions of the SAT might wish to reconsider his or her chances of admission to that institution. An additional score, known as the "selection index," is computed for scholarship consideration by doubling the verbal score on the PSAT/NMSQT and adding the sum to the math score. To become a National Merit Scholarship semifinalist, the selection index must total in the vicinity of 190, with actual cut-off scores varying among the different states in order to obtain the top 1% of scholarship qualifiers from each state.

American College Testing (ACT)

The other national college testing admissions program is that of the American College Testing program (ACT), established in 1959 and based in Iowa City, Iowa. The ACT tests tend to be used more often by colleges in the Midwest and less often by those on the East Coast. The current revision, termed the Enhanced ACT Assessment (American College Testing Program, 1989a), consists of four academic tests, an interest inventory, and a questionnaire regarding student backgrounds and plans. The academic tests take 2 hours and 55 minutes to complete and are designed to assess academic ability in four areas: English, mathematics, reading, and science reasoning. Scores are obtained on each of the four academic tests and their seven subscales, along with a total composite score. The means for college-bound students on the Enhanced ACT scales are set at 18, with a standard deviation of 6 and a range of 1 to 36. The standard error of measurement is approximately 2 for the academic tests and 1 for the composite score.

A preliminary ACT battery, the P-ACT+, has been developed for 10th-grade students (American College Testing Program, 1989b). It consists of (a) four academic tests of 20 to 45 minutes each, yielding ACT standard scores of 1 to 36 with a mean of 18, (b) a brief interest inventory, (c) a study skills assessment inventory, and (d) a student information section.

Validity of Scholastic Aptitude Tests

The ACT and the SAT are approximately equal in their ability to predict college grades. Thousands of studies have been conducted assessing the ability of these tests to predict grades, with the typical correlation ranging in the vicinity of .30 to .50 for freshmen grade point averages (GPAs). Correlations tend to be higher at institutions with more heterogeneous freshmen classes and lower among homogeneous student bodies, particularly at the very highly selective institutions with restricted ranges of student scores.

Most studies have found that high school grades are the best predictors of college GPAs, but that scholastic aptitude tests are able to improve the prediction over high school GPAs or high school ranks alone. That scholastic aptitude test scores would add to the prediction of college success is not surprising. The particular high school GPA that a student obtains is dependent upon a number of factors—the general competitiveness of the high school attended, the grading curve used in that high school, the types of courses taken, as well as other personal factors. Thus a 3.2 high school GPA achieved by a particular student who has taken all college preparatory subjects in a school with a low grading curve and where the majority of classmates are college-bound represents a very different level of achievement than that obtained by a student from a high school in a lower socioeconomic area who has taken a number of vocational or commercial courses. A national college admissions test represents a common task for all students and therefore can operate as a correction factor for the high school GPA. In addition, for the student with low grades but with substantially higher scholastic aptitude test scores than what would be expected from those grades, the scores may suggest hitherto unrecognized academic potential. These scores may represent a "second chance" for such a student.

Test scores tend to be greatly overemphasized by many parents and their college-bound students. It is only at the most highly selective institutions that very high scores are generally required for admission. Students with good high school grades can obtain admission to most colleges unless their test scores are extremely low.

When scholastic aptitude test scores are interpreted to students and their parents, the standard error should be taken into account. On the SAT-V and SAT-M, the standard error is in the vicinity of 30 or 35, suggesting that two thirds of the time the student's true score will fall within 30 to 35 points in one direction or the other from the obtained score. For the ACT, with a standard error of approximately two points, two thirds of the time students' true scores could be expected to fall within two points on either side of their obtained ACT standard scores.

Although the number of colleges and universities in this country that require very high ACT or SAT scores is not large, with the exception of certain public colleges and universities located in a few states, almost all 4-year institutions claim to maintain some type of a selective admissions policy. This selectivity varies greatly. Some public institutions will take any student in the top half of his or her high school class or one who obtains a test score at least equivalent to that level. Others take only those in the top quarter, or in the top three quarters, or have other means of selection using formulae with high school rank or high school grades and Scholastic Aptitude Test scores. A few private institutions admit perhaps only one in five applicants from an already very selective applicant pool. There are many other private colleges that, although maintaining that they are "selective" in their admissions, in fact will admit almost every high school graduate who applies. The result is a great variation in the abilities of the average or typical student on various campuses.

It is definitely not true in this country that a particular grade point average earned at one institution is equivalent to that of another and that college degrees are equivalent from wherever they are obtained (Hood,

1968). Although some differences in levels of competition among colleges are recognized to at least a limited extent by the general public, and perhaps to a greater degree by those in higher education, the actual differences are far greater than all but the most sophisticated observers of American higher education imagine. Levels of competition vary so greatly among institutions that a student obtaining an honors grade point average of 3.4 at one institution could easily fail out of a much more competitive institution.

These differences can be understood by examining the scholastic aptitude scores in various institutions. Scholastic aptitude test scores of entering freshmen at particular institutions of several different types are shown in Table 6–1. This table includes ACT-English and College Board SAT-Verbal scores as rough equivalents. It should be recognized that the equivalence between these two tests shown in this table were based on a large and relatively heterogeneous population, but at a single institution. Populations at particular institutions of varying ability levels and with differing proportions of the two sexes may result in concordance tables that differ substantially from this one. The equivalent scores given in this table should be read as only rough equivalents and not as exact mathematical equivalents. The scores given for the different types of institutions represent a specific institution and are provided here as general examples and do not represent the typical or median institution of that type.

By comparing scores in this table it can be seen that, for example, the median student at the Ivy League institution falls at about the 95th percentile of students at the Midwestern state university. At the same time, the median student at the Midwestern university falls in the lower one or two percent of students at the Ivy League institution. Furthermore, the norms for students at the Midwestern university fall well above those for college-bound students nationally. The median student at the Midwestern university falls at about the 70th percentile of the national college-bound population. The median student at this private liberal arts college is practically never found in an Ivy League school and falls in the bottom quarter among students at the Midwestern state university. The median student at the Southern state college (an accredited institution) is found only in the lower one or two percent of students at the Midwestern state university, and very few students at this private liberal arts college score that low. The highest scoring student at the Southern state college does not reach the mean at the Midwestern state university, and only a handful of students at the Ivy League university obtain scores as low as the highest student at the Southern state college. Thus, between the Southern state college and the Ivy League institution, there is virtually no overlap among the scores of their students.

In assisting college-bound students in their decision making about the institutions they might choose, these types of differences should be considered. Information regarding the levels of academic competition at particular institutions can be found in certain college guides such as *The Comparative Guide to American Colleges* (Cass & Birnbaum, 1989), *Profiles of American Colleges* (Barrons Educational Series, 1990), and *The College Handbook* (College Entrance Examination Board, 1989). Anyone involved in col-

TABLE 6–1

Percentiles of Students With Certain Scholastic Aptitude Test Scores (Verbal) in Different Types of Institutions

ACT-English Standard Score	SAT-V Standard Score	ACT National Norms English %ile	An Ivy League Univ. (SAT-V) %ile	A Midwest State U. (ACT-E) %ile	A Small Liberal Arts Coll. (ACT-E) %ile	A Southern State College (SAT-V) %ile
33	760		95			
32	715		80	99		
30	670		60	94	98	
29	645	99	45	90	95	
27	600	96	23	74	89	
24	525	87	3	44	71	99
20	420	56		14	34	91
18	380	41		8	19	76
12	280	13		1	2	44
6	205	1				11
1	200					2

Note. Institutions shown were selected to show the great variation among them and are not meant to be representative of those types.

lege counseling should obtain a guide that contains information regarding high school ranks and test scores of students at different institutions. Armed with the knowledge that the standard deviation on an academic aptitude test at a given institution is likely to be in the vicinity of two thirds or three quarters that of the standard deviation of the instrument (four or five points on the ACT or 60 to 75 points on the SAT), and with the mean score given in one of the college guides, a counselor can easily calculate a rough estimate of the point at which the student is likely to fall in regard to academic aptitude at that institution. Combining this with a knowledge of the student's achievement level in high school, the general level of competition that a student will find at a given institution can be estimated. Combined with other information about the student, his or her chances of obtaining admission at that institution can also be estimated. A student might therefore be encouraged to apply to several different institutions, including one or two where chances for admission and satisfactory performance are very favorable.

The level of competition a student is likely to meet if admitted should also be discussed. Although there are many, including parents, who feel that a student should attend the highest status institution to which he or she can be admitted, some evidence suggests that for many students this will not be the wisest move. A study conducted a number of years ago (Werts & Watley, 1969) indicated that, holding ability constant, those students who attended an institution where they fell in the bottom portion of the students at that institution were less likely to go on and attend graduate or professional school than those students who had attended an institution where they were closer to or above the middle of the distribution.

When students transfer from college to college, much of the difference in the grade point averages obtained at the new institutions can be accounted for by differing levels of competition. Students transferring from community colleges to more competitive 4-year institutions often experience a drop in grades known as "transfer shock." Students transferring from more competitive institutions to less competitive ones will, on the average, see their grade point averages increase.

Case Example

Tom is just beginning his senior year in high school and he and his parents are having a conference with his guidance counselor. He has a 2.9 grade point average in the academic program in his high school and received scores ranging from 18 to 22 for a composite score of 19 on the ACT battery that he took the previous spring. His parents want to talk about colleges and universities that he should investigate and his chances of getting admitted to them. Included in their consideration is an Ivy League institution that their nephew attends.

The counselor reports to them that his score on the ACT is about an average score for college-bound students in this country. When he takes the SAT a few weeks hence, if he obtains comparable scores, they are likely to be in the 400s. She suggests that unless he were class valedictorian or a star athlete (which he is not) he has little chance of being admitted to a highly competitive institution. She tells them that because the state university admits any high school graduate who is in the top two fifths of his or her graduating class, and because he is at the 65th percentile, he would be admitted to the state university. He would, however, rank toward the bottom at that institution, both in terms of high school record and test scores, and could find it difficult to achieve more than barely passing grades.

Because he is undecided as to a career or a major, he is planning to enter a general liberal arts program and therefore has a wide range of institutions to choose from. At some 4-year institutions, he would fall well above the mean and at others well below the mean. At the particular small college he is considering, he would be below the middle but still above the bottom third. His chances of success there would be better than at a number of other institutions that he and his parents have considered.

GRADUATE AND PROFESSIONAL SCHOOL ADMISSIONS TESTS

Graduate Record Examination

The Graduate Record Examinations (GRE) (Educational Testing Service, 1987) are administered by the Educational Testing Service of Princeton, New Jersey. They consist of two separate types. The GRE Aptitude Test consists of three portions, verbal (GRE-V), quantitative (GRE-Q), and analytical (GRE-A). The verbal portion of the Aptitude Test includes analogies, antonyms, sentence completion, and reading comprehension items. The quantitative portion requires mathematical reasoning and an interpretation of graphs and diagrams, and includes items dealing with arithmetic, algebra, and geometry. The analytical portion includes analytical reasoning questions and logical reasoning questions designed to measure the ability to apply abstract reasoning to a set of given conditions or facts. The GRE Subject Tests are available in 20 different academic areas, such as physics, psychology, and Spanish.

Scores on each of the three portions of the aptitude test are reported in standard scores, with a mean of 500 and standard deviation of 100. The scores were standardized on a group of college seniors who took the test in 1952, and scores are equated to this reference group in order that scores remain constant over time. More recent means for students taking the test were in the vicinity of 480 on the verbal and 520 on the quantitative portions. The GRE Aptitude Tests have been shown to have consistently high internal consistency reliabilities reported at a level of .90 or above.

The GRE Subject (Advanced) Tests are required less often by graduate institutions or by graduate departments than the Aptitude Test. They are each 2 hours and 50 minutes in length and have been developed by committees of faculty members in the appropriate academic departments working with the Educational Testing Service staff. The results are also reported on a standard scale resembling that of the Aptitude Test with a mean of 500; however, the actual mean, range, and standard deviation of scores are different for each of the advanced tests. Certain of the advanced tests provide subscores for specific subject matter areas within the larger test, for example, a subscore on European history and one on American history within the history examination.

The GRE is used in selecting students for admission into graduate school and into specific graduate departments. Norms on the tests therefore vary greatly among institutions and among specific departments. A physics department could require substantially higher scores on the quantitative section than on the verbal section whereas requirements by an English department would be the opposite. An art department might pay little attention to either. Because of these differences, use of GRE test scores to assist students in selecting institutions and departments where they are likely to be admitted and are likely to be successful is difficult without knowledge of the norms in specific graduate institutions and departments.

Using the GRE scores to predict success in graduate school is particularly difficult for a number of reasons. There is likely to be the problem of restriction in range within particular departments, because GREs and undergraduate GPAs are the major criteria on which students are selected for graduate programs, thus eliminating low scores. In addition, graduate school GPAs may be highly restricted in range because grades of A and B are often the only grades given. For a typical department, however, GRE scores plus undergraduate grade point averages still provide a better prediction of academic success than any other readily available variables.

The Miller Analogies Test (MAT)

The Miller Analogies Test, published by the Psychological Corporation (1987a), is a second test often used for the selection of graduate students. The test consists of 100 complex analogy items drawn from the subject matter across a number of academic fields. Although the test is administered with a 50-minute time limit, it is largely a power test. It includes items of considerable difficulty so that resulting scores are purported to differentiate reliably among persons of superior intellect. It is available in a number of parallel forms, with reliabilities in the general magnitude of .90. Familiarity with the kinds of items on this type of test can significantly affect scores, with substantial improvement resulting in a second attempt on an alternate form. As with the GRE, norms among graduate students in different institutions and different departments vary widely, and knowledge of normative data in relevant comparison groups is a necessity if predictive information based on the scores is to have any value. The problems of predictive validity of graduate school success discussed for the GRE are also present for the Miller Analogies Test.

Professional School Tests

A number of different aptitude tests have been developed by different professions for selection into their professional schools. In many cases these tests are universally required for admission to these schools. Such tests include the Medical College Admissions Test (MCAT) (Association of American Medical Colleges, 1977), the Dental Admission Testing Program (DAT) (Division of Educational Measurements, 1984), the Law School Admission Test (LSAT) (Law Schools Admissions Services, 1988), and the Graduate Management Admission Test (GMAT) (Educational Testing Service, 1983). These aptitude tests are typically developed and administered by one of the national testing programs such as the American College Testing Program (ACT) or the Educational Testing Service (ETS).

These tests usually include items similar to those found on scholastic aptitude tests, including measures of verbal and numerical ability. In addition they usually contain subtests with items relevant to the particular profession. The Law School Admission Test includes measures that attempt to assess reasoning ability and writing competence. The Graduate Management Admission Test includes a quantitative section, the Dental Admission Test includes perceptual ability scores, and the Medical College Admission Test includes scores in such areas as biology, chemistry, and physics, as well as quantitative material.

Scores on each of the tests are reported with very different types of standard scores, with different means and standard deviations. For example, the Medical College Admission Test yields standard scores ranging from 1 to 15, with a mean of approximately 8 and standard deviation of approximately 2.50. The Law School Admission Test reports scores ranging from 10 to 50, with a mean of approximately 30 and a standard deviation of approximately 8. The Graduate Management Admission Test, used by most graduate schools of business, reports standard scores that are similar to those on the GRE, with a range of 200 to 800 and a mean of 500.

ADMINISTERING AND INTERPRETING ACADEMIC APTITUDE TESTS

Test Anxiety

In administering aptitude and achievement tests, it is generally considered a good procedure to attempt, while building rapport, to reduce test anxiety. Small but significant negative relationships have been found between test anxiety and scores on these types of tests. This relationship, of course, does not necessarily mean that high levels of anxiety cause lower test scores. Often those who have done poorly on these types of tests in the past are likely to experience more anxiety. Some studies suggest that a moderate amount of test anxiety can actually benefit test scores, whereas a high level of anxiety may be detrimental.

These results have been obtained when tests have been given under experimental conditions of high tension and of relaxed situations. For example, in one study (French, 1962) students took the test under normal conditions when the scores were to be reported to the institutions to which they applied, and a second time on an equivalent form under instructions that the test results were to be used only for research purposes and not otherwise reported. The results showed essentially equal performance under both the anxious and relaxed conditions. The only difference was that certain students under the anxiety conditions attempted more of the mathematical items and therefore achieved slightly higher scores on that subtest than they did under the relaxed conditions. Apparently under the relaxed conditions they "gave up" a little earlier and therefore achieved slightly lower scores. In general, testing procedures that are well organized, smoothly run, and that reassure and encourage should help to reduce the anxiety felt by highly anxious test takers.

Coaching

The effect of coaching or practice on test scores is a controversial one that has received much attention and has been the subject of a number of studies. Obviously practice or coaching that provides the answers to, for example, an individual IQ test such as the Stanford-Binet or WISC would invalidate the results as an accurate assessment. On the other hand, completion of a high school course in mathematics that results in a higher score on a mathematics achievement test probably actually reflects the student's knowledge of mathematics outside of the testing situation. The distinction therefore must be made between broad training and specific training or coaching focused on specific test items.

Coaching has been particularly controversial because of the existence of commercial coaching programs designed to raise scores on admissions tests such as the College Entrance Examination Board's Scholastic Aptitude Test (SAT), the Graduate Record Examination (GRE), or the Medical College Admission Test (MCAT). These coaching programs advertise and almost promise substantially better test performance for those who enroll in their programs. Many of the studies reported have substantial weaknesses that usually include the absence of a noncoached but equally highly motivated control group that is comparable to the coached group in all important ways, including performance on initial tests.

The College Entrance Examination Board (CEEB) has been particularly concerned for two reasons. First, if coaching could help students to improve their scores substantially, then the test results for all students would lose some validity. Second, the commercial coaching programs charge substantial fees and can represent a waste of money if coaching yields little improvement. In a number of CEEB's studies investigating different types of coaching methods among different types of students, well-controlled studies indicate that coaching is unlikely to produce substantial gains on the SAT (Messick, 1981). All students' scores seem to increase on a second testing, most of which can be accounted for by the general development that has occurred as students take additional high school courses.

A small amount of increase is perhaps due to a practice effect—familiarity with the types of problems and the problem-solving skills required. As a result, most of the testing programs—the College Board, the American College Testing Program, and the various professional school testing programs—now provide considerable information about the tests, including booklets with a number of practice test items. Thus all applicants have the opportunity to take practice tests and to become familiar with the types of items that appear in these testing programs. In addition to those provided by the testing programs, a number of test familiarization books have been published, with practice examinations in all of these areas. Usually entitled "How to take the . . . Examination," these books can be found in many bookstores. For certain tests such as the SAT, these materials are not limited to printed booklets but also include a variety of audiovisual and computer software materials.

It should be remembered that although specific coaching provides little improvement in test performance over that achieved by a little familiarization and practice (and this is particularly true on the verbal portions of these tests), additional training in the form of coursework is likely to result in improvement. In addition, a general review of the subject matter covered can substantially increase scores. For example, a student who has not taken any mathematics during the last 2 years in high school can improve scores on the mathematics portion of the Scholastic Aptitude Test by review of the courses in algebra and geometry that were taken earlier. A college senior who has not taken any mathematics in college since the freshman year can also improve his or her scores on the quantitative portion of the Graduate Record Examination by a review of the mathematical and algebraic concepts learned in high school and as a college freshman.

Counselors and human development professionals often receive questions from students, parents, and those involved in the selection and interpretation of such scores regarding the efficacy of coaching programs and other review procedures. They need to be cognizant of the various studies of the effects of different types of training and other activities on test performance.

ACADEMIC ACHIEVEMENT TESTS

Hundreds of thousands of achievement tests are administered each year, primarily in educational institutions ranging from kindergarten through graduate and professional schools. Some are administered for licensing and certification in trades and professions, or in medical specialties, or for the selection and promotion of postal workers. Achievement tests differ from aptitude tests in that they attempt to assess the results of some relatively standardized or specific set of experiences. Aptitude tests are more typically used for prediction purposes and do not assume previous standardized learning experiences. The distinction between achievement and aptitude tests is not absolute, however. Some aptitude tests are based on some generally standardized prior experience, whereas some achievement tests are designed to measure some generalized educational experiences that are not especially uniform in nature (Anastasi, 1988). For example, the American College Testing Program test serves as a scholastic aptitude test to predict success in college; however, its items represent subject matter areas taught in all high school curricula.

Achievement tests vary from the brief achievement test administered by a teacher to evaluate the learning that has taken place from a single lesson to the major nationally available achievement test programs produced by the major commercial test publishers. These achievement test batteries are generally designed across a number of grade levels from kindergarten through the 12th grade. The test batteries provide profiles of scores in various academic skill areas. They tend to be based more on the "three R's" in the early grades and measure more information and knowledge in academic areas at the secondary school levels. The tests are generally carefully written in regard to content, with items written by teachers and consultants and examined by expert reviewers. The items are then subjected to considerable analyses of item difficulty, and attempts are made to eliminate gender and ethnic bias.

Representative Tests

Some of the more commonly used national achievement test batteries include (a) the Iowa Tests of Basic Skills/Iowa Tests of Educational Development (b) the Stanford Achievement Tests, (c) the Metropolitan Achievement Tests, (d) the California Achievement Tests, and (e) the Sequential Tests of Educational Progress. The first three are briefly described as examples of these test batteries.

Iowa Tests of Basic Skills

The Iowa Tests of Basic Skills (ITBS) (Hieronymus & Hoover, 1986) are a battery of achievement tests covering grades kindergarten through 8. The tests are designed to measure basic educational skills and include reading, mathematics, language, and study skills.

Iowa Tests of Educational Development

The Iowa Tests of Educational Development (ITED) (Feldt, Forsyth, & Alnot, 1989) were designed for use at the high school level. There are seven tests in the battery measuring achievement in the different areas considered appropriate for high school. The scores reported are based on standard scores, with a mean of 15 and a standard deviation of 5 in a total range of 0 to 30. Standard scores are given for each of the seven tests and an overall composite score; percentile ranks are also reported for various subgroups of students. Results can be used in counseling for making decisions about high school programs and college planning.

Stanford Achievement Tests

The Stanford Achievement Tests (SACHT) (Gardner et al., 1985) are designed for grades 1 through 9. The Stanford Early School Achievement Test (SESAT) is available for kindergarten and first grade and the Test of Academic Skills (TASK) for grades 9–13. The test batteries are available for a number of different levels, and each battery consists of a number of different tests. Scores are reported in terms of percentile ranks and stanines along with grade equivalents.

Metropolitan Achievement Tests

The Metropolitan Achievement Tests (MAT) (Prescott, Balow, Hogan, & Farr, 1987) provide overlapping batteries from kindergarten through grade 12. The battery consists of a varying number of subtests in basic skill areas which, at the upper levels, can be supplemented by tests of knowledge in specific academic areas. Several kinds of scores including percentile ranks, stanines, and grade equivalents are provided.

Reliability and Validity

These achievement tests are highly reliable, with internal consistency reliabilities ranging from .80 to .90 or above for the various individual tests and well above .90 for composite scores based on the complete batteries. The procedures that the authors and publishers of each of the sets of tests have established for ensuring content validity are thorough and detailed. The item pools have been administered to large samples, and sophisticated item analyses to provide internal consistency and to detect gender and cultural biases are used. Although the results of these test batteries are often grossly misinterpreted by users, considerable pains have been taken to provide the results in understandable language and formats.

Most students take standardized achievements tests at regular intervals during their first 12 years of schooling, and these tests are used for a variety of purposes. They are used in a diagnostic way to identify the strengths and weaknesses of specific skills and achievements in individual students. As a result of such diagnoses, students can be selected for specific types of instructions, either remedial or advanced in nature, and the tests therefore are used as a part of the regular guidance and counseling program in an institution. Counselors thus become involved in interpreting the results to the students themselves, to their parents, and to teachers and other professionals.

Achievement tests are also used (and often misused) in attempts to evaluate the quality of the curricula and instruction within courses, programs, schools, or school systems.

The tests can provide information regarding what has been actually taught in a course or curriculum, for use in the evaluation of the extent to which educational goals have been met. They can also be used to assess change in performance over time within a school or school district and are used to compare the achievement of schools in a district or a district's performance as compared with national norms. Although the public is asking for accountability in education, and this accountability usually involves achievement test results, there are many important factors and complex issues that make such comparisons difficult and often invalid. The complexity of such accountability is often not well understood.

Achievement tests are usually evaluated based on content validity criteria—that is, the extent to which the test includes content similar to that which those tested are expected to have experienced. The validity of aptitude tests is usually predictive, based on the extent to which success in whatever it is the aptitude test attempts to measure can be predicted from the test results. Whereas achievement tests attempt to measure what has already been learned or knowledge or skills that have been attained, aptitude tests attempt to measure a potential ability, although such ability is usually related to that which has been developed up to the time of testing.

College-Level Achievement Tests

Three testing programs by which individuals may be awarded college credit other than by enrolling in college courses are the College-Level Examination Program (CLEP) and the Advanced Placement Program (APP) administered by the College Entrance Examination Board (CEEB) and the Proficiency Examination Program (PEP) administered by the American College Testing Program (ACT). The CLEP contains (a) general examinations that assess college-level achievement in five basic liberal arts areas usually covered during the first two undergraduate years, and (b) subject examinations each taking 90 minutes to complete, along with an optional essay portion. These examinations cover a wide range of popular college-level courses. The APP provides college-level course materials and examinations in different subjects for high school students who wish to qualify for college credits and advanced placement in college courses. PEP tests are also available in a wide range of arts and sciences, business, and education courses. Those in nursing have been particularly widely used to grant college and university credit in this field.

STUDY HABITS INVENTORIES

Counselors and human development professionals in high schools and colleges often work with students who are having difficulties with their coursework or are not achieving academically up to their potential. In working with such students, a study habits inventory is often useful; first, to allow students to understand how adequate their study habits are as compared with those of other students; second, as a teaching tool, as the items on such inventories have useful instructional value; and third, to point out particular weaknesses, useful in discussing specific activities for improvement.

The Wrenn Study Habits Inventory (Wrenn, 1941) is a brief checklist of 28 items containing study habits that distinguish high and low scholarship students. It can be used from grades 10 through 16 and can be accompanied by a booklet designed to assist students in improving their study techniques.

The Survey of Study Habits and Attitudes (Brown & Holtzman, 1984) is a 100-item inventory in two forms: a high school form and a college-level form. It contains four subscales entitled Delay Avoidance, Work Methods, Teacher Approval, and Educational Acceptance. The inventory yields scores on each of these scales along with several additional scores obtained through combinations of these scales. It also includes a counseling key that can be laid over the answer sheet to assist the counselor in focusing on various critical items.

Through the use of such self-rating inventories counselors and human development professionals can assist students in improving their academic performance by examining their various study attitudes and by assisting them to design more effective study strategies.

COGNITIVE DEVELOPMENTAL THEORIES

In addition to the learning of substantive knowledge that takes place in school, college, work, and daily life, other types of cognitive development such as rationality, intellectual tolerance, and intellectual integrity are now beginning to be assessed as well. One of these areas is ethical development as conceptualized by Kohlberg (1969, 1971), building on the structuralist view articulated by Piaget (1965). Kohlberg's theory holds that moral values are first external, then conventional in upholding and maintaining the social order, and at the highest levels maintained through individually held principles. Rest (1974) developed a paper-and-pencil instrument using Kohlberg's hypothetical moral dilemmas called the Defining Issues Test (DIT) to assess this type of cognitive development.

Based in part on the work of both Piaget and Kohlberg, Perry (1970) developed a cognitive developmental scheme of positions of intellectual development that take place during adolescent and adult years. Perry's theory is composed of nine different positions representing a continuum of development that can be clustered into four general categories—dualism, multiplicity, relativism, and commitment in relativism. Assessing cognitive development on Perry's scheme has been difficult, although five different measures have been constructed that attempt to place individuals along these positions. Three (Kitchener & King, 1981; Moore, 1988; and Baxter-Margolda & Porterfield, 1988) require free responses that must be classified using trained raters—thus making for high costs in terms of money and convenience. Two inventories that make use of objective-style responses to assess cognitive development are the Scale of Intellectual Development (SID) (Erwin, 1983) and the Parker Cognitive Development Inventory (PCDI) (Parker & Hood, 1986). Although these inventories are in a form that could be utilized by counselors, more validity studies and probable revisions need to be undertaken before they will be ready for use by counselors with individual clients.

Stages of cognitive development represent important concepts for counselors to explore, as these stages influence many of the decisions that clients make and the processes by which they arrive at these decisions. These concepts can provide an understanding of why one client seeks only one "right" answer to a problem whereas another is willing to explore a number of alternatives.

SUMMARY

This chapter dealt with the assessment of academic aptitude and achievement and presented the following topics: (a) the major college admissions batteries along with the meanings and interpretations given to their standard score results, (b) the great range in levels of competition among institutions of higher education, (c) several of the tests required for admission to graduate and professional programs, (d) the effect of such variables as text anxiety and coaching on the performance on such tests, (e) national academic achievement test batteries, and (f) several cognitive developmental theories.

The following points summarize the discussion of these topics:

1. Almost all counselors can expect to be consulted about scholastic aptitude tests, even if they work in settings where they seldom make use of them.

2. Test results on the College Board, National Merit, and ACT College Admissions Tests are often misunderstood and misinterpreted, even by those with some understanding of their standard score distributions.

3. Scholastic aptitude tests contribute by identifying unrecognized academic potential and acting as a correction factor for high school grades resulting from differing levels of competition.

4. There are great differences in the distribution of students in regard to academic aptitude among the different institutions of higher education in this country. These differences can greatly affect both the chances for admission and the chances for success at specific institutions.

5. Academic aptitude tests required for admission to graduate and professional programs typically have similar verbal and quantitative sections, but otherwise vary considerably in subjects that are assessed and in the types of standard scores with which they report results.

6. Although some practice and familiarity with the types of problems and skills required on academic aptitude tests may make slight improvements in scores, extensive coaching has not been shown to produce substantial gains.

7. Academic achievement tests administered widely in primary and secondary schools can provide useful diagnostic information regarding the strengths and weaknesses of specific skills and achievements of students. The results are often used and misused in attempts to evaluate the quality of instruction within classes, schools, and school systems.

8. Cognitive developmental theories can provide useful concepts in working with adolescent and postadolescent clients, but instruments to assess these stages need considerable additional refinement to be useful to most counselors and human development professionals.

Section III

Career and Life Planning Assessment

CHAPTER 7

Measures of Career Development

According to career development theory, people pass through a series of stages during the course of their lives (Super, 1957, 1984). Each stage involves a number of developmental tasks, such as adjusting to school, choosing a career, and obtaining employment, that a person must master to be able to move successfully to the next stage.

Measures that focus on the *process* of career development are discussed in this chapter. These measures, which enable counselors and human development professionals to assess a client's progress through the developmental stages, include both *attitudinal* and *cognitive* factors (Super & Thompson, 1979; Thompson, Lindeman, Super, Jordaan, & Myers, 1981, 1982). Attitudes toward career planning include such matters as how much thinking and planning a person has done concerning a career choice, what types of efforts a person has undertaken to learn more about careers, and the extent to which a person has been able to make and to clarify a career choice. Cognitive factors refer to decision-making skills and information about the world of work.

The measures of career development discussed in this chapter are important in evaluating readiness for career planning. This type of information should be considered before emphasis is placed on the nature of the career choice itself. Factors that pertain to the *content* of career development, such as work values, career interests, and special abilities, will be considered in subsequent chapters.

ATTITUDES TOWARD CAREER PLANNING

Each of the instruments discussed in this section assesses client concerns in regard to career planning.

Adult Career Concerns Inventory (ACCI)

The ACCI measures the career concerns of adults from the standpoint of Donald Super's theory of career development (Super, Thompson, & Linde-

TABLE 7–1
List of Scales and Sample Items From Adult Career Concerns Inventory

Stage and Substage Scales	Sample Item From Each Stage
Exploration stage	
Crystallization	Clarifying my ideas about the type of work that I
Specification	would really enjoy.
Implementation	
Establishment stage	
Stabilization	Settling down in a job I can stay with.
Consolidation	
Advancing	
Maintenance stage	
Holding	Maintaining the occupational position I have
Updating	achieved.
Innovating	
Disengagement stage	
Decelerating	Developing easier ways of doing my work.
Retirement planning	
Retirement living	

Reproduced by special permission of the publisher, Consulting Psychologists Press, Inc., Palo Alto, CA 94306, from *Adult Career Concerns Inventory* by Donald E. Super, Albert S. Thompson, and Richard H. Lindeman. © 1985. Further reproduction is prohibited without the publisher's consent.

man, 1988). Super's theory postulates four stages of career development in the adult years, each of which subdivides into three developmental tasks.

As indicated in Table 7–1, the ACCI provides scales for each stage and substage specified by Super's theory. It contains 61 items altogether—15 items to measure each of the four stages or, when subdivided, 5 items to measure each of the 12 substages. The one additional item pertains to the client's status in regard to career change.

Instead of setting career maturity as a goal, a concept that does not fit adults who may have already successfully pursued a career or alternative activity, the authors of the ACCI use *career adaptability* as the criterion for effective career planning. Adults who are in the process of career change can be expected to recycle through some of the early developmental stages.

Each item on the ACCI describes a career concern. Table 7–1 lists sample items from each stage. Clients rate each item on a 5-step scale ranging from *No Concern* to *Great Concern* based on their present situation. Most clients complete the ACCI, which requires an eighth-grade reading ability, within 15 to 30 minutes. Answers can be hand scored or computer scored.

The manual reports preliminary norms for each sex and for different age groups (Super et al., 1988). Besides making normative (interindividual) comparisons, the test authors also stress the importance of ipsative (intra-individual) comparisons. Ipsative comparisons enable the counselor and the client to identify the predominant developmental tasks facing the person.

The test scores show a high degree of internal consistency. Factor analytic studies support the construct validity of the ACCI. Such studies have consistently identified factors similar to the four developmental stages that provide the framework for the ACCI (Super et al.).

The ACCI helps to clarify the nature of the developmental tasks of greatest concern to the client at the present time. This information needs to be supplemented with other information regarding the client's attitudes toward work and the client's career planning skills and knowledge. Although limited in its scope, the ACCI fills a gap not met by other measuring instruments (Herr & Niles, 1988).

Assessment of Career Decision Making (ACDM)

The ACDM, which is based on Vincent Harren's model of career decision making (Harren, 1979), provides an assessment of important attitudinal factors associated with career development. In its current version (Form F), it contains 94 items scored on nine scales (Buck & Daniels, 1985). Three of the scales assess decision-making styles; the remaining six scales evaluate progress in resolving developmental tasks common to young people.

The Decision-Making Styles (DMS) scales measure the extent to which clients employ rational, intuitive, or dependent styles in making career decisions. The Decision-Making Tasks (DMT) scales assess three developmental tasks faced by most young people: adjusting to school, choosing a major, and choosing a career. Adjusting to school is measured by one broad scale, School Adjustment, and three subscales, Satisfaction with School, Involvement with Peers, and Interaction with Instructors. The last two DMT scales, Major and Occupation, measure career development on a continuum ranging from the exploration stage of development to the commitment stage.

The ACDM can be used with either high school or college students. If it is used with high school students who do not plan to attend college, the 20 items pertaining to the Major scale should be omitted. The ACDM must be scored by the publisher. Counselors receive an informative computer-based test interpretation; however, they do not have firsthand access to normative tables or scoring procedures.

Coefficients of internal consistency ranged from .49 (Intuitive scale) to .86 (Occupation and Major scales), with a median value of .72 for a sample of 264 high school students. Besides the Intuitive scale, the three School Adjustment subscales also had alpha reliabilities less than .70. These figures indicate that scores on these four scales are rather heterogeneous and may be somewhat difficult to interpret. Counselors should be cautious in interpreting differences between scores for scales with low reliability coefficients. For example, scores on the School Adjustment subscales should be at least 16 to 17 points (*T*-scores) different from each other before the difference can be considered to be significant (Johnson, 1987).

Factor analytic studies support the arrangement of the profile in three groups of scores. Three factors (decision-making style, school adjustment, and career decision-making progress) that closely resemble the three parts of the ACDM consistently emerge from factor analytic studies.

The ACDM contributes most to the counseling process with its Decision-Making Styles scales (Prediger, 1988). These scales provide the most new information to clients. Information obtained from the other scales can be helpful in counseling, particularly to the counselor in understanding the client; however, clients are more likely to be aware of the nature of their scores in these areas.

Career Decision Scale (CDS)

The CDS was developed by Samuel Osipow and his colleagues to help identify the antecedents of career indecision (Osipow, Carney, & Barak, 1976). It comprises two scales: a 2-item Certainty scale and a 16-item Indecision scale. The 16 items on the Indecision scale represent 16 different reasons for career indecision based on the authors' interview experiences with clients. The CDS was the first published instrument to provide this type of information for counselors (Slaney, 1988).

The target population for the CDS includes high school and college students in the process of deciding on a career. Because of its brevity, the CDS can be quickly administered (about 10 minutes) and scored (2 minutes). The manual provides normative data for high school students, college students, and continuing education students.

Counselors and human development professionals are encouraged to study individual items to help identify the sources of career indecision for clients. For each item, clients indicate on a 4-point scale to what extent the item accurately describes their situation. Besides serving as a counseling aid, the CDS can be used as a criterion measure to determine the effectiveness of various career development interventions.

The test-retest reliabilities for the total scores on the CDS are reasonably high; however, test-retest reliabilities for individual items are low. Although individual item responses can provide a springboard for counseling, counselors should keep in mind that the responses could easily change on retesting.

Although the CDS has some shortcomings, principally in the interpretation of the meaning of its scores, it has received positive evaluations from its reviewers for its ease of use, its applicability in counseling and research, and its extensive research support (Harmon, 1985; Herman, 1985; Slaney, 1988).

My Vocational Situation (MVS)

The MVS attempts to identify the nature of problems that may be contributing to career indecision (Holland, Daiger, & Power, 1980). Holland et al. attributed difficulties in decision making to three main factors: (a) problems of vocational identity, (b) lack of information about careers, and

(c) environmental or personal obstacles. The MVS includes scales to measure client concerns in each of these areas. The MVS provides diagnostic information regarding career planning problems that should be helpful in selecting the most appropriate type of treatment for the client.

The first scale on the MVI, the Vocational Identity (VI) scale, contains 18 items (e.g., "I need reassurance that I have made the right choice of occupation") that must be answered *True* or *False*. True responses suggest problems with one's vocational identity. Normative data indicate that high school students mark about seven True answers on the average whereas college students usually mark about two or three True responses. Individuals with a large number of True responses compared with people of their age may profit from career workshops, personal counseling, or additional work experiences.

The two remaining scales, Occupational Information (OI) and Barriers (B), each consist of one question with four parts. The OI scale provides data concerning the client's need for occupational information (e.g., how to obtain training or find a job in one's chosen career), and the B scale points out barriers (e.g., lack of needed abilities or family support) that may be impeding career development. These scales can be used as checklists to suggest specific steps that counselors can take to assist their clients in the career planning process.

When used as a checklist, the MVS can be completed by clients in the waiting room before the first counseling interview, in the same manner as other problem checklists described in chapter 4. Counselors can quickly identify clients with vocational identity problems by counting the number of True responses to the first 18 items. They can also determine specific needs of clients by simply noting those items with Yes responses on the OI or B scales. Items with such responses can be pursued in individual counseling to determine their significance for the client.

CAREER PLANNING COMPETENCIES

Although a number of standardized inventories focus on career planning competencies, few merit endorsement for counseling use at this time. The Career Skills Assessment Program (CSAP), which was constructed by the College Entrance Examination Board (CEEB) for use in career education classes at both the high school and college levels, shows the most promise (CEEB, 1978).

The CSAP includes six units, which represent the major topics taught in career education classes. The units can be used as a package or independently of each other. Each unit was designed so that it could be administered in one class hour, although the tests themselves are untimed.

Besides a total score, each unit provides scores for a number of specific skill areas as indicated below:

1. Self-Evaluation and Developmental Skills: 60 items, 5 scores
2. Career Awareness Skills: 60 items, 4 scores
3. Career Decision-Making Skills: 60 items, 7 scores
4. Employment-Seeking Skills: 70 items, 5 scores

5. Work Effectiveness Skills: 60 items, 7 scores
6. Personal Economics Skills: 60 items, 7 scores

Altogether, the CSAP contains 370 items in its six units to measure a total of 259 specific educational objectives.

Most of the units require a ninth-grade reading level. The Personal Economics Skills unit requires an 11th-grade reading level; the Career Awareness Skills unit demands a reading ability at the college level. Reading ability of the students must be taken into account when administering the CSAP. Although the tests are untimed, approximately 10% to 20% of the students fail to finish the items for each unit. Students with low reading levels will encounter difficulties understanding some of the items.

All six exams can be scored by the examinees themselves. In this manner, students receive immediate feedback concerning their performance in the different units. Accompanying materials explain the reasons for the preferred answer. In essence, the students are "taught the test." The CSAP serves as a combined assessment and instructional program; however, counselors or educators must assist students in their use of the materials. Students may become bored or overwhelmed with the materials if left to their own initiative.

The total scores for each unit show high levels of internal consistency. The CSAP has been validated primarily in terms of its content validity. Items were written to match specifications prepared by experts from the field of career education. All items reflect material taught in various career education courses.

Performance on the CSAP units correlates highly ($r = .65$ to $.70$) with verbal ability (CEEB, 1978). For this reason, the CSAP may be less appropriate for students who lack verbal skills. Job samples may work better for such students as a means of evaluating their career skills and motivating them to improve their knowledge in this area (Wiggins, 1985).

For most students, the CSAP should serve well as a measure of achievement in the different domains of career education. It identifies areas of weaknesses and provides educational materials to deal with these weaknesses.

MEASURES OF CAREER MATURITY

Measures of career maturity provide a broad assessment of career development. They include indices of both career planning attitudes and career planning competencies. The two most thoroughly developed measures of career maturity are the Career Development Inventory (CDI) and the Career Maturity Inventory (CMI) (Crites, 1984). Both instruments have their roots in the Career Pattern Study, a project headed by Donald Super in the 1950s that analyzed the dimensions of career development for school children.

Career Development Inventory (CDI)

Donald Super and his associates began work on the CDI more than 20 years ago (Myers et al., 1972). They designed the CDI "to assess students' readiness to make sound educational and vocational choices" (Thompson, Lindeman, Super, Jordaan, & Myers, 1981, p. 7). The present version of the CDI includes two forms. The School Form (grades 8 through 12) was published in 1979; the College and University Form was published 2 years later in 1981.

Part I of the CDI, which includes 80 items, provides two scales each for Career Development Attitudes (CDA) and Career Development Knowledge and Skills (CDK). Career Planning (CP) plus Career Exploration (CE) both indicate attitudes toward career development. Decision-Making (DM) plus World-of-Work Information (WW) both reveal knowledge and skills related to career development. A Career Orientation Total (COT) score, the best single measure of career maturity from the CDI, combines the scores for all four subscales.

Part II of the CDI evaluates the client's knowledge of the occupational field to which he or she is most attracted. The Knowledge of Preferred Occupational Group (PO) scale uses the same 40 multiple-choice items for each occupational group. The correct response for each item (e.g., employment opportunities or educational requirements) will vary depending upon the occupational field. Part II differs from Part I because of its emphasis on occupational knowledge that pertains to a particular occupational field instead of occupations in general. This part of the CDI should not be administered to students below the 11th grade under ordinary circumstances.

The answer sheets must be machine scored by the publisher. For each form, results are reported as standard scores with a mean of 100 and a standard deviation of 20. The manuals provide separate percentile tables by sex and year in school for both forms (Thompson et al., 1981, 1982). Although the normative samples are diverse in their makeup, the authors acknowledge that they do not represent a cross-section of high school or college students in the United States. They encourage test users to build local norms, which the test publisher will provide when the number of students completing the CDI exceeds 100.

The reliabilities for the combined scales (CDA, CDK, and COT) are adequate; however, the reliabilities for some of the individual scales are surprisingly low (Locke, 1988). The test-retest reliability coefficients were particularly low for the PO, WW, and DM scales for high school students tested over 2- and 3-week intervals. The standard errors of measurement for these scales equal 14 to 16 points (approximately three fourths of a standard deviation).

The CDI can claim content validity by virtue of the fact that items for each scale were selected by expert judges to be representative of the different dimensions of Super's model of career development. It also possesses construct validity in that the scores for most of the scales increase for each age group in the manner suggested by Super's model (Thompson et al., 1981).

As noted by its authors, the CDI should be helpful in counseling individuals, in planning guidance programs, and in evaluating programs and research. Locke (1988, p. 179) concluded that the CDI "should yield data

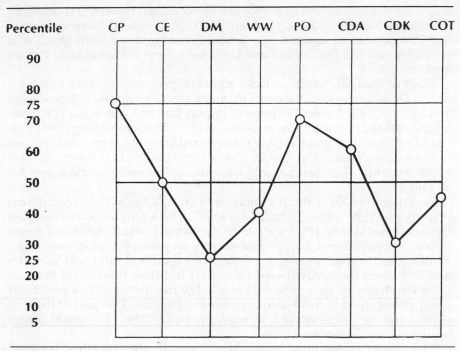

FIGURE 7–1
Career Development Inventory Profile for MJ, a 10th-Grade Female

decidedly useful to high school and college students who desire diagnostic or survey information relating to future educational plans."

Case Example

The User's Manual presents the case of MJ, a 10th-grade female student, to illustrate the interpretation of a CDI profile (see Figure 7–1). The test authors make the following comments about her profile (Thompson et al., 1981, p. 9):

MJ's score on CP is consistent with her score on PO, but inconsistent with her scores on CE, DM, and WW. MJ reports that she has engaged in appropriate career-planning activities and feels knowledgeable about occupations. She has in fact acquired accurate information about her preferred occupational group.

However, her scores show that she does not know as much about the world of work or occupations in general as she reports, that she has engaged in only an average amount of career exploration, and that she apparently knows very little about what to consider in making vocational *choices. Although MJ's profile appears at first sight to be encouraging, careful examination raises important questions, the importance of which is confirmed by her slightly below-average COT score. Her high score on PO may indicate premature specification of an occupation rather than thoughtful selection based on a genuine readiness to choose. Evaluation of her vocational choice in the light of other information (e.g., school record and test scores) may show that her vocational preference is not only premature and poorly grounded but also unrealistic and inappropriate.*

In terms of next steps, the authors suggest a planned intervention that focuses on those areas where MJ showed the greatest need for improvement, including decision-making skills, information about the world of work, and perhaps career exploration. Possible interventions include individual counseling, structured learning exercises, or exploratory experiences.

Career Maturity Inventory (CMI)

The CMI is based on John Crites's (1978) model of career development. According to his model, career maturity encompasses a hierarchy of factors. He hypothesizes a general factor of career maturity similar to the "g" factor in intelligence testing, several group factors, and a large number of specific factors. The group factors pertain to both the process of career planning (attitudes and competencies) and to the content of career planning (consistency and realism of career choice).

The CMI resembles the CDI in its focus on the career planning process variables. It includes a set of scales for both career planning attitudes and career planning competencies in a manner similar to the CDI. It differs from the CDI in regard to the specific scales that it subsumes under each factor.

The specific scales for both parts of the CMI are listed below:

Attitudes Toward Career Decision Making—75 items
- Decisiveness
- Involvement
- Independence
- Orientation
- Compromise
   Total (Screening Form)

Competence In Career Decision Making—100 items
- Self-Appraisal
- Occupational Information
- Goal Selection
- Planning
- Problem Solving

In contrast with the CDI, the CMI includes only one composite score—the Attitude Total scale. The Attitude Total scale can also be administered separately as a 50-item screening inventory.

The CMI has been standardized on students in grades 6 through 12. Separate-sex norms are provided. An adult form of the CMI is also available. Most people complete the CMI within 2 hours. It can be machine-scored or hand-scored.

Crites selected items for the CMI in terms of theoretical specifications and age and grade differentiations. Validity studies show that students in higher grades score higher on the scales than do students in lower grades.

The CMI presents the following advantages: It is based on a carefully constructed theory of career development, it includes a number of specific measures of career development not available elsewhere, and it has been thoroughly researched. In terms of disadvantages, the scales do not sharply differentiate among students in adjacent or nearby grades, the scales lack sufficient reliability to detect small changes in maturation, and the construct validity of the instrument needs elaboration (Zytowski, 1988; Frary, 1988).

USE OF CAREER DEVELOPMENT MEASURES IN COUNSELING

Several guidelines concerning the use of career development measures in counseling are listed below:

1. Use the various measures of career development to determine readiness for career planning. Estimate the client's stage of development both in terms of attitudes and competencies. Plan counseling activities that can enhance the client's level of development.

2. Use items from the career development measures themselves as a means of teaching clients about the different aspects of career maturity. "Teaching the test" can help clarify the meaning of career development and suggest topics for homework.

3. Assign career development measures to clients to stimulate their thinking about career issues. The measures can help focus the attention of clients on matters related to career planning.

4. Assess the clients' decision-making style. Teach the problem-solving model to clients who wish to improve their decision-making ability. Help clients to evaluate career myths or distorted beliefs about careers that may be interfering with their career development (Ellis, 1988; Mitchell & Krumboltz, 1987).

5. Distinguish between indecision and indecisiveness. Clients who are indecisive will probably need personal counseling in addition to assistance for career planning. Use individual items from career decision-making scales as a checklist to identify factors contributing to indecision. Explore these factors in counseling with the client.

6. Administer career development measures to classes or groups of students to help determine needs for different types of educational or counseling interventions. For example, information from career development measures could be used in planning activities for career orientation courses or career exploration counseling groups.

7. Ask students or clients to retake career development measures as counseling or education progresses to assess changes in dealing with developmental tasks. Use career development measures as criteria for evaluating the effectiveness of career counseling programs.

SUMMARY

1. Measures of the career development process include both attitudinal and cognitive factors. These measures are most important for determining the client's readiness for various counseling or educational interventions.

2. The Assessment of Career Decision Making enables counselors to distinguish among different decision-making styles including rational, intuitive, and dependent styles. Counselors should help clients assess the nature and the effectiveness of their preferred style.

3. Several instruments have been designed to detect sources of a client's problems in selecting a career. These instruments can serve as a springboard for discussing critical issues in counseling sessions.

4. Very few instruments have been developed to provide valid and reliable measures of career planning competencies. The Career Skills Assessment Program shows the most promise for this purpose.

5. The Career Development Inventory and the Career Maturity Inventory both provide comprehensive measures of career maturity in terms of attitudes and competencies. They can be particularly helpful in planning and evaluating career guidance programs.

CHAPTER 8

Measures of Work and Personal Values

Counselors and human development professionals often need to help clients to evaluate their motivations in regard to work or other aspects of living. Measures of both values and interests can be helpful for this purpose. Values define what a person thinks is *important*, whereas interests refer to what an individuals *likes* to do. According to Nevill and Super (1986b, p. 3), "values are the objectives sought in behavior," whereas "interests are the activities in which the values are sought." Measures of values are considered in this chapter; measures of interest will be discussed in the next chapter.

VALUES INVENTORIES

Values can be assessed either by a values inventory or a values clarification exercise. Inventories of both work and personal values will be considered in this section.

Inventories of Work Values

The two most popular instruments for assessing work values are the Minnesota Importance Questionnaire and the Work Values Inventory.

Minnesota Importance Questionnaire (MIQ)

The MIQ asks individuals to evaluate 20 different work needs or values in terms of their importance in an ideal job (Rounds, Henly, Dawis, Lofquist, & Weiss, 1981). The 20 needs derive from studies of job satisfaction based on the theory of work adjustment developed by Rene Dawis and Lloyd Lofquist (1984). In the theory of work adjustment, worker satisfaction is predicted by correspondence between worker needs and occupational rewards, assuming that the person has sufficient ability to succeed at the job. The 20 needs have been reduced to six broad factors (called values) by means of factor analysis. Table 8–1 provides a list of the 20 needs, the statement that measures the need, and the six values that summarize the 20 needs.

TABLE 8–1
Description of Scales and Item Content of the Minnesota Importance Questionnaire

Value (Need Factor)	Need Scale	Need Statement
Achievement	Ability utilization	I could do something that makes use of my abilities.
	Achievement	The job could give me a feeling of accomplishment.
Comfort	Activity	I could be busy all the time.
	Independence	I could work alone on the job.
	Variety	I could do something different every day.
	Compensation	My pay would compare well with that of other workers.
	Security	The job would provide for steady employment.
	Working conditions	The job would have good working conditions.
Status	Advancement	The job would provide an opportunity for advancement.
	Recognition	I could get recognition for the work I do.
	Authority	I could tell people what to do.
	Social Status	I could be "somebody" in the community.
Altruism	Coworkers	My coworkers would be easy to make friends with.
	Social service	I could do things for other people.
	Moral values	I could do the work without feeling that it is morally wrong.
Safety	Company policies and practices	The company would administer its policies fairly.
	Supervision—human relations	My boss would back up the workers (with top management).
	Supervision—technical	My boss would train the workers well.
Autonomy	Creativity	I could try out some of my own ideas.
	Responsibility	I could make decisions on my own.

Note. From *Manual for the Minnesota Importance Questionnaire: A Measure of Vocational Needs and Values* (pp. 3–4, 7) by J. B. Rounds, Jr., G. A. Henly, R. V. Dawis, L. H. Lofquist, and D. J. Weiss. Reproduced by permission of Vocational Psychology Research, University of Minnesota, Copyright 1981.

Two forms of the MIQ exist. One contains 190 pairs of items by which the respondent can compare every need with every other need. The other form is a simplifed version that requires the respondent to rank five different needs arranged in 21 sets. Most people prefer the simplified version, which usually takes about 20 minutes to complete. Computer scoring, available through the publisher, is recommended.

The MIQ measures intraindividual variability, that is, its scores show the range of work needs within the individual. The raw scores are converted to z-scores with a mean of 0 and a standard deviation of 1. The z-scores are adjusted for the client's tendency to make a large number of either positive or negative responses so that the scores can be compared with those of other individuals. By means of the adjustment, all negative scores indicate values that are unimportant to the individual, whereas all positive scores indicate needs that are important to the individual.

All profiles are checked for consistency by means of the Logically Consistent Triad (LCT) score. The LCT score shows the percentage of logically consistent answers made by the client. To be logically consistent, one who has chosen item A over item B and item B over item C should rank item A over item C. If the LCT percentage drops to less than 33, counselors should check to see if the client understood and followed the instructions. LCT scores are used in setting error bands for each score to indicate how much the score might change upon retesting.

The MIQ has a fifth-grade reading level; however, it should not be used with individuals younger than age 16. Needs are not well defined for most people until at least age 16.

Work needs as measured by the MIQ can be compared with the rewards or reinforcements provided by different occupations by means of Occupational Reinforcer Patterns (ORPs). The ORPs indicate to what extent different types of reinforcements can be obtained from a particular occupation (Borgen, Weiss, Tinsley, Dawis, & Lofquist, 1968; Rosen, Weiss, Hendel, Dawis, & Lofquist, 1972). An ORP is determined by asking a number of supervisors from an occupation to complete the Minnesota Job Description Questionnaire (MJDQ). The MJDQ lists 20 rewards offered by jobs that match the 20 needs assessed by the MIQ. For example, the work environment for personnel clerks provides the following reinforcements according to supervisors from that occupation (Rosen et al., 1972, p. 104):

- Have work where they do things for other people
- Have a company which administers its policies fairly
- Have steady employment
- Do not have the position of somebody in the community
- Do not tell other workers what to do
- Do not do their work alone

ORPs for representative occupations are listed in the Minnesota Occupational Classification System II (MOCS II) (Dawis, Lofquist, Henly, & Rounds, 1979).

The test authors have organized the ORPs into six clusters based on the predominant factor (value) scores. For example, Cluster A includes occupations that score high on Achievement and Autonomy values and moderately high on Altruism. Sample occupations include Architect, Dentist, and School Teacher.

An individual's MIQ scores are correlated with the ORP for each occupation to determine the degree of similarity between the worker's needs and the rewards offered by different occupations. Correlation coefficients (also referred to as Correspondence or C-scores) above .50 indicate similarity of individual and job characterisitics. C-scores between .10 and .50 show some similarity. C-scores less than .10 indicate no similarity. According to the test authors (Rounds et al., 1981), if the correlation is .50 or greater between an individual's MIQ score and an ORP, the individual stands at least 7 chances out of 10 of being satisfied in that occupation.

Counselors need to be more concerned about profile reliability for the MIQ than they do about scale reliability because of the emphasis on rank order of scores for clients. For most people, the shape of the MIQ profiles will be very similar upon retesting after a few weeks' interval (Hendel & Weiss, 1970).

Research indicates that when individuals work on jobs providing rewards that match their needs, they will be happy. For example, Elizur & Tziner (1977) found that when social workers expressed needs (high social service, responsibility, and variety needs; low compensation, authority, and social status needs) that matched the reinforcements provided by their work, they were more likely to report satisfaction as defined by the Minnesota Satisfaction Questionnaire. Similar results have been reported in other validity studies (Benson, 1988).

Case Example

Kevin, a 29-year-old college graduate in marketing, wished to consider new career possibilities. He had been employed in sales positions since graduating from college 7 years earlier. Kevin sought counseling at a continuing education counseling service at a nearby university. He completed the MIQ during the course of his counseling contacts.

He obtained his highest MIQ scores on the following scales: Ability Utilization = 3.5; Achievement = 2.7; Responsibility = 2.7; and Autonomy = 2.5. His sales position was not enabling him to express these values as much as he would have liked. He especially felt the need to obtain work in which he could make better use of his abilities and obtain a sense of accomplishment.

His scores on the six value factor scales were highest for Achievement (3.1) and Autonomy (2.4). These values match the reinforcements provided by occupations in Cluster A (Achievement-Autonomy-Altruism) in the MIQ scoring scheme. He expressed an interest in the following types of occupations included in this cluster: social services, health sciences, and recreation. He obtained correspondence (C) scores of .79 for Dentist and .71 for Lawyer, both of which he planned to explore in greater detail. The MIQ helped him to identify occupational possibilities that met his work values.

Work Values Inventory (WVI)

The WVI was developed by Super in 1970 for career development research and counseling. Its 15 scales measure the satisfactions desired from work itself (intrinsic values) or satisfactions sought from work as a means to an end (extrinsic values). The 15 values or goals include altruism, esthetic, creativity, intellectual stimulation, achievement, independence, prestige, management, economic returns, security, surroundings, supervisory relations, associates, way of life, and variety.

Each scale contains three items with five response options ranging from 1 (Unimportant) to 5 (Very Important). Most people can complete the WVI in 10 to 20 minutes. Hand scoring requires 5 to 10 minutes. The manual provides separate norms for boys and girls for each grade from grade 7 through grade 12, but no norms for college students or adults.

According to factor analytic research conducted by Bolton (1980), the 15 WVI scales can be reduced to six factors that account for most of the variance. Three of these factors measure intrinsic values (Stimulating Work, Interpersonal Satisfaction, and Esthetic Concerns), and two tap extrinsic values (Economic Security and Comfortable Existence). A sixth factor (Responsible Autonomy) reflects both intrinsic and extrinsic values. Five of the six WVI factors resemble the MIQ factors. In addition, the MIQ contains a status factor, which the WVI lacks, whereas the WVI includes an esthetic factor that is missing on the MIQ.

Inventories of Personal Values

The Study of Values has been used most frequently for assessing personal values (Zytowski & Warman, 1982; Sell & Torres-Henry, 1979); however, it has been some time since this instrument has been revised (Allport, Vernon, & Lindzey, 1960). Two new instruments, the Values Scale and the Salience Inventory, both seem to be promising measures of personal values.

Study of Values

The Study of Values measures the relative strength of an individual's values in six areas: theoretical, economic, aesthetic, social, political, and religious. The instrument contains 45 items that ask respondents to make choices between or among the various types of values. Emphasis should be placed on intraindividual comparisons in interpreting the test results. Because the reading level is somewhat difficult, the Study of Values is most appropriate for college students or advanced high school students. Scores on the scales significantly differentiate among people in different types of settings (e.g., seminary, medical school, business school) in expected directions; however, most of the differences are relatively small.

Values Scale (VS)

Since developing the WVI, Super has collaborated with vocational psychologists from a number of different countries as part of the Work Importance Study to construct both the Values Scale and the Salience Inventory (Nevill & Super, 1986a, 1986b). The VS provides a broader measure of values than the WVI does. It possesses 21 scales, which represent all 15 values measured by the WVI plus six additional values: physical activities, physical prowess, risk, advancement, personal development, and cultural identity.

Each VS scale contains five items with four response options ranging from 1 (of little or no importance) to 4 (very important). All items are prefaced by the phrase, "It is now or will in the future be important for me to . . ." Sample items include "use all my skills and knowledge," "be physically active in my work," and "know that I can always make a living." For each scale (except Working Conditions), at least two of the five items pertain to nonwork situations, and two others pertain to work. Most people complete the inventory in 30 to 45 minutes. The VS, which is intended for people aged 13 and older, requires an eighth-grade reading level. It can easily be scored by hand within a few minutes.

The authors are in the process of developing national and cross-cultural norms for the VS. At the present time, the VS should be used only for intraindividual comparisons; that is, to help clients to determine the relative strengths of their values when compared with each other. It should be used as an interview aid, not as an established measure of personal values.

Salience Inventory (SI)

The SI measures the importance of different life roles for individuals in the context of Super's life-career rainbow model (Super, 1980; Nevill & Super, 1986a). Five life roles are each assessed from three different perspectives. The importance of study, work, home and family, leisure, and community service are evaluated from the standpoint of the individual's participation, commitment, and value expectations. The SI yields 15 scores (five roles × three measures of importance for each role). The instrument, which includes 170 items rated on a 4-point scale, requires about 30 to 45 minutes to complete. It can be hand-scored easily without the use of templates.

The SI provides significant information for counseling. At the present time, the instrument can be used to help clients to assess the relative importance they place on different aspects of their lives. Counselors and human development professionals can use the SI to identify and explore role conflicts within clients or between clients and their environment. The SI can be particularly valuable in aiding clients to take into account cultural differences. Because the SI was developed as part of an international project, it should generate normative data for a wide range of cultures.

The SI and the VS both fall short of acceptable standards for standardized tests in a technical sense, but both instruments can provide valuable assistance to counselors who would like to have a vehicle for discussing values with clients (Harmon, 1988; Zytowski, 1988). The structure provided by such instruments should help clients in values clarification and values implementation.

Use of Values Inventories in Counseling

The following points pertain to the use of all values inventories in counseling:

1. Use a measure of values when a client wishes to clarify work or life goals and objectives. Integrate measures of values with measures of interests in attempting to understand client motivation for work or other activities.

2. Use the scales or factors from a values inventory to provide a meaningful structure by which clients can consider their values. A structure of this sort enables the client to describe the nature of values expressed in various activities.

3. Ask clients to estimate their own profile. Ask them to separate those needs that are most important for them from those that are least important. This approach will teach clients to apply a values structure to their own situation.

4. Try to estimate the client's profile. This type of exercise helps the counselor to become more familiar with both the values inventory and the client. The counselor is forced to organize his or her thinking about the client's values in a systematic fashion.

5. Compare the client's and the counselor's estimates with the actual profile from the values inventory. If they do not match, try to determine the reasons for the discrepancies. Clarify the meaning of both estimated and measured values.

6. To what extent do the values scores agree with the client's experiences? Clients should report satisfaction with previous occupations and activities that provide rewards that agree with their needs and values.

7. Ask clients to interpret individual items in regard to their situation. What do the items mean to them, particularly those items that they may be most concerned about?

8. Look at the relationship between values scores and rewards provided by different occupations or activities. Use the Minnesota Occupational Classification System II (MOCS II) to obtain a list of occupations that provide rewards appropriate to clients' values. If an occupation is not listed in MOCS II, ask clients to estimate the rewards offered by that occupation based on their best judgment. Clients can gather additional information about an occupation or other activities through reading and informational interviews to help them in making these judgments.

9. Consider work values within a larger context of life values. Help clients to consider a range of values that may be expressed within a variety of situations.

10. Use the results from values inventories to stimulate self-exploration. The results should not be used as a basis for decision making except in conjunction with other data that take into account interests, abilities, previous experiences, and opportunities.

11. Keep in mind that values can change. As values or needs are satisfied, other needs that have not been satisfied become more important. Counselors may need to help clients to review their needs as their situations change.

VALUES CLARIFICATION EXERCISES

Values clarification exercises are strategies that enable clients to identify and to make comparisons among their values. Compared with values inventories, they require clients to engage in self-assessment at a deeper level that takes into account actual behavior as well as preferences. The exercises ask clients to review their beliefs and behaviors in response to different situations. They encourage clients to assume a more active role in exploring and expressing their values. They possess all of the advantages of qualitative assessment procedures noted in chapter 1.

Simon, Howe, and Kirschenbaum (1978) provided 79 strategies to help clients to identify and to clarify their values. The first strategy, for example, asks clients to list 20 things they love to do. For each activity, they are then asked to consider when the last time was that they participated in this activity, if it is something that they do with others or alone, how much the activity costs, how important that activity is compared with other activities, how much planning the activity requires, and whether or not this is a new activity for the person within the past 5 years. The exercise requires clients to analyze their activities in terms of the values expressed. A client's values are clarified in terms of what the client does more than by what the client says.

Most career planning workbooks contain several values clarification exercises (e.g., Blocher, 1989; Carney & Wells, 1987; Figler, 1979). The workbooks help clients to integrate information derived from the values clarification exercises with other information about themselves and with occupational information. Typical exercises include the values auction, values card sort, and guided fantasy.

Values clarification exercises can be used in conjunction with values inventories. The scales from the values inventory can provide a structure for analyzing the types of values expressed in one's work experiences or one's career choice. The counselor can then help clients to consider the amount of satisfaction that they have gained (or could expect to gain) from the expression of these values. This type of information should be helpful to clients in career and life planning.

Kinnier and Krumboltz (1984, p. 317) summarized the basic processes underlying most values clarification strategies. These include the following: (a) identify and analyze the specific values related to an issue, (b) examine past experiences, preferences, behaviors, and decisions related to the present issue, (c) investigate how others view the issue, (d) test or confront yourself about tentative choices, positions, or resolutions, (e) find personal environments that are conducive to thinking clearly about the issue, and (f) make a "best" tentative resolution, values statement, or policy and live in accordance with it. They suggest that these procedures be used throughout one's life in a continuous process of values clarification and implementation.

SUMMARY

1. Values refer to one's objectives or goals in work or other settings. Counselors usually assess client values by means of values inventories or values clarification exercises.

2. The Minnesota Importance Questionnaire is the most thoroughly researched measure of work values. Counselors can compare client values with work rewards by means of the Minnesota Importance Questionnaire and the Minnesota Occupational Classification System.

3. Two new inventories by Donald Super and his associates extend the measurement of values to nonwork situations. These inventories enable counselors to assess personal as well as work values and to compare the relative importance of different life roles for individuals.

4. Values clarification exercises require clients to identify and to compare their values with their behaviors. As such, they can be particularly valuable in stimulating exploration and development of client values.

CHAPTER 9

Assessment of Interests

Since 1909, at least, when Frank Parsons published his classic book, *Choosing a Vocation*, counselors have tried to devise ways in which to assess people's career interests. Interest inventories, which ask clients to report their likes and dislikes for various activities, have proven to be particularly useful for this purpose. Four interest inventories that counselors and human development professionals use frequently are discussed in this chapter, together with guidelines for their selection and interpretation.

TYPES OF INTEREST INVENTORIES

Interest inventories can be classified in a variety of ways: by age level, occupational level, or by type of item, for example. In many ways the most useful distinction pertains to type of scale. Two types of interest scales predominate. The first type measures the strength of one's interests in broad fields of activity, such as art, mechanical activities, or sports. These scales are frequently described as *general or basic* scales. They are *homogeneous* in nature because they refer to one type of activity. For this reason they are relatively easy to interpret.

In contrast, the second type of scale assesses the similarity of one's interest patterns with those of people in specific occupations. These scales, usually called *occupational* scales, are *heterogeneous* in terms of item content. The scales include a variety of items that distinguish between the interests of people in a particular occupation and those of people in general. Because of the mixed item content, scores on these scales are more difficult to interpret.

The first type of scale is usually constructed by a rational process. The scales are designed to include items that logically fit together. Examples include Occupational Theme scales and Basic Interest scales on the Strong Interest Inventory. Internal validation procedures such as factor analysis are usually undertaken to ensure that the item content of the scales is relatively pure. Scales of this type usually belong to a closed system of scales; that is, the system includes all the scales that are necessary to represent all the different types of interests (Clark, 1961).

Scales of the second type are based on those items that differentiate between the interests of people in an occupation and people in general.

Item selection depends on an empirical process (observed differences between groups), not on theoretical or logical considerations. External validation procedures such as discriminate analysis are frequently employed to determine the effectiveness of the scales in differentiating between the interests of people employed in different occupations. Empirical scales are usually part of an open system; no one set of scales is established to represent the universe of occupational interests. New scales must be constructed as new occupations emerge or as old occupations change.

Both types of scales contribute to the career or life planning process. Because they are easy to interpret, the basic interest scales can be used in a variety of situations where counseling contact may be limited. The basic interest scales can also be helpful in interpreting the scores on the occupational scales when both types of scores are available. The occupational scales, on the other hand, provide a means of comparing one's interest patterns as a whole with those of people in different occupations. These scales include in a single score the information that is distributed over a number of basic interest scales.

In most cases, counselors should use interest inventories that provide broad measures of interest with high school age or younger students. Not only are such scales easier to interpret, but they also preclude young students from focusing too early on specific occupations before they have had sufficient opportunity to explore different occupations. Inventories that show scores for specific occupations are most appropriate for college students or other adults.

SELECTION OF INTEREST INVENTORIES FOR COUNSELING

Counselors most often use interest inventories to aid clients with academic or career planning. Interest scores can be used to help clients to explore or discover new academic or career possibilities, to decide among various alternatives, or to confirm a previous choice. The scores can also be used for considering ways in which a job might be modified to produce greater job satisfaction or for planning leisure time activities. As indicated by Hansen and Campbell (1985), interest scores can also be used as a catalyst for discussions between client and parents or other significant people in the client's life.

The following guidelines should help counselors and human development professionals to decide when to use an interest inventory with a client. First, counselors should keep in mind that interest inventories measure likes and dislikes, *not* abilities. Most studies show a negligible relationship between inventoried interests and tested abilities (Campbell, 1972). The interest inventories can identify careers or work situations that clients should find satisfying, but they do not indicate how successful the person would be in those settings.

Second, clients should be positively motivated to participate in the assessment process. Clients are more likely to benefit from taking an interest inventory if they express an interest in the results beforehand (Zytowski, 1977). They are also more likely to present an honest picture of their interests or intentions if they clearly understand and accept the purpose for testing (Gellerman, 1963). Large changes in interest scores can occur when clients change the manner in which they approach the test. Sometimes clients answer items in terms of what they think other people (especially parents) would like them to say in regard to their abilities or opportunities. Clients may answer the questions hastily or insincerely, especially if they take the inventory as part of a classroom administration. Test scores will be less valid and reliable under such circumstances.

Third, general interest inventories are of limited value for people who must make rather fine distinctions, such as choosing between civil and electrical engineering. Special purpose inventories such as the Purdue Interest Questionnaire for engineering and technical students (LeBold & Shell, 1986) or the Medical Specialty Preference Inventory for medical students (Savickas, Brizzi, Brisbin, & Pethtel, 1988; Zimny & Senturia, 1976) can provide some assistance in such cases. Under any circumstance, interest inventories must be supplemented with other information about the person and his or her situation, including abilities, values, previous work experiences, and job availability, before a decision is made.

Fourth, interest inventories may be inappropriate for people with emotional problems (Brandt & Hood, 1968). Disturbed people make more negative responses and endorse more passive interests than do people who are not disturbed (Drasgow & Carkhuff, 1964). Personal issues can interfere with decision making. Counselors usually must address the emotional difficulties before career planning can take place.

Fifth, scores on interest inventories can show significant changes for clients who are young or after long time periods (Johansson & Campbell, 1971). As a rule of thumb, counselors should consider readministering an interest inventory if it has been longer than 6 months since the client last completed one. Interests are most likely to change for people under age 20 who have experienced large changes in their situation (e.g., new work or school experiences).

Sixth, interest scores should be particularly helpful for clients who are undecided about their career plans. Research indicates that interest inventories predict occupational membership just as accurately for college freshmen who are undecided as they do for those who are decided (Bartling & Hood, 1981). Interest inventories can be used as a means of identifying a number of occupational possibilities for such students to explore.

Finally, counselors may wish to use an interest card sort instead of an interest inventory if they are interested in the underlying reasons for the client's choices (Dolliver, 1982). The card sort functions as a structured interview. As originally designed by Tyler (1961), clients sort cards with occupational titles on them into piles of "Would Choose," "Would Not Choose," and "No Opinion." They then subdivide the three piles into smaller piles based on their reasons for placing the cards into those piles. This technique helps counselors to understand the reasons for a client's choice. The counselor and the client together look for themes in the client's preferences that can guide the career exploration process. Examples of such card sorts include the Missouri Occupational Card Sort, the Missouri Occupational Preference Inventory, the Non-sexist Vocational Card Set, the Occ-U-Sort, and the Vocational Explorational and Insight Kit (Dolliver, 1982).

POPULAR INTEREST INVENTORIES

Four of the most popular interest inventories used for career or life planning are discussed in this chapter. These measures include the Strong Interest Inventory, Kuder General Interest Survey, Kuder Occupational Interest Survey, and Career Assessment Inventory. Other interest inventories frequently used in counseling will be considered in chapter 10.

Strong Interest Inventory (Strong)

The 1985 Strong is the most recent version of a series of interest inventories that began with the publication of the Strong Vocational Interest Blank (SVIB) by E. K. Strong, Jr., in 1927 (Hansen & Campbell, 1985). The Strong replaces the Strong-Campbell Interest Inventory (SCII), a merged version of the male and female forms of the SVIB, created by David Campbell in 1974 and revised with the help of Jo-Ida Hansen in 1981 (Campbell & Hansen, 1981).

The Strong has become one of the most frequently used, thoroughly researched, and highly respected psychological measures in existence (Borgen, 1988; Layton, 1985; Westbrook, 1985). Counselors at university counseling centers report that they use the Strong more than any other psychological test (Sell & Torres-Henry, 1979). In a recent survey (Watkins, Campbell, & McGregor, 1988), counseling psychologists indicated that they were more likely to select the Strong for a psychological test battery than any other test.

The Strong produces scores on several administrative indexes, three sets of interest scales, and two special scales. Most clients complete the inventory in 25 to 35 minutes. The Strong must be scored by means of a computer program by Consulting Psychologists Press or one of its agents.

A Strong profile for a 21-year-old female college junior is shown in Figure 9–1. Ellen sought counseling for help in considering academic major and career alternatives. Her grade point average was too low to gain acceptance into the School of Physical Therapy, the academic major of her first choice. Ellen's profile will be discussed in the course of considering the different sections of the inventory.

Administrative Indexes

The Strong consists of 325 items separated into seven sections. For each of the items in the first five sections (Occupations, School Subjects, Activities, Leisure Activities, and Types of People), clients indicate whether they *Like*, are *Indifferent* to, or *Dislike* that particular item. The sixth section, Preferences Between Two Activities, requires clients to choose which of two activities they like better. The last section, "Your Characteristics," asks clients to describe their personality by marking *Yes*, *?*, or *No* to various statements (e.g., "Usually start activities of my group").

The Administrative Indexes show the response percentages for each of the seven sections of the inventory. Information concerning the distribution of a client's response percentages is helpful in interpreting a client's interest scores. Most clients divide their responses about equally among the three possible answers for each section.

Ellen was somewhat unusual in her answers in that she marked very few Indifferent responses (see bottom of profile shown in Figure 9–1). She seemed to have stronger opinions about the items than most people, at least for the first four sections of the test. Her interests may be less subject to change than those of someone who marked a large number of Indifferent responses. She also marked a larger percentage of Dislike responses than she did Like responses.

In addition to response percentages, the administrative indexes on the Strong also include Total Responses, which simply shows the number of items that the client answered, and Infrequent Responses, which is used to help determine if the client properly understood and cooperated with the inventory instructions. Ellen's score on Total Responses is 325, which indicates that she answered all 325 items. The profile becomes suspect if this score falls below 305 (Hansen & Campbell, 1985).

A score on the Infrequent Responses scale is of concern only if it falls below zero. This scale consists of item responses infrequently selected (less than 7% of the time) by men or women in the standardization sample. The maximum possible scores on this scale are 8 and 7 for men and women, respectively (Hansen & Campbell, 1985). Infrequent responses by clients are subtracted from the maximum score. Ellen obtained a score of 7 on the Infrequent Response scale—the highest score possible for her sex. This indicated that she made no unusual responses to any of the items. This score supports the validity of her responses.

General Occupational Theme (GOT) Scales and Basic Interest Scales

The Strong contains two sets of general or homogeneous scales: the GOT scales and the Basic Interest scales. These scales have been developed by a combination of logical and statistical means to ensure that all of the items for each scale represent a single type of interest.

The GOT scales provide a summary or overview of the Strong profile as well as a framework for interpreting the other scales. Each of the six GOT scales contains 20 items selected to fit Holland's (1985) descriptions of the six types of occupational personalities. Holland concluded that people could be broadly classified according to six types of interests (or abilities) as shown in Figure 9–2. This figure shows the nature of the relationship among the six categories. The closer the categories are to each other, the more highly they are interrelated.

The 23 Basic Interest scales function as subscales for the six GOT scales. They were grouped into the six GOT categories based on correlations between the two sets of scales. Each of the GOT scales subsumes three or more of the Basic Interest scales except for the Conventional GOT scale. The authors of the Strong speculate that the Conventional category represents a rather narrow band of interests (Hansen & Campbell, 1985).

FIGURE 9–1
Strong Interest Inventory Profile for Ellen, a Counseling Center Client

FIGURE 9–1   *Continued*

PAGE 2

AGE: 21   SEX: Female

DATE TESTED:
Jan 20, 1989

DATE SCORED:
Jan 25, 1989

OCCUPATIONAL SCALES

STANDARD SCORES

SOCIAL

		Standard Scores
GENERAL OCCUPATIONAL THEME – S	30 40 50 60 70	F M
Moderately High (61)		

			Std F	M
SA	(AS)	Foreign language teacher	39	(AS)
SA	SA	Minister	37	40
SA	SA	Social worker	45	44

BASIC INTEREST SCALES (STANDARD SCORE)

TEACHING — Very High (68)

S	S	Guidance counselor	41	49
S	S	Social science teacher	31	41
S	S	Elementary teacher	43	52

SOCIAL SERVICE — High (66)

S	S	Special education teacher	49	56
SRI	SAR	Occupational therapist	44	47
SIA	SAI	Speech pathologist	53	51

ATHLETICS — Moderately High (53)

SI	(ISR)	Nurse, RN	63	(ISR)
SCI	N/A	Dental hygienist	62	N/A
SC	SC	Nurse, LPN	59	60

DOMESTIC ARTS — Average (53)

(RIS)	SR	Athletic trainer	(RIS)	57
SR	SR	Physical education teacher	43	38
SRF	SE	Recreation leader	41	37

RELIGIOUS ACTIVITIES — Average (49)

SE	SE	YWCA/YMCA director	50	44
SEC	SCE	School administrator	32	33
SCE	N/A	Home economics teacher	44	N/A

ENTERPRISING

GENERAL OCCUPATIONAL THEME – E	30 40 50 60 70
Moderately Low (39)	

E	ES	Personnel director	28	28
ES	E	Elected public official	16	16
ES	ES	Life insurance agent	18	11

PUBLIC SPEAKING — Moderately Low (41)

EC	E	Chamber of Commerce executive	21	8
EC	EC	Store manager	21	22
N/A	ECR	Agribusiness manager	N/A	26

LAW/POLITICS — Moderately Low (38)

EC	EC	Purchasing agent	19	14
EC	E	Restaurant manager	13	29
(AR)	EA	Chef	(AR)	24

MERCHANDISING — Low (36)

EC	E	Travel agent	19	37
ECS	E	Funeral director	35	39
(CSE)	ESC	Nursing home administrator	(CSE)	41

SALES — Moderately Low (41)

EC	ER	Optician	26	31
E	E	Realtor	15	20
E	(AE)	Beautician	47	(AE)

BUSINESS MANAGEMENT — Moderately Low (42)

E	E	Florist	31	23
EC	E	Buyer	10	21
EI	EI	Marketing executive	9	21
EIC	ECI	Investments manager	14	15

CONVENTIONAL

GENERAL OCCUPATIONAL THEME – C	30 40 50 60 70
Moderately Low (40)	

C	C	Accountant	28	14
C	C	Banker	29	9
CE	CE	IRS agent	21	32

OFFICE PRACTICES — Average (50)

CES	CES	Credit manager	23	11
CES	CES	Business education teacher	28	23
(CS)	CES	Food service manager	(CS)	38

(ISR)	CSE	Dietitian	(ISR)	50
CSE	(ESC)	Nursing home administrator	41	(ESC)
CSE	CSE	Executive housekeeper	39	31

CS	(CES)	Food service manager	46	(CES)
CS	N/A	Dental assistant	60	N/A
C	N/A	Secretary	36	N/A

C	(R)	Air Force enlisted personnel	39	(R)
CRS	(RC)	Marine Corps enlisted personnel	32	(RC)
CRR	CR	Army enlisted personnel	36	27
CIR	CIR	Mathematics teacher	42	40

ADMINISTRATIVE INDEXES (RESPONSE %)

OCCUPATIONS	39	L %	6	I %	55	D %
SCHOOL SUBJECTS	39	L %	0	I %	61	D %
ACTIVITIES	47	L %	6	I %	47	D %
LEISURE ACTIVITIES	36	L %	3	I %	62	D %
TYPES OF PEOPLE	54	L %	29	I %	17	D %
PREFERENCES	20	L %	47	= %	33	R %
CHARACTERISTICS	21	Y %	29	? %	50	N %
ALL PARTS	38	%	11	%	50	%

CONSULTING PSYCHOLOGISTS PRESS
577 COLLEGE AVENUE
PALO ALTO, CA 94306

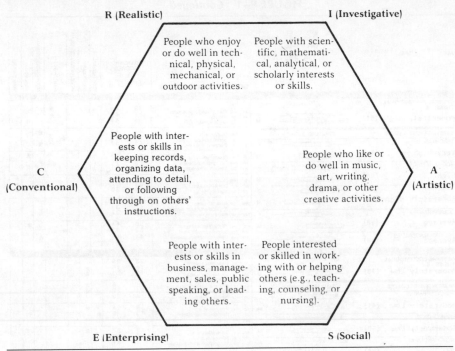

Note. From *Making Vocational Choices: A Theory of Vocational Personalities and Work Environments* (2nd ed., p. 29) by John L. Holland. © 1985. Adapted by permission of Prentice Hall, Inc., Englewood Cliffs, New Jersey.

FIGURE 9–2
Holland's Classification of Personality Types

Both the GOT and Basic Interest scales have been standardized by the use of *T*-scores so that the general reference sample of 300 men and 300 women will obtain a mean of 50 and a standard deviation of 10. The *T*-scores are based on combined-sex norms; however, the test authors provide bar graphs beside the scales on the profile sheet to indicate how the scores are distributed for each sex (see Figure 9–1).

Separate-sex norms are needed because of the large sex differences shown in the preferences for the Strong items. Men and women in the general reference samples differed in their Like or Dislike responses by at least 16 percentage points for 109 of the 325 items on the Strong (Hansen & Campbell, 1985). Men showed greater preference for mechanical activities, military activities, athletics, and adventure; women expressed more interest in domestic activities, art, music/dramatics, and writing. Separate-sex norms make it easier for people to show interest in nontraditional activities for their sex. For example, women who major in science do not express as much mechanical curiousity as do men who major in science, but they are just as successful as men in their coursework (Goldman, Kaplan, & Platt, 1973). If they were held to the same standards of expressed interests as men, they would be less encouraged to enter a scientific field despite the fact that they could be just as successful.

High scores on both the GOT and Basic Interest scales are based on Like responses whereas low scores are based on Dislike responses. If clients make a large number of Like responses, they will obtain relatively high scores on these scales; if they mark a large number of Dislike responses, their scores will be on the low side. Ellen's scores run below average on both sets of scales because she marked a relatively large number of Dislikes (see Administrative Indexes).

A large number of likes indicates broad interests; a large number of dislikes indicates fairly focused interests. In either case, the interest scores should be interpreted in relationship to one another. That is, clients should give careful consideration to their highest scores regardless of their absolute level.

The GOT and Basic Interest scales are highly reliable both in terms of internal consistency and test-retest consistency over extended time periods. Both sets of scales possess a high degree of content validity because of the manner in which they were constructed. The items for each scale were systematically selected to ensure that they would be representative of the interest domain to be measured. Empirical validity studies indicate that both sets of scales effectively discriminate among people employed in different types of occupations (Borgen, 1972; Hansen & Campbell, 1985).

The GOT scores can be used to arrive at a Holland code to summarize a persons's interests. To determine Ellen's Holland code, we must identify her three highest scores on the GOT scales. When we take sex norms into consideration, her highest scores are Social (S), Investigative (I), and Realistic (R), in that order. Therefore, her Holland code is SIR.

The Basic Interest scales are short scales, so scores can be significantly affected by responses to a few items. The scales range in length from 5 to 24 items. The typical (median) scale includes 11 items (Hansen & Campbell, 1985). The Military Activities scale, for example, contains only 5 items, 3 of which pertain to marching.

As a counseling technique, it is usually helpful to ask clients to look at their four or five highest and lowest scores on the Basic Interest scales. Do they agree with this description of their interests? Can they think of ways in which they could combine the activities represented by their highest scores in a career or life plan? Ellen received her highest scores on the Medical Science, Medical Service, Teaching, and Social Service scales. These interests support her desire to enter a health-related occupation.

Occupational Scales

The Strong profile provides scores for 102 Occupational scales for men and 105 Occupational scales for women. The same occupations are represented for both men and women with very few exceptions.

The Occupational scales were developed by selecting items that significantly differentiated between the interests of men or women in the occupation and men or women in general. The typical scale contains 50 to 60 items selected in this manner. Members of occupational criterion groups used to develop the Occupational scales usually possessed the following characteristics:

- Employed in the occupation for 3 years or more
- Satisfied with their work
- Between the ages of 25 and 55 (this excludes both young and old members of the occupation, who may not be typical of the membership in that occupation)
- Belong to a primary professional or business organization associated with membership in that occupation
- Perform typical duties of members of the occupation

The number of people in the occupational criterion groups ranged from 60 to 420. All of the groups exceeded 100 members except for female electricians, female carpenters, and male and female medical illustrators. Information regarding the specific characteristics of each occupational criterion group can be obtained from the Strong *Manual* (Hansen & Campbell, 1985, pp. 105–154).

The Occupational scales have been normed so that men or women in the occupation (depending on which sex was used for constructing the scale) obtain a mean *T*-score of 50 with a standard deviation of 10. Men and women in general obtain mean *T*-scores of approximately 20 to 35 for most scales. Scores of 40 or 45 should be looked upon as "high" scores, that is, as scores that show similarity of interests with those of people employed in the occupation.

Some clients receive few or no high scores on the Occupational scales. In such cases, it is best to interpret the scores relatively. That is, counselors should pay attention to the client's highest scores even if they are less than 40. Research indicates that clients with undifferentiated (or "flat") profiles will usually produce differentiated profiles over time. In a study conducted by Athelstan (1966) on an earlier version of the Strong, 85% of college students who had a flat profile as freshmen obtained a differentiated profile by the time they were seniors. Furthermore, the profile became differentiated in the direction indicated by the freshman scores. Scores that had been only slightly high at that time became significantly higher by the senior year. Students with flat profiles may need additional time and experience to clarify their interests.

Scores of less than 25 on the Occupational scales indicate dissimilarity of interests compared with people in the occupation. Often profiles will contain one or two negative scores that students sometimes find puzzling. A negative score shows that the student obtained a score more than five standard deviations below the mean compared with people in the occupation group. Negative scores are most likely to occur for those Occupational scales with uncommon interest patterns, such as Physicist or Art Teacher.

Separate-sex scales have been established to take into account differences in social conditioning. The Strong printout gives the client's scores for both the male and female Occupational scales, but only plots the score on the Strong profile for the same-sex Occupational scales. Scores on the two sets of scales are highly correlated; but men tend to obtain higher scores on cross-sex scales for occupations that have traditionally appealed to men, such as Army Officer, whereas women tend to get higher scores on cross-sex scales for occupations that women have usually preferred, such as Interior Decorator (Johnson, 1977). Surprisingly, scores on cross-sex scales seem to be as valid as scores on same-sex scales in predicting future occupational membership (Dolliver & Worthington, 1981).

In contrast with the GOT and Basic Interest scales, high scores on the Occupational scales are based on both Like and Dislike responses. People can obtain high scores because they share the same dislikes as people in the occupation as well as the same likes. In essence, high scores on the Occupational scales point to occupations where individuals can pursue those activities they enjoy and avoid those they dislike.

Some Occupational scales include a large number of items with positive weights for Dislike responses. These scales include Bus Driver, Farmer, Fine Artist, Florist, and Marketing Executive scales for both sexes. People in these occupations possess rather narrow or focused interests. If clients mark a large number of Dislike responses, they will probably obtain elevated scores on these scales. On the other hand, high scores on some Occupational scales are influenced primarily by Like responses. These scales include a large number of occupations from the Social, Enterprising, and Conventional categories. Such occupations seem to appeal to individuals with broad interests.

The Occupational scores are highly reliable particularly for older people (age 20 and beyond) and over short time periods (less than 1 year). Even over very long time periods (10 to 20 years), the Occupational scales produce similar results for most people based on research conducted with earlier versions of the Strong (Johansson & Campbell, 1971).

Concurrent validation studies show that the Occupational scales significantly differentiate between people in the occupation and people in general (Hansen & Campbell, 1985). A number of longitudinal research studies have been conducted to examine the predictive validity of the Strong. These studies indicate that between 55% and 70% of the people who take the Strong will become employed in occupations congruent with their high scores on the Occupational scales (Brandt & Hood, 1968; Dolliver, Irvin, & Bigley, 1972; Dolliver & Will, 1977; McArthur & Stevens, 1955; Trimble, 1966; Strong, 1955). Scores on the Occupational scales show greater validity when they are supported by scores on the Basic Interest scales that are most relevant (Johnson & Johansson, 1972).

When Occupational scores agree with expressed interests (career choice stated at the time that the Strong was completed), the predictive accuracy of Occupational scores significantly increases (Bartling & Hood, 1981). When Occupational scores disagree with expressed interests, the latter are more accurate. Expressed interests take into account factors that go beyond the characteristics measured by the Strong, such as values, abilities, and opportunities. McArthur and Stevens (1955), found that Harvard students from upper-class families frequently followed family traditions in choosing occupations (e.g., law, medicine, or business) instead of basing their choices on their measured interests. Counselors should recognize the limitations of an instrument such as the Strong. It provides helpful information about the client's interests, but it needs to be incorporated with other relevant information.

According to several studies, people report greater job satisfaction when their occupation matches the type of occupation suggested by their Strong scores than when it does not; however, the relationship tends to be modest (Brandt & Hood, 1968; McArthur, 1954; Strong, 1955; Trimble, 1966). Presumably, factors other than interests, such as salary, opportunities for advancement, and relationships with supervisors or coworkers, account for much of one's satisfaction or dissatisfaction.

Scores on the Occupational scales can be interpreted by referring to both the GOT scales and to the Basic Interest scales. For example, Ellen obtained "Very similar" scores (55 or greater) on nine of the Occupational scales normed on women. Each of these scales (Radiologic Technologist, Physical Therapist, Respiratory Therapist, Pharmacist, Dietitian, Nurse-RN, Dental Hygienist, Nurse-LPN, and Dental Assistant) pertains to a health-related occupation. The Occupational scores can be readily interpreted in terms of the elevated Social and Investigative GOT scores and the high Medical Science, Medical Service, Teaching, and Social Service Basic Interest scores that Ellen received. These scores help clarify the nature of the occupational interest patterns represented by the Occupational scales.

Special Scales

The Strong includes two special scales that measure personality factors related to educational and career planning. These two scales, Academic Comfort (AC) and Introversion-Extroversion (IE), were both developed by empirical means, that is, by selecting the items that differentiated between the interest patterns of people in identified groups. The AC items differentiated between students who had obtained high grades and those who had received low grades in a liberal arts curriculum at the University of Minnesota. The IE items differentiated between people who had been identified either as introverts or extroverts by means of the Minnesota Multiphasic Personality Inventory.

The AC scale has been used to predict academic level or educational persistence whereas the IE scale has been used to help clients to determine to what extent they may wish to work with people versus things. The AC scale was standardized so that a sample of men and women with PhD degrees would obtain a mean of 60 and a standard deviation of 10. The IE scale was standardized so that men and women in general will obtain a mean score of 50 with a standard deviation of 10 (Hansen & Campbell, 1985).

Scores on both scales correlate highly with scores on the GOT scales. The AC scale holds much in common with the Investigative and Artistic GOT scales, whereas the IE scale overlaps to a large extent with the Social and Enterprising scales (Prediger & Johnson, 1979, p. 37). People who score high (above 50) on the AC scale possess theoretical interests and enjoy learning for its own sake. People who receive low scores (below 40) on this scale evince applied or practical interests and view education as a means to an end. Graduate students in applied fields such as business or counseling often obtain low scores on the AC scale. Scores on this scale can change substantially for students during their years in college. Campbell (1977) reported that scores on the AC scale increased about 10 points for the typical student during 4 years of college.

High scores (above 55) on the IE scale indicate lack of interest in social or enterprising activities; low scores (below 45) show preference for such activities. People who mark a large percentage of Dislike responses will often obtain high scores on the IE scale.

Campbell (1972) noted that the nonoccupational scales "are not simple to use in counseling and *their use should be restricted to professionally trained people who are aware of their pitfalls*" (p. 195, italics in the original). Because of the high correlations with the GOT scales, and because of the danger of misinterpreting the special scales, counselors can usually best interpret the special scales by referring directly to the GOT scales. Ellen's scores, for example, were close to average on these two scales, which coincides with the level of her scores on the related GOT scales.

Interpretation of Client Profile

Much of Ellen's profile has been discussed in preceding paragraphs. As a means of obtaining some focus, we asked Ellen to select the four or five occupations on the SCII profile that had the most appeal to her. We asked her to look particularly at the scales for which she received high scores, but not to exclude any occupations. She chose the following occupations: Physical Therapist, Occupational Therapist, Nurse, Social Worker, and Special Education Teacher. She had obtained scores showing similarity between her interests and those of people employed in these occupations in each case. We then discussed ways in which she could obtain more information about these career possibilities, which included visiting departmental representatives on campus for each of the academic majors in these fields, interviewing people employed in these fields, reading about the occupations in the *Occupational Outlook Handbook* and related materials, and possibly taking a course in these areas or obtaining volunteer work in a related field.

She was pleased to obtain information from her Strong profile that suggested a number of possibilities other than Physical Therapy. The Strong enabled her to evaluate her interests systematically in regard to different career fields, which was the type of information that she needed at the time.

Kuder General Interest Survey (KGIS), Form E

Frederic Kuder developed a number of interest inventories, beginning in the 1930s, that have had a large impact on counseling. The various forms of the Kuder interest inventories, when considered together, are among the most popular assessment procedures used by counselors. The two most widely used forms at the present time are the Kuder General Interest Survey

(KGIS), Form E, and the Kuder Occupational Interest Survey (KOIS), Form DD. Both forms have been revised recently (Kuder, 1988; Zytowski, 1985). The KOIS will be discussed in the next section.

Since 1942, all forms of the Kuder interest inventories have presented items as forced-choice triads. Clients must select which of three types of activities they prefer most and which they prefer least. For example, one forced-choice triad includes the following items: "Repair a broken lock," "Look for mistakes in a typewritten report," and "Add columns of figures." The use of forced-choice triads controls for response styles such as acquiescence (marking *Like* to most items) and deviation (making extreme responses to most items).

The forced-choice item format affects the interpretation of the results. The scores must be interpreted in regard to each other. A high score indicates that the person likes that type of activity more than other activities compared with members of the norm group, but it does not indicate the absolute magnitude of the interest.

The KGIS represents a revision of the Kuder Preference Record-Form C (Vocational), a broad measure of interest patterns widely used by counselors for many years. The reading level required for the inventory was reduced from the ninth grade to the sixth grade so that it could be used with middle school students and with adults who have limited reading ability.

Scales

The KGIS includes the same 10 general interest areas assessed by the Kuder Preference Record-Form C (Vocational). The 10 scales were carefully constructed to be relatively independent of each other. Few of the scale intercorrelations exceed .30. The scales are similar to the Holland scales found on many interest inventories as indicated below:

Holland scales	*Comparable KGIS scales*
Realistic	Outdoor and Mechanical
Investigative	Scientific
Artistic	Artistic, Literary, and Musical
Social	Social Service
Enterprising	Persuasive
Conventional	Clerical and Computational

The V-score (Verification score) can be used to identify answer sheets that may have been answered carelessly, insincerely, or improperly. This scale includes items that are rarely marked by clients who are trying to answer honestly and who have paid careful attention to the instructions. Profiles with V-scores equal to or above 15 should be reviewed with clients for possible problems.

A relatively large number of young people obtain elevated V-scores. According to the manual, 25% of middle school boys and 12% of middle school girls obtain V-scores of 15 or higher. Such scores may reflect immaturity in regard to development of interests. As a general rule, the KGIS should not be interpreted for such students. These students should be readministered the KGIS at a later point in their educational program.

Answer sheets may be self-scored or scored on the computer. One research study indicated that errors were fairly common on self-scored answer sheets (Lampe, 1985). Counselors should check to make certain that hand-scored answer sheets have been scored correctly. Most people can complete the revised instrument in 45 to 60 minutes. Additional time should be provided if students are asked to score their own answer sheets.

The publishers provide supplementary material to aid in interpretation of the results. The *Job and College Majors Charts* (available from CTB/McGraw-Hill test publishers) list a number of occupations and college majors that match the various scales, both singly and in combination.

Norms

New norms for the KGIS were assembled in 1987. Separate-sex norms are used for middle school (grades 6 through 8) and high school (grades 9 through 12) students. The manual states that norms for college students and for adults will be published later. Research with Native Americans indicates that separate norms may be necessary for some minority groups or subcultures (Epperson & Hammond, 1981). The manual encourages test users to develop local norms if they believe that their student or client population may differ from the published norms.

Reliability and Validity

The KGIS scales possess adequate test-retest reliability for most purposes. The median reliabilities are close to .80 for both middle school boys and girls and for high school boys and girls tested twice over a 2-week period.

In a 25-year follow-up study, Zytowski (1974) found that 53% of students tested as 14-year-olds were engaged in an occupation related to their highest scores on the Kuder Preference Record-Form B, an earlier version of the KGIS. He also found that people who were employed in occupations consistent with their interests reported greater job satisfaction than did individuals working in occupations inconsistent with their interests. Similar results have been found in other validity studies conducted with previous versions of the KGIS (Levine & Wallen, 1954; Lipsett & Wilson, 1954; McRae, 1959).

Although the studies mentioned above support the validity of the Kuder instruments, they also show a wide range of outcomes for individuals with similar interest profiles. Zytowski (1974), for example, noted that nearly one third of the students in his sample were employed in occupations that were consistent with their lowest interest scores. Similarly, he found that the majority of the people in his study reported job satisfaction even when they were in occupations not predicted by their interest scores. The interest scores provide valuable information, but they should be looked upon as just one of a number of factors to be considered in academic or career planning.

Kuder Occupational Interest Survey (KOIS), Form DD

In contrast with the KGIS, which uses homogeneous scales to measure interests in broad categories, the KOIS employs heterogeneous scales to assess interests in specific occupations. The KOIS, which was established in 1966, was preceded by the Kuder Preference Record-Form D (Occupational). Kuder had constructed Form D with Occupational scales in 1956 in a manner similar to that used with the Strong Vocational Interest Blank.

Kuder used the same items for the KOIS that appeared on Form D, but radically changed the scoring procedure. Instead of selecting items that differentiated between members of an occupation and people in general, Kuder calculated correlation coefficients (called lambda coefficients) between an individual's responses to each of the 100 triads and the mean responses of occupational members to each of the 100 triads. High lambda coefficients (.45 or better) indicate that the individual's interests are similar to those of people in the occupational criterion group.

Occupational scales based on lambda correlations offer a number of advantages. Not only are they are easier to construct and simpler to interpret than scales based on the use of a general reference group, but they also seem to be more effective in correctly identifying members of different occupational groups. Kuder and Diamond (1979, pp. 29–31) found that lambda scores produced significantly fewer errors of classificiation than did Strong's system in a study that involved the use of both types of scales. In a related study, Zytowski (1972) noted that KOIS scales exceeded Strong scales in avoiding gross errors of classification.

The KOIS has a sixth-grade reading level, but should not be used with students until they are in the 10th grade because of the specificity of the scores. Most people complete the KOIS within 30 minutes. The answer sheets must be scored by computer to calculate the lambda coefficients. The publisher provides an interpretive booklet to aid clients and counselors in understanding the test results. An audiotape that can be used by students to interpret the results is also available.

The KOIS yields five types of scores—dependability measures, vocational interest estimates, college majors, occupations, and experimental scales—each of which is discussed below.

Dependability Indices

The dependability, or validity, measures for the KOIS include the V-score (should be greater than 44), the number of unreadable responses (should be less than 15), and the magnitude of the highest lambda correlation coefficients (should be greater than .39). The V-score for the KOIS was derived in the same manner as the V-score for the KGIS (described above), but the scoring has been reversed so that a low score instead of a high score indicates a possible validity problem. Lambda coefficients less than .40 indicate interest patterns that are not well differentiated. Profiles that have their highest lambda correlations between .30 and .40 should be interpreted with caution. If the highest lambda correlation coefficient does not exceed .30, the profile should not be interpreted at all. Such results can be attributed to chance. Computer-based test interpretations for the KOIS advise respondents of the validity of their reports in terms of the dependability indices.

Vocational Interest Estimates (VIEs)

The VIEs, which were added to the KOIS in 1985, are abbreviated versions of the general interest scales found on the Kuder General Interest Survey. They are called "estimates" instead of scales because of their brevity.

The manual recommends that the VIEs be used to help interpret scores on the College Major and Occupational scales. For example, members of the criterion group for the male High School Counselor scale scored high on the Social Service, Literary, and Science scales. Inspection of the relative magnitude of an individual's scores on these scales should be helpful in interpreting that person's score on the male High School Counselor scale. For the female High School Counselor scale, the highest VIE scores were Persuasive, Social Service, and Literary. Differences between scores on the two High School Counselor scales can be considered in terms of differences of scores on the relevant VIEs.

Although the VIEs profiles are relatively stable for most people, some of the individual VIEs suffer from low internal consistency reliabilities (Zytowski, 1985). For this reason, counselors should be cautious in interpreting the meaning of scores on the VIEs.

Occupational and College Major Scales

The 1985 version of the KOIS includes a total of 98 Occupational scales (66 based on men and 32 based on women) and 42 College Major scales (23 based on men and 19 based on women). New scales need to be added and old scales need to be updated, a process that is currently underway (Jepsen, 1988).

All of the Occupational and College Major scores are expressed as lambda coefficients, which, as described above, show the degree of relationship between one's interests and those of people in different college majors or occupations. The lambda coefficients are interpreted in terms of their rank order. Scales with lambda coefficients that are within .06 points of the highest score (the 99% confidence band) should be given "primary consideration" by clients. All scores within .06 points of each other can be considered to be equivalent. Differences of less than .06 should be attributed to chance.

Men and women are scored on all scales, but scores for the female scales are listed separately from scores for the male scales. Most people will obtain higher scores on scales based on their own sex; however, the rank order of the scores for matching male and female scales will usually be similar (Zytowski & Laing, 1978).

Profile scores show high levels of reliability for both sexes at both the high school and college levels. Median test-retest profile reliabilities over short time periods for the Occupational scales equalled or exceeded .90 for all studies reported in the manual. Zytowski (1976b) also found relatively stable results for college students over a 12-year period.

Kuder studied the validity of the Occupational and College Major scales in differentiating among the interests of 3,000 individuals drawn from 30 "core" occupations and college majors. Two thirds of the 3,000 respondents in his study obtained their highest score on their own Occupational or College Major scale. All but 10% of the total group obtained scores on their own scales that were within .06 points of their highest score (i.e., in their top group of scores). The typical scale showed very little overlap of scores with the other scales. Most overlap occurred with scales that were highly related, such as Clinical Psychologist and Social Caseworker. The scales effectively differentiated among the interests of people engaged in a variety of occupations or college majors.

The scores can also be used to predict future occupation or college major with a fair degree of success. In a 12- to 19-year longitudinal study of 882 high school and college students, Zytowski (1976a) found that 51% of the people were employed in occupations that would have been suggested to them by their KOIS Occupational scores. Approximately 55% of the high school students who went to college majored in a subject that corresponded with their high scores on the KOIS College Major scales. The predictive validities for the two sets of scales compare favorably with those reported for the Occupational scales on the Strong. Zytowski found that the predictive validities for the Occupational scales increased when any of the following conditions were met: (a) the person entered one of the occupations listed on the KOIS profile; (b) the person had a relatively large number of occupations listed within his or her top group of occupations; (c) the person went to college; or (d) the person entered a technical or scientific occupation or high-level occupation.

In a reanalysis of the data discussed above, Zytowski and Laing (1978) found that the male and female scales predicted equally well for both sexes as long as the scores were ranked separately by sex. These results suggest that counselors can use scores from opposite-sex scales for counseling purposes when same-sex scales do not exist.

Experimental Scales

The Kuder Occupational Interest Survey also includes eight experimental scales, which can contribute to research but possess dubious value for counseling. These scales were designed to measure interest maturity (Father minus Son score or Mother minus Daughter score) and the tendency to give socially desirable responses (Men minus Men-Best-Impression scores and Women minus Women-Best-Impression scores). There has not been enough research support for these scales to justify their use in counseling.

Career Assessment Inventory

The Career Assessment Inventory (unofficially abbreviated as "CAI") was constructed in 1975 by Charles Johansson to measure career interests at the technical and skilled trades level. At that time, it complemented the Strong, which was designed to evaluate interest patterns of men and women considering business or professional occupations. Since that time, both instruments have changed. The Strong now includes a number of scales for occupations that require less than a college education. In 1986, the Career Assessment Inventory was expanded so that it now contains a large number of scales for occupations that require a 4-year college degree or advanced training in a professional program (Johansson, 1986).

The Career Assessment Inventory consists of three types of items— Activities, School Subjects, and Occupations—each of which employs a five-step response format (L = like very much, l = like somewhat, I = indifferent, d = dislike somewhat, and D = dislike very much). This type of format, as opposed to a forced-choice format, produces fewer objections from test takers and also permits the collection of large quantities of data that can be interpreted without the difficulties inherent in forced-choice answers. Most of the items (200 of 370) describe various types of activities (e.g., "Work with small hand tools" and "Greet visitors from out-of-town"). The most recent version of the inventory provides brief definitions for each of the items that use occupational titles. For example, the term Biologist is followed by the phrase "Studies plants and animals."

The CAI is patterned after the Strong in most respects. It includes the same types of scales: Administrative indices, Nonoccupational scales (called Special scales on the Strong), General Theme scales (identical to the General Occupational Theme scales on the Strong), Basic Interest scales, and Occupational scales. It differs from the Strong in some of its details, such as the number of scales in each category. It is most different from the Strong in its use of combined-sex norms for the Occupational scales.

Administrative Indices

The Administrative indices (or indexes as they are called on the Strong) include Total Responses (number of items answered out of 370), Response Percentages (percentages of L-l-I-d-D responses for the different types of items), and a Response Consistency scale. The latter scale replaces the Infrequent Response index that appeared on previous editions of the inventory. The Response Consistency scale checks consistency of responses to pairs of similar items (e.g., "Sell life insurance" and "Life Insurance Salesperson"). This scale is scored by subtracting the number of inconsistent responses one makes from a constant. In this way, a negative score can be used to indicate a possible administrative problem. Research indicates that the large majority of profiles obtained by means of random responding can be detected by this method. This scale should help to identify individuals who may be either unable or unwilling to complete the instrument according to instructions.

Nonoccupational Scales

The four Nonoccupational scales all appeared on earlier versions of the CAI. The Fine Arts-Mechanical scale consists of those items that show large sex differences. High scores (T-scores greater than 57) indicate interests in mechanical, skilled trades, and outdoor activities. Low scores (T-scores less than 43) reflect interests in fine arts, cultural, food service, and clerical activities. Johansson (1986) suggested that the scale may be helpful in counseling clients who wish to consider occupations that are atypical for their gender.

The Extroversion-Introversion scale consists of items that correlate highly with other measures of extroversion-introversion. All of the items on this scale are based on "like very much" or "like somewhat" responses. Individuals with a large percentage of such responses will probably score high on this scale. Scores on the scale are highly correlated with scores on the Social General Theme scale.

The Educational Orientation scale is similar to the Academic Orientation scale on the Strong, with which it is highly correlated. It differs in that it is based on those items that differentiate between college-educated and noncollege groups instead of between good and poor students. That is, it was specifically designed to predict educational level instead of academic achievement. Research indicates that the scale effectively differentiates among individuals or occupations at different educational levels. Educational Orientation scores correlate highly with Investigative and Artistic scores on the General Theme scales.

Finally, the Variability of Interests scale, which consists of 25 unrelated items, was created to measure the breadth of one's interests. As with the Extroversion-Introversion scale, all of the items on the Variability of Interests scale are scored in the positive direction. Individuals who mark a large number of "like" responses can be expected to get a high score on this scale.

Scores on the Nonoccupational scales are more difficult to interpret than scores on the other scales of the CAI. Counselors can gain the same type of information regarding clients by studying the Administrative Indexes (especially number of likes and dislikes) and the scores on the General Theme Scales. The latter scores are less subject to misinterpretation than are scores on the Nonoccupational scales. Counselors may acquire some insights regarding clients from the Nonoccupational scales, but in most cases, counseling time can be spent more fruitfully by exploring scores on the remaining scales.

General Theme Scales

As with the Strong, the General Theme scales of the CAI provide a structure for interpreting the other scores on the instrument. The six scales measure the six types of vocational personalities identified by Holland (1985) (see Figure 9–2) that are common to many interest inventories. Each scale contains 25 items.

The scales are relatively pure in terms of their item content. The internal consistency reliablility coefficients for the six scales all exceed .90. Test-retest studies show that scores on the General Theme scales are highly consistent over relatively long time periods for college students and adults.

Basic Interest Scales

The 25 Basic Interest scales provide a means of subdividing the General Theme scales into more specific types of interests. The manner in which this takes place is similar to that of the Strong with a few exceptions. The

CAI includes more Basic Interest scales in both the Realistic and Conventional General Theme categories than does the Strong. The greater emphasis on these categories reflects the CAI's history of attempting to measure technical, skilled trades, and clerical occupational interest patterns.

Even though the scales are relatively short (median length is 11 items), they possess high test-retest reliability. Scores on the CAI Basic Interest scales show high correlations with scores on similar scales on the Strong (Johansson, 1986). The two sets of scales produce similar results.

Occupational Scales

The Career Assessment Inventory yields scores for 111 different Occupational scales. The same scales serve both men and women. Only "core" items that differentiated between the interests of both men and women in the occupation and men and women in general were included on the scales. Items that showed significant differences for only one sex were rejected. For this reason, the scales contain fewer items (median length = 37 items) than do the Occupational scales on the Strong (median length = 56 items). The reliability and validity coefficients are slightly lower than they would be if longer scales were used; however, use of the combined-sex scales greatly simplifies interpretation of the results.

As with the Strong, the CAI Occupational scales have been coded according to Holland's classification system. The two systems produce similar results for comparable occupational scales in most cases.

The Occupational scales have been normed so that people in the occupation will obtain a mean score of 50 with a standard deviation of 10. Scores above 45 represent high scores. Approximately two thirds of the people in the occupation obtain scores of 45 or above. People not in the occupation obtain means of 20 to 30 for most of the scales. Interpretation of the Occupational scores for men and women is aided by bar graphs on the CAI profile that show the middle third of the scores for each sex of people not in the occupation.

Despite the use of fewer items, the CAI Occupational scales seem to be as reliable and valid as comparable scales on the Strong. The CAI scales clearly distinguish among the interest patterns of people employed in different fields. For the typical scale, workers in the occupation average about two standard deviations above the mean of workers not in the occupation. The CAI matches the success of the Strong in this regard.

Because it is relatively new, the CAI lacks the extensive research base that has been established for both the Strong and the Kuder inventories. Nonetheless, it seems to be a sound instrument that has profited from the work conducted on other interest inventories. It has now begun to generate considerable research data in its own right, especially with the 1986 revision.

Case Example

Tom requested counseling to help him decide on a training program. He had already taken some coursework in his community college, but lacked a career direction. The counselor assigned the Career Assessment Inventory to Tom to assess his interests in regard to various career possibilities.

Tom obtained high scores (T-score greater than 57 or 75th percentile) on the Realistic General Theme scale and on each of the following Basic Interest scales within the Realistic field: Carpentry, Athletics/Sports, Manual/Skilled Training, and Mechanical/Fixing. He also received a high score on the Performing/Entertaining scale from the Artistic field. When his likes and dislikes were compared with those of people in different occupations, he obtained high scores (45 or greater) on each of the following scales: Drafter, Painter, Carpenter, Firefighter, Pipefitter/Plumber, Architect, Piano Technician, Card/ Gift Shop Manager, and Surveyor.

After studying his results, he expressed an interest in exploring the following occupations: Drafter, Photogrammetrist or Cartographer (suggested by the Occupational Outlook Handbook *as occupations similar to Drafter and Surveyor), Painter, Carpenter, and Architect. He planned to read about these occupations and to visit with advisers who could provide information about training programs in these fields. The CAI thus helped him to focus his career exploration efforts.*

INTERPRETATION OF INTEREST INVENTORIES IN COUNSELING

Suggestions for interpreting interest inventories to clients include the following:

1. Check to make certain that the client has answered a sufficient number of items and to ensure that the client has understood and followed the directions. Total response and infrequent responses indexes should be helpful for this purpose.

2. Give the interest profile to clients just prior to their counseling session so that they will have time to read the results and formulate questions before meeting with the counselor. Allow clients time to study their printouts in a comfortable place. Clients should come early for their appointments to do this so that they will have ample time to discuss their results and other matters in the counseling session. After a client has studied the printout, follow the steps listed below.

3. Keep the purpose for assigning the inventory in mind. Review this purpose with the client before interpreting the results.

4. Ask clients about their reactions to the inventory before interpreting the results.

5. Note the percentage distribution of Like, Indifferent, and Dislike responses for interest inventories with this type of response format. Remember that high scores on general or basic interest scales are based on Likes, whereas low scores on these scales are based on Dislikes. If clients mark a disproportionate number of any one of the responses, be sure to interpret scores relatively; that is, give greatest consideration to the highest scores, regardless of their absolute level.

6. Interpret the general (homogeneous) scales first. Help clients to de-

termine their Holland code. Use these scales as a framework for interpreting the occupational scales.

7. Use separate-sex norms in interpreting scores on the interest scales. The separate-sex norms take into account the differences in the socialization process for men and women, which can affect the validity of the scales.

8. Interpret the occupational scores as measuring similarity of interest patterns compared with those of people in the occupation. Emphasize that the scores reflect interests rather than abilities. The scores can be used to help predict job satisfaction, but not job success.

9. Do not overinterpret small differences in scores between scales. If *T*-scores fall within 8 to 10 points of each other, do not consider them to be significantly different from each other for most scales.

10. Refer to Dislike as well as Like responses in interpreting high scores on occupational scales. Clients can obtain high scores for some occupational scales simply by sharing the same dislikes that people in the occupation possess.

11. Relate the scores to other information, such as work experience, academic background, career plans, and other test data concerning the client. Work together with the client in attempting to integrate the results.

12. Deemphasize scores on special scales unless these are particularly relevant. The same type of information can be obtained from the general scales in a more understandable fashion.

13. Bring into consideration occupations that are not on the profile by using Holland's occupational classification system (Gottfredson & Holland, 1989). Try to think of occupations that bridge the client's interests. Be sure to actively involve the client in the process.

14. Ask clients to identify four or five occupations suggested by the interest inventory that they would like to investigate. Suggest sources of occupational and educational information, including the *Occupational Outlook Handbook*, career pamphlets, informational interviews, and volunteer work.

SUMMARY

1. Interest inventories differ in the types of scales they use. General scales, which measure interests in different types of activities, provide scores that can be easily interpreted. Occupational scales, which measure the similarity between one's interests and those of people in employed in different occupations, yield scores that summarize one's interest patterns.

2. Counselors should carefully consider the circumstances for assigning an interest inventory to a client. These circumstances include the purpose for testing, the client's motivation for taking the inventory, the client's emotional adjustment, and the availability of other interest scores, among other matters. Card sorts should be used to explore underlying reasons for career preferences.

3. The Strong Interest Inventory, which contains both general and occupational scales based on Holland's theory of career choice, represents

the most thoroughly developed interest inventory for people considering business or professional occupations.

4. The Kuder General Interest Survey, which contains only general scales, is well suited for use with middle school and high school students or for people whose interests are uncrystallized.

5. The Career Assessment Inventory includes a large number of scales for people interested in technical, clerical, or skilled trades occupations. It closely resembles the Strong in the nature of its construction.

6. Counselors should use all of the scales on an interest inventory in combination to understand a client's profile. The administrative scales, especially response patterns, should be reviewed. The general scales should be used to help interpret the occupational scales.

CHAPTER 10

Comprehensive Assessment Programs for Career and Life Planning

Comprehensive assessment programs measure a combination of one's values, interests, and aptitudes. Most programs include a means for identifying academic, career, or social environments that would be compatible with a person's preferences and abilities. Comprehensive assessment programs differ in terms of their emphasis on self-ratings or standardized testing procedures. Both types of programs are discussed in this chapter.

SELF-RATING CAREER AND LIFE PLANNING PROGRAMS

Self-rating career and life planning programs suggest occupations or activities for clients to consider based on the client's self-analysis. They include self-assessment inventories, computer-based programs, and career education workbooks. These programs primarily help clients organize their thinking about themselves and various opportunities. They have been validated primarily in terms of their success in encouraging people to explore various occupations and in enabling individuals to make progress in their career decision making.

Research shows that *informed* self-assessments can predict future performance as least as accurately as standardized tests in many situations (Norris & Cochran, 1977; Shrauger & Osberg, 1981). Self-assessments will be most accurate when clients know specifically what aspects of their behavior are being predicted, when questions are phrased as directly as possible, when the counselor helps the client to recall previous behavior in similar situations, and when clients are motivated to cooperate (Shrauger & Osberg).

Self-Assessment Inventories

Comprehensive self-assessment inventories counselors frequently use include the Self-Directed Search, the Career Decision-Making System, and the Vocational Interest, Experience, and Skill Assessment.

Self-Directed Search (SDS)

The SDS, which is based on Holland's (1985a) theory of vocational choice, can be self-administered, self-scored, and self-interpreted. Although it is sometimes classified as an interest inventory, the SDS is actually an inventory of both one's interests and abilities. Holland refers to it as a career counseling simulation. It consists of sections that ask respondents to indicate their liking for activities (66 items) or occupations (84 items) as well as sections that inquire about competencies (66 items) and abilities (12 self-rating scales). By making comparisons between ratings for similar types of activities, counselors and human development professionals can learn to what extent clients perceive discrepancies between their interests and their abilities.

The SDS can be used with people between the ages of 15 and 70. A special edition, Form E (for easy), should be used by adolescents and adults with limited reading ability (fourth-grade level or above). Most people complete the SDS within 40 to 50 minutes.

Each part of the SDS includes an equal number of items from each of the six Holland categories (Realistic, Investigative, Artistic, Social, Enterprising, and Conventional) as described in chapter 9. Based on the test taker's responses, a three-letter Holland code is derived that can then be compared with the Holland code for various occupations or college majors. *The Occupations Finder*, a booklet that accompanies the SDS, lists over 1,300 occupations according to their Holland code and the amount of education required. Holland codes for each of the 12,860 different occupations defined in the *Dictionary of Occupational Titles* and its supplements are provided in a separate publication (Gottfredson & Holland, 1989). Codes for more than 900 college majors are given in *The College Majors Finder* (Rosen, Holmberg, & Holland, 1987). Finally, two-letter Holland codes for over 750 leisure activities have been published recently (Holmberg, Rosen, & Holland, 1990).

The codes that Holland and his colleagues have assigned to different occupations are based primarily on judgments of job analysts. These codes may differ from the codes assigned by authors of interest inventories based on actual test scores. For example, college or university faculty member is coded as an SEI (Social-Enterprising-Investigative) occupation by Gottfredson and Holland (1989), whereas college professor is coded as an I (Investigative) occupation for both men and women on the Strong (Hansen & Campbell, 1985). In most cases, the codes based on the two types of systems agree. When they disagree, codes derived by means of actual data should be given greater weight.

Unlike most interest inventories, Holland uses raw scores in interpreting tests results. He has been criticized for this approach in that it reinforces sexual stereotypes (Hanson, Noeth, & Prediger, 1977). With the use of raw scores, men are more likely to obtain high scores on the Realistic and Enterprising scales, and women are more likely to score high on the Artistic and Social scales than they would if standardized scores based on separate-sex norms were used. Holland defends his approach because he says it reflects the real world, namely, that men and women are in fact attracted to different types of occupations.

Holland (1987) recommends that the SDS be supplemented with another inventory that he has developed, My Vocational Situation (MVS), which measures aspects of vocational identity not measured by the SDS (see chapter 7). Clients with a clear vocational identity probably need relatively little assistance from counselors. The SDS may be sufficient for such clients. Clients who score low on the Vocational Identity scale (indicating difficulties in self-perception) are more likely to need individual counseling or other interventions, such as career seminars or volunteer experiences, in addition to the SDS. Similarly, clients who show a need for occupational information or who face external barriers to their career development, such as lack of money, parental disapproval of their career choice, or lack of ability to complete a training program, probably could profit from individual counseling. The SDS may also be supplemented with the Vocational Exploration Insight Kit (VEIK) for clients who desire a more intensified assessment (Holland, Birk, Cooper, Dewey, Dolliver, Takai, & Tyler, 1980).

Case Example

Joan, a college sophomore, completed both the SDS and the MVS to help her in career exploration after she was dropped from her academic program on account of poor grades. She had been majoring in biology, with plans to become a dentist, but she had lost interest in this career goal some time ago. She planned to reconsider her career plans during the next 3 to 4 months, then reapply to the university the following semester. According to the SDS, her Holland code was ESI (Enterprising-Social-Investigative). In discussing these results, she indicated that she wished to consider the possibility of pursuing a career in business with an emphasis on the environment. The MVI indicated that she lacked occupational information. She planned to take advantage of the time that she would not be in college to explore this type of career direction by talking with people in the field, reading relevant materials, and obtaining volunteer or paid employment in a related field.

Career Decision-Making System (CDM)

The CDM, by Harrington and O'Shea (1988), asks clients to rate themselves in terms of career fields, school subjects, school plans, job values, abilities, and interests. Greatest emphasis is placed on interests, which are assessed by means of 120 items. Each of the six Holland interest categories are represented by 20 items. Clients score their own answer sheets by simply counting the number of responses in each category. Raw scores (instead of standardized scores) are used in the same manner as in the SDS. (The authors have published a set of norms for the interest scales in the manual for those who wish to use them.)

The results are used to suggest career clusters that clients may wish to investigate. The CDM has received favorable reviews from guidance experts as a system for the delivery of comprehensive career planning services (Bauernfeind, 1987). It is a simple, yet relatively thorough, instrument that is well integrated with the counseling literature.

Vocational Interest, Experience, and Skill Assessment (VIESA)

VIESA (pronounced "Veesa") is a self-scored, short form of the ACT Career Planning Program (described later in this chapter). Level 1 of VIESA should be used with students in grades 8 through 10; Level 2 is appropriate for 11th graders through adults. VIESA has no time limits, but most students can complete all of the exercises in 45 minutes.

VIESA enables clients to assess their interests, experiences, and skills by a series of exercises based on the World-of-Work Map (see Figure 10–1) (American College Testing Program, 1988b). The map shows the relationships among 23 job families grouped into 12 interest fields. The arrangement of interest fields on the map closely resembles that of the Holland hexagon (see Figure 9–2 in chapter 9).

The job families and interest fields differ from each other in regard to two basic dimensions: data versus ideas and people versus things. Each of the exercises for VIESA are scored in terms of these two dimensions. Students use their scores for each exercise to locate on the map those occupations that match their characteristics.

For example, students who express an interest in activities related primarily to people and secondarily to data would be directed to regions 1 and 2 on the map. They would be encouraged to investigate occupations in social and government services, education and related services, and personal customer services (job families U, V, and W, respectively) as ones that fit their interests.

Because of its brevity, VIESA lacks the reliability and validity of the ACT Career Planning Program from which it is adapted. Essentially, VIESA should be looked upon as a "well designed teaching module" that can serve as a catalyst for career investigation and self-exploration (Mehrens, 1988).

Computer-Based Programs

A number of computer-based career and life planning programs have been developed in recent years. These programs assist clients in self-assessment, environmental assessment (i.e., educational and occupational information), and decision making. The self-assessment modules usually ask clients to evaluate their interests, values, and skills. Based on the self-evaluations, the computer generates a list of appropriate occupations.

Two popular programs are SIGI+ (System of Interactive Guidance and Information), a product of the Educational Testing Service, and DISCOVER II, a creation of the American College Testing Program. Both programs are comprehensive, interactive, and simple to use, and both are updated each year. Students and counselors react positively to both programs (Kapes, Borman, & Frazier, 1989).

Research indicates that use of computer-based programs leads to increased retention of career information and to greater certainty of occupational choice (Pyle, 1984). The programs are most effective when they

WORLD-OF-WORK MAP
(2nd Edition)

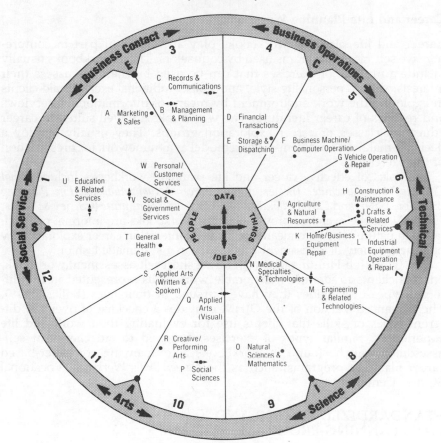

About the Map

- The World-of-Work Map arranges job families (groups of similar jobs) into 12 regions. Together, the job families cover all U.S. jobs. Although the jobs in a family differ in their locations, most are located near the point shown.

- A job family's location is based on its primary work tasks—working with DATA, IDEAS, PEOPLE, and THINGS. Arrows show that work tasks often heavily involve both PEOPLE and THINGS (◄•►) or DATA and IDEAS (⬍).

- Six general areas of the work world and related Holland types are indicated around the edge of the map. Job Family Charts (available from ACT) list over 500 occupations by general area, job family, and preparation level. They cover more than 95% of the labor force.

FIGURE 10–1
World-of-Work Map Used in ACT's Career Planning

are used in conjunction with a counselor (Kapes et al., 1989; Roselle & Hummel, 1988).

Career and Life Planning Workbooks

Career and life planning workbooks play an important part in comprehensive self-rating programs used by counselors. These workbooks usually include a number of exercises that can be used by clients to assess their interests, values, personality style, and skills. Additional exercises aid clients in exploring the work environment by means of informational interviews and reviews of career literature. The workbooks are well suited to career education classes or career exploration groups. They usually employ a decision-making or problem-solving model as a framework for presentation of the exercises.

Examples of effective career and life planning workbooks include *What Color Is Your Parachute?* (Bolles, 1989), *Career Actualization and Life Planning* (Blocher, 1989), and *Career Planning: Skills to Build Your Future* (Carney & Wells, 1987). All of the exercises provided in the workbooks are informal or qualitative in nature. They are meant to stimulate interest in career exploration by offering a variety of assessment procedures in a systematic fashion.

The Quick Job-Hunting Map (QJHM), a short self-assessment workbook, enables clients to identify transferable work skills represented in the different types of activities they have pursued in their lives (Bolles, 1979). The Advanced Version of the QJHM provides a checklist of over 150 different types of skills that clients use for evaluating their work and life experiences. Similar types of exercises designed to aid clients in self-assessment can be found in workbooks accompanying computer-based career planning programs, such as the *Career Skills Workbook* (Vocational Studies Center, 1989).

STANDARDIZED CAREER AND LIFE PLANNING PROGRAMS

As indicated by their name, standardized career and life planning programs employ a series of standardized tests to assess individual and environmental characteristics. Five of the most often used programs—ACT Career Planning Program, DAT Career Planning Program, Vocational Information Profile, Armed Services Vocational Aptitude Battery, and Career Occupational Preference System—will be discussed in this section. These measures are usually validated in terms of work or academic performance.

ACT Career Planning Program (CPP)

The CPP provides a series of measures at two levels (grades 8 through 10 and grade 11 through adult) (American College Testing Program, 1983). The measures include an interest inventory, an experiences inventory, a self-rated abilities report, and timed abilities tests. It is an extended, standardardized version of VIESA described earlier in this chapter. The entire program requires 173 minutes of testing and administration time, which can be divided into three testing sessions if necessary.

The Unisex edition of the ACT Interest Inventory (UNIACT), which serves as the measure of interest, consists of 90 items chosen to represent the six interest fields identified by Holland (1985a). Each of the six fields (Technical, Science, Arts, Social Service, Business Contact, and Business Operations) is assessed by means of 15 items. All items yield equivalent responses for men and women; items that showed significant sex differences were eliminated. For this reason, combined-sex norms can be used. The client's interests are compared with the activities represented in different clusters of occupations by means of the World of Work Map (shown in Figure 10–1).

The Work-Related Experiences Inventory contains six scales that match the six categories of the interest inventory. Sample items from Level 2 of the CPP include "Identified star constellations by name" and "Performed in a variety show." Students answer "Never," "Only once or twice," or "Several times" for each item. Counselors can use this information to review both the depth and the range of experience in situations related to work activities. The experience scales add to the validity of the interest scales. The measured interests of students possess greater predictive validity when they are supported by relevant experiences than when they are not (American College Testing Program, 1988a).

The Self-Rated Abilities Questionnaire asks students to rate themselves in nine broad categories that are difficult to measure with existing tests of abilities. The Abilities Test Battery includes six timed measures of ability: Reading Skills, Numerical Skills, Language Usage, Mechanical Reasoning, Space Relations, and Clerical Speed/Accuracy. Each of the six tests is somewhat speeded. Counselors should take into account the speed at which the student worked in interpreting the meaning of the test scores. Norms have been established for the 8th, 10th, and 12th grades; norms are needed for community college students and adults, however.

The test-retest reliabilities were only moderately high over short time periods (2 to 5 weeks) for secondary school students. The median reliabilities ranged from .76 to .82 for the three types of measures (interests, experiences, and abilities) (American College Testing Program, 1988a). Scores for each scale should be interpreted as falling within one of five categories: high, moderately high, average, moderately low, or low. More precise measurement is not feasible given the level of reliability. In regard to validity, the CPP scores effectively differentiate among individuals pursuing various educational and occupational objectives.

DAT Career Planning Program

The DAT Career Planning Program consists of the Differential Aptitude Tests (DAT) and the Career Planning Questionnaire (CPQ). The DAT, originally published in 1947, was most recently revised in 1981 as Forms V and W (Bennett, Seashore, & Wesman, 1981). It contains eight separate tests: Verbal Reasoning, Numerical Ability, Abstract Reasoning, Clerical

Speed and Accuracy, Mechanical Reasoning, Space Relations, Spelling, and Language Usage. The eight tests, designed for students in grades 8 through 12, require 3 hours to complete. Although all the tests are timed, they function primarily as power tests except for the Clerical Speed and Accuracy test. The tests can be hand-scored or computer-scored. The computer-scored option produces a Career Planning Report with career recommendations.

The CPQ asks students to state their interests in different school subjects, their occupational preferences, and the amount of education they plan to obtain (Super, 1981). Information from the CPQ is used together with the DAT scores to evaluate the student's top three career choices. If a career choice is not supported by educational plans, tested abilities, or school interests, the student is so informed.

The norms were revised for the fourth edition. Members of the norm groups represent students from different parts of the country, different socioeconomic classes, and different ethnic groups. The norm tables have been subdivided in terms of sex and grade. Significant sex differences persist on five of the eight tests. Girls score higher on Language Usage, Spelling, and Clerical Speed and Accuracy; boys score higher on Mechanical Comprehension and Space Relations. For occupations that tend to be dominated by one sex, students use the norm group that matches the sex of most of the people in the occupation (Pennock-Roman, 1988).

The tests possess high internal consistency and alternate form reliability. Test scores are reported as percentile bands that take test error into consideration.

The DAT has been validated primarily in terms of educational criteria. Very few studies have been done involving the use of occupational criteria. Typically, DAT scores have been correlated with course grades from a variety of subjects. In most cases, combined scores on Verbal Reasoning plus Numerical Ability (VR + NA) produce the highest correlations with course performance. Except for Clerical Speed and Accuracy, test scores are highly intercorrelated, so that differential prediction (the goal of the DAT) is questionable.

The validity of the interpretations provided by the Career Planning Report is unknown. These interpretations, which depend on the wisdom of experts in the field, are probably more accurate than those that would be made by most counselors, but no evidence has been produced to support this assumption.

The DAT can also be administered and scored by microcomputer. This version, called the Computer Adaptive Edition (DAT Adaptive), administers only the items that are most appropriate for the student's ability level. By the use of item response theory, the computer is able to eliminate questions that would be too difficult or too easy for the student as the student progresses through each test. When the adaptive version is used, testing time can be cut in half. Research indicates that scores obtained in this manner are just as reliable and valid as scores based on the complete test.

The Psychological Corporation (1990) is in the process of developing a new edition of the DAT (Form C) together with a new interest measure, the Career Interest Inventory, both of which can be used with adults as well as secondary school students. Additional information regarding these instruments can be obtained by writing to the publisher.

Case Example

The Career Planning Report for Richard, a ninth-grade student who se-lected "Business-Administration" as his first career choice, reads as follows:

Most people who do this kind of work have had the amount of ed-ucation you plan to get. Also they have aptitudes like yours. However, the school interests you reported are different from those of most workers in this area. While this occupational choice seems reasonable in terms of your educational plans and tested abilities, you may want to consider some field of work closer to your stated interests. (Psychological Cor-poration, 1987b, p. 181)

Richard, who planned to graduate from college, had stated an interest in technical subjects, mathematics, and biology. His DAT percentile scores ranged from 35th percentile (Spelling) to 75th percentile (Numerical Ability) com-pared with other ninth-grade boys. His Verbal Reasoning plus Numerical Ability (VR + NA) score, which is the best predictor of academic or career success in most cases, was 75th percentile. The Career Planning Report suggested the following career fields as ones that matched his educational plans, measured abilities, and school interests: Business-Analytic, Business-Sales and Promotion, Visual and Performing Arts, and Medically Related.

Vocational Information Profile

The Vocational Information Profile takes advantage of the extensive re-search conducted by the United States Employment Service on career ap-titudes and interests (National Computer Systems, 1984). It provides a well organized and comprehensive report of career possibilities for clients to consider. It integrates scores from the 12 scales on the United States Em-ployment Service (USES) Interest Inventory with scores from the nine scales on the General Aptitude Test Battery (GATB).

USES Interest Inventory

The USES Interest Inventory consists of 162 items arranged in 12 categories (U.S. Department of Labor, 1981). The 162 items describe various activities (e.g., "Draw cartoons for newspapers," and "Diagnose and treat vision problems") that are answered Like, Not sure (?), or Dislike. The items represent all worker-trait groups and occupational groups in the *Dictionary of Ocupational Titles* (Droege & Hawk, 1977). Factor analysis of the original item pool revealed 11 factors for both male and female samples: Artistic, Scientific, Plants and Animals, Protective, Mechanical, Industrial, Business Detail, Selling, Accommodating, Humanitarian, and Leading and Influ-encing. The best items were retained to form interest scales of 10 to 15 items each for the 11 factors. A 12th scale, Physical Performing, was added to represent a small group of occupations that did not fit any of the other 11 fields.

The USES Interest Inventory classification is similar to that of Holland (1985a). The main distinction occurs in extra divisions provided by the USES Interest Inventory for the broad Social and Realistic Holland categories. The similarity of the two systems means that most of Holland's work can be applied to the USES Interest Inventory.

The main advantage of the USES Interest Inventory lies in the ease with which it can be related to the world of work. The same 12 interest fields measured by the USES Interest Inventory are used in the Guide for Occupational Exploration (GOE) (Harrington & O'Shea, 1984) to classify all occupations defined by the *Dictionary of Occupational Titles* (U.S. Department of Labor, 1977).

For some situations, the USES Interest Check List (U.S. Department of Labor, 1979) serves as an alternative to the USES Interest Inventory. The Interest Check List is essentially an interview aid. It consists of 210 sample tasks that have been keyed to the 66 work groups listed in the GOE. It does not require scoring or any type of specialized training to interpret. It is most appropriate for clients who are relatively certain of their career choice. For such clients, it provides an organized structure for them to convey their interests to the counselor. The information provided by the Interest Check List is not as reliable or valid as that provided by the USES Interest Inventory. The counselor should use the USES Interest Inventory with clients who need help in clarifying a career direction.

General Aptitude Test Battery (GATB)

The GATB was first published by the U.S. Department of Labor in 1947 to be used by counselors in state employment services. It is controlled by the federal government, but its use has since been expanded to Veterans Administration offices and hospitals, vocational counseling offices, and high schools and community colleges (U.S. Department of Labor, 1982). Because the battery is used in some settings to select or recommend job applicants for employment, test security is important. Counselors outside of the employment service must have special training and permission to use the battery. In high schools it is sometimes administered to graduating seniors who do not plan on further education and who expect to enter the local employment market upon graduation. In community colleges it is used for counseling and guidance and occasionally for selection into the vocational programs in those institutions.

The battery yields nine aptitude scores based on 12 separate tests. The nine aptitudes comprise three cognitive (general learning ability, verbal aptitude, and numerical aptitude), three perceptual (spatial aptitude, form perception, clerical perception) and three psychomotor (motor coordination, finger dexterity, and manual dexterity) factors.

The tests are highly speeded. Ten of the 12 tests are paper-and-pencil tests; two tests require special apparatus. The battery of 12 tests can be administered in approximately 2.5 hours. The nine aptitude scores are expressed as standard scores with a mean of 100 and a standard deviation of 20. In addition to adult norms, 9th- and 10th-grade norms are also available.

As a result of validity studies conducted by the U.S. Employment Service, cut-off scores have been established for aptitudes that are important for success in various occupations. The cut-off scores have been used to determine occupational ability patterns (OAPs) for different work groups. All of the occupations in the *Dictionary of Occupational Titles* have been classified into 66 work groups, most of which are represented by OAPs. The OAPs have been used for counseling and job referral by employment service agencies and other agencies at which the GATB has been administered. Recent research by the U.S. Employment Service indicates that combined linear scores predict work success more effectively than the multiple cutoff (OAP) scores do (McKinney, 1984). The U.S. Employment Service is currently in a state of transition between the use of the two procedures.

Test-retest or alternate form reliabilities generally range from the .80s to the .90s, with the paper-and-pencil tests yielding higher reliabilities than the dexterity tests. The test reliabilities are affected by both the speed and the accuracy of the respondent. Counselors should be aware that the GATB may not adequately assess the aptitudes of those who, for one reason or another, are unable to work very quickly.

Large numbers of empirical studies have been carried out, with some of them showing substantial validity coefficients for certain types of jobs. The typical validity coefficients fall in the neighborhood of .40. These validities have been obtained for individual tests or for a combination of several aptitudes. Unfortunately, the GATB suffers from the same problem noted for the DAT; that is, differential prediction is limited because of the high correlations among the subtest scores. If clients qualify for one OAP, they often qualify for many others as well.

Keesling and Healy (1988) suggested that clients compare GATB scores with their own estimates of their abilities. If discrepancies occur, the client may wish to consider such matters as (a) how speed may have affected the test results, (b) what type of work or educational experience formed the basis for the self-estimate, and (c) what comparison group was used to make the self-estimate. They believe that the GATB scores help clients to make "reasoned estimates" of their abilities compared with working adults.

Case Example

John B. obtained his highest interest score on the Artistic scale of the USES Interest Inventory (National Computer System, 1984). This scale represents eight specific types of artistic interests as shown in the Guide to Occupational Exploration. *Aptitude for six of the eight artistic fields can be assessed by means of the GATB Occupational Ability Patterns (all but elemental arts and modeling). According to John's GATB scores, he possesses high aptitude for work in visual arts, performing arts (dance), and craft arts. He shows medium aptitude for literary arts and performing arts (drama) and low aptitude for performing arts (music).*

The computer printout for the Vocational Information Profile lists sample jobs for each of the fields for which clients obtain high interest scores and high or medium aptitude. In John's case, sample jobs included sculptor, set designer, industrial designer, choreographer, dancing instructor, dancer, graphic arts technician, patternmaker, artbrush artist, book editor, copy writer, lyricist, stage manager, actor, and narrator for the five artistic fields for which he obtained high or medium aptitude scores. John also obtained high scores on the Selling and Leading-Influencing interest scales. The computer printout listed additional career possibilities for him in each of these areas.

Armed Services Vocational Aptitude Battery (ASVAB)

ASVAB, which is administered and interpreted without charge by representatives of the Armed Services, provides scores on 10 individual scales and seven composite indexes. Test results are used by the military for recruitment and research; school counselors use the results to help students with educational and vocational planning. Testing time, including instructions, takes approximately 3 hours. More than 1 million students complete the tests each year. Besides the aptitude tests, ASVAB also includes a workbook, *Exploring Careers*, containing exercises that help students to identify their interests, values, and achievements. In this sense, ASVAB qualifies as a comprehensive career and educational planning program.

The 10 ASVAB tests and the seven composite scores are shown below (U.S. Military Entrance Processing Command, 1985).

Individual Tests. General Science (GS), Arithmetic Reasoning (AR), Word Knowledge (WK), Paragraph Comprehension (PC), Numerical Operations (NO), Coding Speed (CS), Auto and Shop Information (AS), Mathematics Knowledge (MK), Mechanical Comprehension (MC), and Electronics Information (EI).

Composite Scores. Academic Ability, Verbal, Math, Mechanical and Crafts, Business and Clerical, Electronics and Electrical, and Health, Social, and Technology.

Students receive only the composite scores. Counselors obtain both the individual scores and the composite scores for their students. The ASVAB authors provide extensive supplementary materials that can be used to help interpret the results. Separate norms are available for men and women.

In contrast with the GATB, the ASVAB tests possess sufficient time limits to allow most of the test takers to complete each section. Only 2 of the 10 tests, Numerical Operations and Coding Speed, qualify as speed tests. For this reason, the results can be interpreted in a rather straightforward manner. They represent abilities, as defined by the test content, independent of speed of responding.

According to recent test reviews, the military has significantly improved ASVAB. Earlier versions received negative reports in the professional literature (Cronbach, 1979; Weiss, 1978). A panel of test experts concluded that the recent version of the ASVAB (Form 14) was "highly satisfactory" both in terms of its psychometric characteristics and interpretive materials (Bauernfeind, 1988).

Internal consistency coefficients are high for all of the composite scores that are reported to students; however, counselors should be cautious about interpreting the individual scale scores. Several of the reliability coefficients for the individual scales are low (.50s and .60s), particularly for women.

ASVAB composite scores significantly correlate with success in the areas for which they were designed. However, they lack differential validity. The composite scores are so highly intercorrelated (median intercorrelation = .87) that meaningful distinctions cannot be made among the scores. If students score high on one composite score, they will probably also score high on the other six composite scores. From this point of view, the battery could be substantially shortened (e.g., reduced to Academic Ability composite score) and still be just as predictive of success for most students (Jensen, 1988). Prediger (1987) found that the differential validity of the ASVAB composite scores could be significantly improved by the use of self-estimates of abilities in nine areas (e.g., Leadership/Management, Meeting People, and Creative/Literary).

According to present plans, new versions of the ASVAB (Forms 18a, 18b, 19a, and 19b) will be available in the fall of 1991 (J.G.S. Wiggins, personal communication, July 13, 1990). At that time, the composite score will be replaced by one general ("g") score and two factor scores (verbal and math). The current workbook will be revised to include Holland's Self-Directed Search. As part of the revision, the test authors plan to improve the usefulness of the ASVAB for exploring civilian careers.

Career Occupational Preference System (COPSystem)

The COPSystem includes measures of interests, values, and abilities as follows (Knapp & Knapp, 1986): (a) the Career Occupational Preference System Inventory (COPS) assesses interests in 14 occupational clusters at different educational levels, (b) the Career Orientation Placement and Evaluation Survey (COPES) measures eight personal values related to the work one does, and (c) the Career Ability Placement Survey (CAPS) measures eight abilities that are important for different types of work.

Several versions of COPS have been developed to take into account different grade levels and reading abilities of the clients. COPS itself may be used with seventh-grade students through adults. COPS-II (Intermediate Inventory), a highly visual, simplified version of COPS based on knowledge of school subjects and activities familiar to younger students, may be used with elementary school children or with adults who have a limited reading ability (fourth-grade level). COPS-R (Form R) provides a simplified version of COPS that more closely parallels COPS than does COPS-II. COPS-R requires a sixth-grade reading level. COPS-P (Professional level) provides an advanced version for college students and adults who may be considering professional occupations. The COPSystem probably contributes most to the counseling process by stimulating clients to explore various career fields. It lacks sufficient validity data to serve as a decision-making tool (Kane, 1989).

USE OF COMPREHENSIVE ASSESSMENT PROGRAMS IN COUNSELING

Several recommendations for the use of comprehensive assessment programs discussed in this chapter are listed below:

1. Use self-rating career and life planning programs such as the Self-Directed Search to promote self-examination and career exploration.

2. Provide self-rating career and life planning programs as an alternative to counseling for people who are unwilling or unable to see a counselor.

3. Use standardized career and life planning programs to obtain data to predict an individual's success in an educational or occupational setting.

4. Disregard small differences between test scores on multiple aptitude tests. Use percentile bands to interpret scores; if percentile bands for two scores overlap, ignore score differences.

5. Use combined verbal and numerical ability measures to predict school or job success. Not only is this measure more valid than the other test scores in most cases, but it also shows less sex difference (Pennock-Roman, 1988).

6. Develop local norms for interpreting results, especially if the results are used to estimate performance in local courses.

7. Consider recommendations listed in materials that accompany comprehensive career planning programs, but proceed cautiously. Obtain supporting material from other sources before making any decisions based on these recommendations. Remember that, for the most part, multiple aptitude tests lack differential predictive validity.

8. Use interviewing aids (such as the Career Planning Questionnaire) provided by career planning programs. Although their reliabilities and validities are unknown, they provide a structure that can be helpful in focusing the interview.

9. Help students with low scores consider how they may improve their scores through appropriate coursework or related experiences.

10. Interpret aptitude scores as measures of *developed* abilities. Exposure to the subject matter represented within the test is necessary for the student to perform well on the test.

11. Use nonlanguage tests, such as the Abstract Reasoning and Spatial Relations from the DAT, for students with limited English language skills to determine general ability to learn new material or to perform tasks where knowledge of English is not required.

12. Consult supplementary materials provided by publishers of comprehensive career planning programs. For example, *Counseling From Profiles* (Bennett, Seashore, & Wesman, 1977), provides case illustrations of the use of the DAT Career Planning Program. Use student workbooks to encourage active participation on the part of clients.

SUMMARY

1. Comprehensive assessment programs for career and life planning provide measures of individual values, interests, and abilities that can be compared with the requirements of different educational and occupational environments.

2. Comprehensive assessment programs differ in terms of their assessment procedures. Some of the programs use self-assessments of all characteristics, including abilities. Others use standardized procedures with objective measures of abilities.

3. The Self-Directed Search represents a comprehensive self-assessment career and life planning program based on a well researched theory of career behavior.

4. The CPP and DAT Career Planning Programs provide the most reliable and valid measures of success in educational settings.

5. The Vocational Information Profile (USES Interest Inventory plus GATB) and ASVAB offer the most reliable and valid indicators of occupational performance.

6. The multiple aptitude tests included in comprehensive assessment programs have not been very effective in differentiating among people in various educational programs or occupations.

Section IV

Personality Assessment

CHAPTER 11

Personality Inventories

The term *personality* is often used to cover a very broad concept. When applied to psychological assessment instruments, however, it is used more narrowly to describe those instruments designed to assess personal, emotional, and social traits and behaviors, as distinguished from instruments that measure aptitudes, achievements, and interests. The instruments discussed in this chapter are generally referred to as self-report personality inventories in which respondents check or rate items they believe are most descriptive of themselves.

A description of the different approaches used to construct these inventories is followed by a description of the 10 inventories most often used by counselors and human development professionals.

INVENTORY DEVELOPMENT

There are four different methods by which personality tests have been constructed (Anastasi, 1988). One that uses a deductive approach is the *logical content method*. In this method the inventory author uses a rational approach to choosing inventory items. Statements related to the characteristic being assessed are logically deduced to be related to the content of the characteristic being assessed. The Mooney Problem Checklist is probably the instrument most often used today that utilizes this method. The principal limitation of this approach is that it assumes the validity of each item—that individuals are capable of evaluating their own characteristics and that their answers can be taken at face value. If a client checks an item related to "not getting along with parents," this approach assumes that that person is having parental difficulties.

The second approach is the *theoretical method*, in which items are developed that contribute to scales consistent with traits consistent with a particular theory of personality. After the items have been grouped into scales, a construct validity approach is taken to determine whether the inventory results are consistent with the theory. Two examples of this approach that are based on Murray's theory of needs are the Edwards Personal Preference Schedule (EPPS) and Jackson's Personality Research Form (PRF). Similarly, the Myers-Briggs Type Indicator (MBTI) is based on Jung's theory of personality types.

149

Two methods make use of empirical strategies to develop personality inventories. The *criterion group method* begins with a sample with known characteristics, such as a group of diagnosed schizophrenics. An item pool is then administered to individuals in the known sample and to a control group—usually a normal population. The items that distinguish the known sample from the normal group are then placed in a scale—similar to the method used to construct the occupational scales on the Strong Interest Inventory. Typically these items are then used on another similar sample to determine whether the scale continues to distinguish between the two groups. This method can also be used with groups that present contrasts on a particular trait. For example, members of fraternities and sororities are asked to judge the five most and the five least sociable individuals in their group, and then items that distinguish between these two groups are used in the development of a sociability scale. The Minnesota Multiphasic Personality Inventory (MMPI) and the California Psychological Inventory (CPI) are both based on the criterion group method of inventory construction.

The *factor analytic* method is the second method using empirical strategy in test development. In this method a statistical procedure is used to examine the intercorrelations among all of the items on the inventory. This technique, which can effectively be completed only on a modern computer, groups items into factors until a substantial proportion of the variability among the items has been accounted for by the dimensions that have resulted. An example of this approach is Cattell's Sixteen Personality Factor Questionnaire (16PF), which resulted from a factor analysis of 171 terms that describe human traits and that were, in turn, developed from a list of thousands of adjectives that in one way or another describe humans. The factor analytic method also includes the use of internal consistency measures to develop homogeneous scales.

Researchers using factor-analytic techniques across a number of personality inventories have synthesized personality traits into five major dimensions nicknamed the "Big Five." These five factors are (1) neuroticism—insecure versus self-confident, (2) extroversion—outgoing versus shy, (3) openness—imaginative versus concrete, (4) agreeableness—empathic versus hostile, and (5) conscientiousness—well-organized versus impulsive (McCrae & Costa, 1986). The four dimensions of the Myers-Briggs Type Indicator are related to each of the last four of these factors, but not to neuroticism. The Minnesota Multiphasic Personality Inventory, on the other hand, contains numerous items related to neuroticism and fewer items relating to the remaining four factors.

SELF-REPORT PERSONALITY INVENTORIES

The Myers-Briggs Type Indicator

Work on the Myers-Briggs Type Indicator (MBTI) (Myers & McCaulley, 1985) was begun in the 1920s by Katherine Briggs when she developed a system of psychological types by conceptualizing her observations and readings. Upon finding much similarity between her conclusions and that of Carl Jung, who was working at the same time, she began using his theory. Together with her daughter Isabel Myers, she developed an inventory now known as the Myers-Briggs Type Indicator. The inventory, in its several forms, was slow in gaining acceptance but is now reported to be the most widely used personality inventory outside of clinical settings.

The MBTI is based on Jung's concepts of perception and judgment that are used by different types of people. Each of the several forms of the MBTI are scored on eight scales (four pairs) yielding four dimensions that reflect individuals' preferences for taking in information, making decisions, and their preferences for dealing with the outer world. Jung's theory proposes that apparently random variations in human behavior can be systematically accounted for by the manner in which individuals prefer to employ their capacities for perception and judgment. The MBTI is a self-reporting instrument designed to identify these preferences.

The first of the four dimensions involves the preference for extroversion versus introversion (E-I). Extroverts prefer to direct their energy to the outer world of people and things, whereas introverts tend to focus energy on the inner world of ideas.

The second dimension measures personal preference for mode of perceiving, and is labeled the sensing-intuition (S-N) dimension. Sensing individuals prefer to rely on one or more of the five senses as their primary mode of perceiving. Intuitive people, on the other hand, rely primarily on indirect perception by the way of the mind, incorporating ideas or associations that are related to perceptions coming from the outside.

The third MBTI dimension is designed to measure an individual's preference for judging data obtained through sensing or intuition by means of either thinking or feeling (T-F). A thinking orientation signifies a preference for drawing conclusions using an objective, impersonal, logical approach. A feeling-oriented individual is much more likely to base decisions on personal or social rationales that take into account the subjective feelings of others.

The fourth dimension measures a person's preference for either a judging or perceiving (J-P) orientation for dealing with the external world. Although individuals must use both perception and judgment in their daily lives, most find one of these orientations to be more comfortable than the other and employ it more often, in the same way that a right-handed person favors the use of the right hand. Persons preferring the judgment mode are anxious to employ either the thinking or feeling mode and come to a decision or conclusion as quickly as possible. The perceptive person is more comfortable continuing to collect information through either a sensing or intuitive process and delaying judgment as long as possible. This fourth dimension was not defined by Jung but represents an additional concept of Briggs and Myers. All possible combinations of the four paired scales result in 16 different personality types.

Split-half reliability studies of the MBTI have generally yielded correlation coefficients exceeding .80 and test-retest correlations ranging from .70 to .85. In terms of the four letter types, reliability data tend to be somewhat discouraging in that an individual's four-letter MBTI type has only about a 50–50 chance of being identical on retesting. On the average, 75% of the persons completing the instrument will retain three of the four dichotomous type preferences on retesting.

Although the four dimensions of the MBTI are theoretically indepen- dent, significant correlations in the vicinity of .30 have been found between the S-N and J-P scales. This finding tends to support Jung's theory, which included only the first three dimensions. Other than the relationship be- tween these two sets of scales, the remaining scales are statistically inde- pendent of each other.

A person's MBTI personality type is summarized in four letters, which indicate the direction of the person's preference on each of the four di- mensions. Thus an ENTJ is an extrovert with a preference for intuition and thinking who generally has a judging attitude in his or her orientation toward the outer world. An ISFP type indicates an introvert with a pref- erence toward sensing and feeling who has a perceptive orientation toward the outer world. The manual provides a summary of the processes, char- acteristics, and traits of each of the 16 types.

In computing the personality type, scores are obtained for each of the opposite preferences and then subtracted to obtain the particular type. A large difference between the two scores indicates a clear preference and yields a higher score on that type whereas a smaller difference yields a low score, indicating a preference on that type that is considered less strong and less clear. Even though the difference is small (and the scoring formula eliminates ties), one or the other letter is included in the four-letter code type.

One of the reasons the MBTI is attractive to many individuals is that there are no good or bad scores nor good or bad combinations of types. A score indicates a preference to use certain functions or behavioral pref- erences, although most individuals have the capacity to make use of the opposite preference as well. Each preference includes some strengths, joys, and positive characteristics and each has its problems and blind spots. In the interpretive materials in the manual, as well as in a number of other publications, the strengths, weaknesses, abilities, needs, values, interests, and other characteristics are provided for scores on each of the scales as well as for the 16 types. Resources include *Gifts Differing* (Myers, 1980b), *People Types and Tiger Stripes* (Lawrence, 1982), *Introduction to Type* (Myers, 1980a), *Please Understand Me* (Kiersey & Bates, 1978), *Type Talk* (Kroeger & Thuesen, 1988), and *Applications of the MBTI in Higher Education* (Provost & Anchors, 1987). Answer sheets can also be mailed to Consulting Psy- chologists Press for computer-based interpretations.

The MBTI is used in a number of counseling situations. It is often used to explore relationships between couples and among family members (chapter 13). It is used to develop teamwork and an understanding of relationships in work situations and in vocational counseling by examining the effects of each of the four preferences in work situations. For example, introverts tend to like a work situation that provides quiet or concentration and may have problems communicating, whereas extroverts like variety in action and are usually able to communicate freely. People with strong thinking preferences are interested in fairness and logic and may not be sensitive to other people's feelings. Feeling types tend to be very aware of other people's feelings and find it difficult to tell people unpleasant things. Thus preferences and strengths on the MBTI can be discussed in terms of occupational functions and work environments, although solid validity data for such use still needs to be obtained.

In addition, the manual lists the types of people found in various occupations from a vast data pool of persons in different occupations who have had the MBTI administered to them. Persons with certain MBTI types are found in substantially higher proportions in certain occupations. All types may enter all types of occupations, but certain types choose particular occupations far more than others. For example, although all types are represented among psychologists, 85% of psychologists are intuitive types and only 15% are sensing types, but they are almost exactly evenly split on the introvert-extrovert dimension. The MBTI is seldom used by itself in career counseling, but is often used along with interest inventories and other psychological test results and adds an additional dimension in vocational counseling.

Individuals who are intuitive, feeling, and perceptive seem to be more likely to seek counseling than individuals with other MBTI types (Mendelsohn & Kirk, 1962; Vilas, 1988). There are counselors who administer the MBTI before counseling has begun and make use of the results, along with the knowledge of their own type, in structuring the counseling process for a particular client.

Because of the wide variety of settings in which counselors use the MBTI, no specific list of guidelines for its use or interpretation is included here. However, because of its popularity and seemingly simplistic interpretation of results, it is often administered and interpreted by those who are overly enthusiastic about its use or who have little background in psychological assessment. Counselors who make use of this personality inventory should be aware not only of its strengths and usefulness in various settings, but also its various weaknesses, including ipsative scoring and lack of criterion-related validity studies in certain settings.

The MBTI should not be used to "label" or narrowly categorize people. Although most people have a preferred personality style that they can learn to use to their advantage, they can also learn to express the less dominant aspects of their personality when appropriate. Counselors can teach clients to become more flexible in the manner in which they respond to different situations.

The California Psychological Inventory

The California Psychological Inventory (CPI) (Gough, 1987) was developed for use with relatively well-adjusted persons. Although the MMPI was used as a basis for development of this inventory (194 of the 462 CPI items), the CPI is designed to measure everyday traits that its author, Harrison Gough, calls "folk concepts," such as sociability, tolerance, and responsibility—terms that people use every day to classify and predict each other's behavior.

The content of the items deals with typical behavior patterns and attitudes with less objectionable content than those of the MMPI. The scales are designed to assess personality characteristics and to aid in the understanding of the interpersonal behavior of normal individuals. Thus the CPI is sometimes termed "the sane person's MMPI."

The 1987 revision contains 20 scales that are organized into four separate clusters (see Figure 11–1):

1. The first cluster is designed to assess interpersonal adequacy of poise, self-assurance, and ascendency and contains seven scales entitled Dominance (Do), Capacity for Status (Cs), Sociability (Sy), Social Presence (Sp), Self-Acceptance (Sa), Independence (In), and Empathy (Em).

2. The second cluster contains measures of socialization, responsibility, and character with seven scales entitled Responsibility (Re), Socialization (So), Self-Control (Sc), Good Impression (Gi), Communality (Cm), Well-Being (Wb), and Tolerance (To).

3. The third cluster contains scales measuring intellectual and academic themes useful in educational counseling. The three scales in this cluster are entitled Achievement via Conformance (Ac), Achievement Via Independence (Ai), and Intellectual Efficiency (Ie).

4. The fourth cluster contains a mixed group of three scales that do not fit well together nor are they highly related to scales in the other three clusters. They include Psychological-Mindedness (Py), Flexibility (Fx), and Femininity-Masculinity (F/M).

Of the 20 CPI scales, 13 were developed by the criterion-group method, four by internal consistency analysis (SP, Sa, Sc, Fx), and three by a combination of these two methods (Gi, Cm, and Wb) (Megargee, 1972).

Three of the scales are validity scales developed to detect faking or other test taking attitudes. "Faking bad" is detected by T-scores of 35 or less on the Well-Being (Wb), Communality (Cm), or Good Impression (Gi) scales. Scores on the Communality scale are based on a frequency count of popular responses, with low scores suggesting that the inventory has been taken in a random or idiosyncratic fashion. When a "fake bad" profile is obtained, the counselor should ask why the individual feels a need to create an impression of serious problems. The person might in fact have very serious problems, or might be malingering for some reason, or the low score might represent a "cry for help." The Good Impression scale is based on responses by normal individuals asked to "fake good" to identify persons who are overly concerned about making a good impression. "Faking good" is suggested by a good impression (Gi) T-score of 65 or more with this score as the highest on the profile. Generally most other scales will also show scores in the positive direction, and it can be difficult to differentiate between an individual with an excellent level of adjustment and one who is "faking good." Here an individual's history can usually help the counselor to differentiate between "faking good" and superior adjustment.

Standard scores (T-scores) are reported on a profile with a mean of 50 and a standard deviation of 10 (see Figure 11–1). High scores tend to

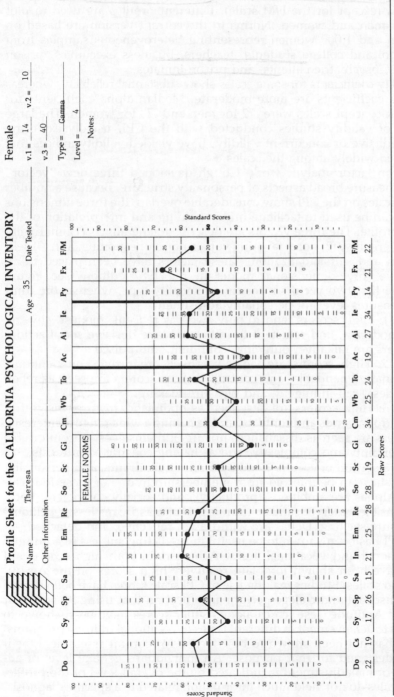

FIGURE 11-1
CPI Profile for Theresa

indicate psychological health and lower scores psychological inadequacy or distress (except for the F/M scale). Different profiles are used to plot scores for men and women. Norms in the current version are based on 1,000 men and 1,000 women representing heterogeneous samples from high school and college students, teachers, business executives, prison executives, psychiatric patients, and prison inmates.

Reliability coefficients for some scales show substantial reliability, whereas for others coefficients are more moderate. Median alpha coefficients for the 20 folk concept scales were .72 for men and .73 for women. The large numbers of validity studies conducted with the CPI, usually exploring either predictive or concurrent validity, have yielded validity indices that have varied widely among the scales.

Based on factor analytic work, Gough developed three new "vector" scales to measure broad aspects of personality structure. Because a number of the 20 scales on the CPI show considerable overlap, the three dimensions (vectors) can be used to facilitate understanding and interpretation of the 20-scale profile. The three vectors are described generally as (1) internality versus externality, (2) norm favoring versus norm questioning, and (3) self-realization and self-actualization. These factors have been placed in an interpretive three-dimensional model in the 1987 edition (see Figure 11–2). The first two vectors measure personality type, whereas the third vector measures levels of personality adjustment.

Vector 1: High scorers tend to be viewed as reticent, modest, shy, reserved, moderate, and reluctant to initiate or take decisive social action. Low scorers are talkative, outgoing, confident, and poised.

Vector 2: High scorers are viewed as well organized, conscientious, conventional, dependable, and controlled. Low scorers are seen as rebellious, restless, self-indulgent, and pleasure-seeking.

Vector 3: High scorers are described as optimistic, mature, insightful, free of neurotic trends and conflicts, and as having a wide range of interests. Low scorers are seen as dissatisfied, unsure of themselves, uncomfortable with uncertainty and complexity, and as having constricted interests.

The intersection of vectors 1 and 2 form four quadrants, and personality characteristics can be inferred from membership in one of these four categories: Alphas are ambitious, productive, and socially competent; Betas are responsible, reserved, and conforming; Gammas are restless, rebellious, and pleasure-seeking; Deltas are withdrawn, reflective, and detached.

The CPI has been shown to be useful in predicting success in a number of educational and vocational areas. Achievers in both high school and college have been shown to obtain relatively high scores on the Ac, Ai, Re, and So scales. Studies making use of CPI scale scores have been shown to predict school and college performance beyond that using IQ scores or Scholastic Aptitude Test scores alone. Other scores have been shown to be related to achievement in different types of vocational training programs. The CPI has not been shown to be effective for clinical assessment, as it was not designed for that purpose. An individual's general level of adjustment or maladjustment is indicated by the overall level of the profile, but the scales do not yield much information related to a specific diagnosis.

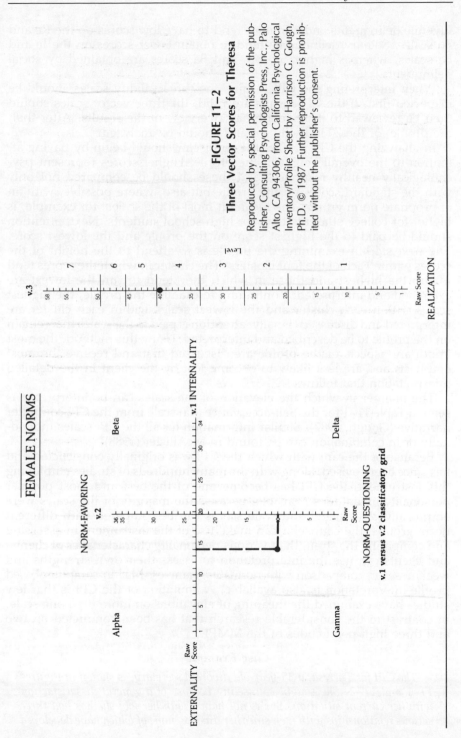

FIGURE 11–2
Three Vector Scores for Theresa

Juvenile delinquents and criminals tend to have low scores on the Re and So scales. Solitary delinquents tend to obtain lower scores on the Ie and Fe scales, whereas higher Sy, Sp, and Sa scores are obtained by social delinquents.

When interpreting the CPI results, the three validity scales should be inspected first. If the CPI results are valid, the three vector scales should then be reviewed to provide a broad overview of the results. After that, the profile for the 20 individual scales should be analyzed.

In analyzing the CPI profile, the counselor should begin by paying attention to the overall height of the profile. Higher scores represent psychologically healthy responses and these should be compared not only with the standard scores on the profile but also, where possible, with an appropriate norm group. The mean on most of the scales, for example, is higher for college students than for high school students. Next, attention should be paid to the highest score on the profile and the lowest score. The next step in examining the profile is to attend to the height of the scores within each of the four clusters. The cluster in which the scores tend to run the highest and those in which they tend to run the lowest are examined and interpreted. Continuing to examine the profile, the highest scales within each cluster and the lowest scales within each cluster are interpreted and discussed. Finally, attention is paid to the scales that remain on the profile to be described and interpreted. Using this method, the most important aspects of the profile are discussed first and receive the most emphasis and are less likely to become lost by the client in the detailed interpretation that follows.

The manner in which the elevation of the scales can be interpreted is seen in Table 11–1 for the Self-acceptance (Sa) scale from the CPI computer narrative (Gough, 1987). Similar information for all the CPI scales individually or in combination can be found in McAllister (1988).

Because of the care with which the CPI was originally constructed and has since been revised, along with the many hundreds of studies employing this instrument, the CPI has become one of the best and most popular personality inventories available. Because the majority of the scales were empirically constructed and scale scores can be compared with different norm groups, the counselor can make use of the instrument in assessing and comparing the strength of various personality characteristics of clients, and clients can use the interpretation to assess their own strengths and weaknesses in comparison with normative samples. Mail-in computer-based profile interpretation is also available. A limitation of the CPI is that few studies have examined the meaning of elevations on more than one scale, in contrast to the considerable research that has been conducted on two and three high point codes of the MMPI.

Case Example

The CPI for Theresa, a 35-year-old divorced secretary, is shown in Figures 11–1 and 11–2. She sought counseling because of a general dissatisfaction with her current situation. She is not happy with her job; she has had three serious relationships with men since her divorce, none of which have developed

TABLE 11–1
Examples of Interpretive Sentences for the CPI Self-Acceptance (Sa) Scale

Score	Interpretation
Above 64.5	Has a strong sense of personal worth, even to the point of being self-centered and egotistic; optimistic concerning personal prospects; articulate and persuasive in dealing with others; socially outgoing and responsive.
59.5–64.5	Is sure of self and at ease in most situations; presents self well; is verbally fluent, versatile in interpersonal relations—can take the initiative or can defer to others.
54.5–59.5	Is at ease and comfortable in most situations; is good at avoiding interpersonal friction and conflict; is usually liked and accepted by others.
45.5–54.5	Is not strongly characterized either by a firm sense of personal worth or its lack; is reasonably self-confident and enterprising; adapts well to most situations; has average or better verbal skills.
39.5–45.5	Is somewhat self-doubting; often behaves in an inhibited and subdued manner; prefers not to engage in direct, personal competition with others; tends to be self-denying.
34.5–39.5	Is anxious when decisions must be made or when action is necessary; tries to avoid any form of interpersonal conflict; doubts own ability and worries about the future.
Below 34.5	Feels inferior to others; either avoids any kind of conflict or gives in; is withdrawn and shy in behavior; sets minimal goals for self and even then often anticipates failure.

Reproduced by special permission of the publisher, Consulting Psychologists Press, Inc., Palo Alto, CA 94306, from California Psychological Inventory/Computer Narrative by Harrison G. Gough, Ph.D. Further reproduction is prohibited without the publisher's consent.

into marriage; and she is often in conflict with her 15-year-old daughter. After graduation from high school, she attended college sporadically for 2 years, earning less than 40 credits and a grade point average of 1.6. She attributes her poor record to a lack of goals and interest in liberal arts subjects and to "too much partying."

The validity scales from Theresa's CPI profile show a tendency to present herself in a negative fashion (Gi = 25). Her personality type, Gamma, suggests self-confidence and social competence together with restlessness, pleasure-seeking, and nonconforming beliefs and behaviors. At level 4 (out of 7 levels) on vector 3 (Realization), she shows average integration and realization of potential. As a Gamma at this level she may feel somewhat alienated from society. At a higher level, she might be seen as creative or progressive; at a lower level, she might be viewed as antisocial.

In general, the scores on Theresa's profile fall near the midpoint, which corresponds with a level 4 score on vector 3. Her two high scores (T-score of 60 or above) indicate that she is "self-sufficient, resourceful, detached" (In) and that she "likes change and variety," that she is "easily bored by routine life and everyday experience," and that she "may be impatient, and even erratic" (Fx) (Gough, 1987, pp. 6–7). Her three low scores (T-score of 40 or below) indicate that she "insists on being herself, even if this causes friction or problems" (Gi), that she is "concerned about health and personal problems; worried about the future" (Wb), and that she "has difficulty in doing best work in situations with strict rules and expectations" (Ac) (Gough, pp. 6–7). Theresa used the information from the CPI together with other information to gain a better understanding of herself and her situation.

The Sixteen Personality Factor Questionnaire

The Sixteen Personality Factor Questionnaire (16 PF) is a personality inventory developed through the factor analytic technique by Raymond B. Cattell and others (Cattell, Eber, & Tatsuoka, 1970). Based on the theory that if a human trait exists, a word in the language would have been developed to describe it, Cattell began from a list of all adjectives that could be applied to humans from an unabridged dictionary and produced a list of 4,500 trait names. These were combined to reduce the list to 171 terms that seemed to cover all of the human characteristics on the longer list. He then asked college students to rate their acquaintances on these terms, and, through factor analysis, arrived at 16 different factors that were developed into the 16 scales.

High and low scores on each of the scales represent opposite characteristics. Thus the scales are labeled by such terms as reserved versus outgoing, humble versus assertive, tough-minded versus tender-minded, and relaxed versus tense. Norms are available based on nine separate norm groups of adults, college students, and high school juniors and seniors, with one set for men, one set for women, and one set for combined-sex groups. Several sets of equivalent forms of the inventory have been developed. In addition, the level has been extended downward to develop a form for junior and senior high school students (the Junior-Senior High School Personality Questionnaire) and another one for use with children aged 8 to 12 (the Children's Personality Questionnaire).

Three different validity scales have been developed, one to detect random responding, one to detect faking good responses (called the Motivational Distortion scale), and a third to predict attempts to give a bad impression (called the Faking Bad scale). Additional adaptations of the 16 PF have been published and promoted for use in marriage counseling, career counseling, and for the assessment of managers.

One approach in using the 16 PF is to compare the client's overall profile with that of typical profiles of certain groups. This approach is aided by the use of computer programs available for such interpretation.

The 16 PF is based on a large amount of research both in the construction of the instrument and in examining its reliability and validity. Test-retest reliability coefficients tend to range from .60 to .85. The reliability coefficients are somewhat low because the scales are made up of relatively few items. A wide variety of validity data are available, including the prediction of academic grades and mean profiles for many groups such as delinquents, neurotics, and for persons in a variety of different occupations.

Eysenck Personality Questionnaire (EPQ)

The EPQ offers a brief, broad, and well-researched measure of personality characteristics (Eysenck & Eysenck, 1975). It yields scores for three personality scales and one validity scale. The three personality scales—Extroversion, Neuroticism, and Psychoticism—measure independent factors that account for most of the variance among different personality measures. The scales were designed to be used primarily with a normal, nonpathological population; however, extreme scores on the Neuroticism or Psychoticism scales usually indicate psychopathology. The Lie scale measures the extent to which a client may have distorted his or her answers to give a good impression. The 90 items on the EPQ describe behaviors that fall primarily within the normal range, not psychiatric symptoms.

For normal clients, the Neuroticism scale can be relabeled as a measure of "emotionality" and the Psychoticism scale as a measure of "toughmindedness." The Lie scale, although it is primarily a measure of dissimulation, also may reflect social naivete.

The EPQ has been validated primarily in terms of factor analysis and related procedures. These analyses attest to the construct validity of the instrument. The statistical analyses show that the scales do represent independent dimensions of personality that are important in describing variations in human behavior. The scales significantly discriminate among different groups (e.g., mental patients, criminals, business leaders, etc.) in the expected manner. The scales possess satisfactory test-retest reliabilities for short time periods and moderately high alpha reliabilities.

Separate age and gender norms are needed. Men score higher on the Psychoticism scale; women score higher on the Neuroticism and Lie scale. Men score higher than women on the Extroversion scale when they are young (less than age 50), but lower than women as they get older. Both sexes obtain lower scores on the Psychoticism and Neuroticism scales as they get older. Scores on the Lie scale are positively correlated with age. A separate form of the EPQ, the EPQ Junior, should be used for younger age groups.

Guilford-Zimmerman Temperament Survey (GZTS)

The Guilford-Zimmerman Temperament Survey (Guilford, Guilford, & Zimmerman, 1978) measures 10 personality factors derived by factor analysis. These factors subdivide into more specific measures (62 different scores can be obtained—the subscales aid in interpretation of scale scores).

The 10 personality factors can be reduced to 4 second-order factors to further simplify test interpretation. These are: (1) Social Activity; (2) Introversion-Extroversion; (3) Emotional Stability; and (4) Paranoid Disposition.

Additional information to help interpret the GZTS scores can be obtained from the guidebook, *Interpretation System for the Guilford-Zimmerman Temperament Survey*, published by the authors (Guilford, Guilford, & Zimmerman, 1976). The book provides "cookbook" interpretations to aid the work of the counselor. Test-retest coefficients are only moderate (.50 over 3 years), indicating that scores can change substantially over time.

Edwards Personal Preference Schedule

One of the better known personality theories is that of manifest needs, as developed by Murray (1938). The Edwards Personal Preference Schedule (EPPS) (Edwards, 1959) was designed to assess those needs. The instrument contains 15 needs, such as Achievement, the need to be successful; Order, the need to have things organized; Autonomy, the need to feel free to do what one wants; and Endurance, the need to keep at a job until it is finished.

The inventory consists of 225 pairs of statements in which each of the items in the 15 scales is paired with each of the items from the other 14. The EPPS uses a forced-choice format in which the subject chooses from each pair of statements the one that is most characteristic of him or her. The paired statements were carefully selected to be equal in regard to social desirability. Although this procedure reduces the influence of the social desirability factor, it does not necessarily eliminate it because social desirabilities of items change when the item is compared with other items in a forced-choice format. In addition, EPPS responses can be faked to yield the desired results when it seems to the subject to be desirable to do so. Because each EPPS statement is paired with each other one, the statements appear over and over again throughout the inventory. Clients often feel the instrument is boring to take, and it seems very lengthy to them. Greater cooperation in completing the instrument can be obtained by warning clients of this fact and pointing out the reasons for the type of format used.

Scores based on both percentile equivalents and *T*-scores are available for large samples of male and female college students and adults. The EPPS is typically interpreted by paying particular attention to the high and low need scores using the description of the Murray needs found in the manual. After the high and low need scores have been discussed, interpretation proceeds to those closer to the mean. It must be remembered that the scores on the EPPS are ipsative in nature. The score represents the strength of a need in relation to the strength of the client's other needs and not in absolute terms. This makes the interpretation of percentile or normative references misleading, as the scores show a comparison of needs for an individual but cannot be compared directly with the strength of needs in others. The percentiles represent comparisons that can be made only within each individual.

Different types of reliabilities generally fall in the range of .60 to .90 depending upon the type of reliability, and vary among the different scales. The ipsative nature of the instrument causes certain problems with regard to validity studies, and the nature of the scales makes it difficult to find external criteria with which to compare EPPS scores, and difficult to handle the scores when reasonable criteria can be found. The format of the EPPS and the problems of interpreting scores confound the problems in making use of the EPPS in counseling situations.

The Personality Research Form

The Personality Research Form (PRF) (Jackson, 1984b) is one of two personality inventories authored by Douglas Jackson that represent a method of test construction using the availability of high speed computers. It also uses Murray's personality theory and yields scores on 20 personality traits. The majority of the scales have labels similar to those of the EPPS. It is designed to be used with normal persons. In addition to the 20 personality scales, there are two validity indices: a Social Desirability scale and an Infrequency scale. High scores on the Social Desirability scale indicate that the clients may be saying socially desirable things about themselves and low scores suggest "faking bad" or malingering by saying undesirable things about themselves. High scores on the Infrequency scale, which is based on items with highly unlikely responses, suggest careless or random responses.

Jackson Personality Inventory

The Jackson Personality Inventory (JPI) (Jackson, 1976) was also developed by Jackson to assess normal personality characteristics but is designed to provide a more practical orientation than the PRF. It consists of 320 true-false items yielding 16 scales measuring traits such as anxiety, energy level, conformity, responsibility, risk taking, and social adroitness. The norms are based on standard scores from a number of college student samples. Each of the 16 scales yields a standard score with a mean of 50 and a standard deviation of 10. The instrument takes approximately 10 minutes to score. High scores represent the traits mentioned by the scales. For example, a high scorer on the Conformity scale is described as susceptible to group influence and pressure and tends to modify behavior consistent with standards set by others. High scorers are described as compliant, agreeing, and cooperative. Low scorers tend not to go along with the crowd and are independent in thought and action. Low scorers are described as individualistic, self-reliant, and contradicting. Reliabilities range from .75 to .95 with a median of .90. Validity data, primarily correlations with appropriate scales on other personality inventories, seem to indicate reasonable validity.

Both of the Jackson instruments represent a contemporary method of constructing psychometrically sound personality instruments, but they are not well known and have not yet received much use in counseling and other applied settings. Jackson has accomplished the construction of psychometrically sound inventories but has not produced the interpretive materials that make them useful in applied settings.

Coopersmith Self-Esteem Inventories (SEI)

Stanley Coopersmith, who devoted a large part of his career to the study of factors related to self-esteem, defined self-esteem as "the evaluation a person makes and customarily maintains with regard to him- or herself" (Coopersmith, 1981, p. 5). He reasoned that people who have confidence in their abilities will be more persistent and more successful in their activities than will those who perceive themselves negatively. He looked upon self-esteem as a global construct that affects a person's evaluation of his or her abilities in many areas. Because of its importance to the individual, in terms both of school or work performance and of personal satisfaction, he believed that counselors and teachers in particular should be aware of deficits in children's self-esteem and that they should be aware of methods for helping to improve self-esteem.

He developed three forms of the Coopersmith Inventory (so-named to avoid influencing responses) to measure self-esteem. The longest and most thoroughly developed form is the School Form. This form, which contains 58 items and six scales, was designed for students aged 8 to 15. An abbreviated version of this form, the School Short Form, was constructed from the first 25 items in the School Form for use when time was at a premium. (The School Form requires about 10 to 15 minutes for most students, whereas the School Short Form can usually be answered in about 5 minutes.) The Adult Form, which also contains 25 items, was adapted from the School Short Form. All items, such as "I'm a lot of fun to be with," are answered *"like me"* or *"unlike me."*

The School Form provides six scores: A total self-esteem score, four scores derived from subscales that measure self-esteem in regard to peers, parents, school, and personal interests, and a score based on a lie scale that checks for defensiveness. The School Short From and the Adult Form yield only one score—the total self-esteem score. Measures of internal consistency show high reliabilities for both the subscores and the total scores. Studies based on the School Form show significant relationships between self-esteem and school performance (Peterson & Austin, 1985; Sewell, 1985).

As a check on the individual's self-report on the SEI, Coopersmith and Gilberts (1982) developed the Behavioral Academic Self-Esteem (BASE) rating scale for teachers to use in evaluating a student's performance in 16 situations. Sample items include "This child is willing to undertake new tasks," and "This child readily expresses opinions." Teachers rate students on a 5-point scale based on the frequency with which they perform the behavior indicated. The BASE provides outside information to check the accuracy of one's self-perception. Counselors can profit from both types of information in helping clients to enhance their self-esteem.

Tennessee Self-Concept Scale

This 100-item instrument yields a number of scales measuring self-concept (Roid & Fitts, 1988). The items assess self-concept in terms of identity, feelings, and behavior on which the items are answered on a 5-point scale ranging from "completely false about me" to "completely true about me." Eight different measures of self-concept are derived in such areas as identity, physical self, moral/ethical self, self-satisfaction, and social self. In addition to the eight self-concept scales, there are two summary scales of total conflict and response defensiveness. The inventory can also be scored for a number of clinical scales with such labels as neurosis, psychosis, and general maladjustment. The instrument is designed for individuals 12 years of age or older and is written at a sixth-grade reading level. A similar instrument designed for younger children is the Piers-Harris Children's Self-Concept Scale, an 80-item instrument designed for children in grades 3 through 12 and written at a third-grade level.

SUMMARY

1. To interpret results of a personality inventory competently, it is necessary to understand both the personality characteristics being assessed and the approach used to develop the various inventory scales.

2. The Myers-Briggs Type Indicator has gained great popularity and is used in many settings in addition to its use by counselors and clinicians.

3. The California Psychological Inventory (CPI) and the 16 Personality Factor Questionnaire (16 PF) are carefully developed inventories with much research backing that assess everyday personality traits.

4. The Edwards Personal Preference Schedule (EPPS) is designed to assess the strength of manifest needs as defined in Murray's Theory of Personality.

5. The Personality Research Form (PRF) and the Jackson Personality Inventory (JPI) are two relatively recently developed personality inventories that use the capabilities of modern computers in their construction.

6. Two inventories useful in assessing self-concept are the Self-Esteem Inventory (SEI) and the Tennessee Self-Concept Scale.

CHAPTER 12

Other Personality Measures and Theories

Techniques used to assess personality include the interview, behavioral observations, and personality inventories, as discussed in the previous chapter. In this chapter three of the most commonly used projective personality measures are discussed briefly because they are seldom used by counselors and human development professionals.

Also described are instruments constructed to assess different environments in which individuals find themselves. The chapter concludes with a summary of the assessment of adolescent and postadolescent psychosocial development.

PROJECTIVE TECHNIQUES

In using projective techniques as a method of assessment, unstructured tasks are presented to the examinee, and responses to these tasks are expected to reflect needs, experiences, inner states, and thought processes. This concept is known as the projective hypothesis—that responses to ambiguous stimuli reflect a person's basic personality. Examinee responses are usually in the form of completed sentences, associations, or descriptive or storytelling responses (Anastasi, 1988).

Because there is an infinite variety of possible responses to ambiguous stimuli, no particular conclusion can be drawn from any single response. Responses may be classified, however, and from a number of responses general impressions and inferences regarding a person's personality may be derived. The administration and scoring of most projective instruments requires considerable training and experience on the part of the examiner. The scoring process may be quite complex or subjective. In addition, even highly experienced examiners frequently disagree in the interpretations and inferences drawn from projective data.

The Rorschach Ink Blot Test

The most widely used projective test has been the Rorschach Ink Blot Test (Goldfried, Stricker, & Weiner, 1971), developed in 1921 by Hermann Rorschach, a Swiss psychiatrist. Placing ink on a piece of paper and folding the paper to form ink blots, he asked people to say what images the ink blots suggested to them and used the responses to assess personality. A series of 10 ink blots have become the standardized stimuli, some of them in gray and several with combinations of colors. Several different methods of administration have been developed, along with various methods to score the responses. Responses are classified and scored according to such criteria as the location of the response on the ink blot, the feature that determined the response, and the content of the response. Traditional methods of measures of reliability and validity are difficult to apply to the Rorschach and other projective instruments, if in fact they are applicable at all. For a number of psychometric reasons, theoretical reasons, and the large amount of time, effort, and experience necessary to interpret the results of this instrument adequately, counselors seldom use the Rorschach Ink Blot Test.

Thematic Apperception Test

The Thematic Apperception Test (TAT) (Murray, 1943) was developed by Christina Morgan and Henry Murray based on Murray's theory of needs. It consists of 30 black-and-white picture cards, most containing one or more human figures, and one completely blank card. Twenty of the 30 cards are presented in a test administration, the selection of the 20 depending on the age and sex of the examinee. The examinee is asked to make up a story about each picture and to include what is currently happening in the picture, what lead up to that situation, how the people in the story feel, and how the story ends. If examinees fail to include any of these elements, they are asked to fill in the information after the initial story has been completed.

When the entire test is administered, it is usually broken down into two sessions on two different days with 10 cards administered at each session. The cards that illustrate more threatening material are usually included in the second session. Many of those who use the TAT do not use all 20 cards but select 10 or 12 of them and administer them in a single session. The TAT is usually not scored in any objective fashion, but the frequency of various themes, the intensity and duration of the stories, and the outcomes are taken into account. It is assumed that the hero in the story is the person with whom the examinee identifies, and the assumption in interpreting the results is that examinees reveal their conflicts, experiences, needs, and strivings in their storytelling responses. The TAT is widely used and has many supporters but has been attacked primarily on psychometric grounds. Subjective interpretations of TAT results often result in different or opposite conclusions even by experienced users. Instead of administering the entire TAT, counselors often select a few cards for use in an early interview. The cards can be used as a method of initially gaining rapport and as a method of encouraging the client to open up and talk during the counseling session. At the same time, the storytelling responses can yield considerable insight into the needs and personality of the client.

The Rotter Incomplete Sentence Blank

In the sentence completion technique, a person is asked to complete a number of sentence fragments that are related to possible conflicts or emotions. The most popular sentence completion test is the Rotter Incomplete Sentence Blank (Rotter & Rafferty, 1950), which consists of 40 sentence fragments. Most of them are written in the first person such as "My mother. . . ." or "What bothers me most is. . . ." There are three forms, one for high school, one for college, and one for adults, and it is expected that attitudes, traits, and emotions will be expressed in the responses. The responses are then scored on a continuum of 6 to 0, from unhealthy or maladjusted through neutral, to healthy or positive responses. Higher scores thus suggest greater maladjustment.

Because sentence fragments are easy to construct, counselors often develop their own incomplete sentence instruments to deal with various types of conflicts and problems presented by clients. Thus one counselor-constructed incomplete sentence instrument will deal with problems and conflicts revolving around educational/vocational decision making, another might deal with family conflicts, another deal with interpersonal conflicts, and yet another with school difficulties.

PERSON-ENVIRONMENT INTERACTION

Other influences on personality include both environmental and developmental factors. Several theories have been advanced regarding the effect of interaction with the environment on persons, and several others regarding the developmental changes that occur as an individual moves through various life stages. Instruments designed to assess the effect of these influences and to substantiate the relevant theories have been constructed, but at this point they are not yet ready for use in individual counseling. Nevertheless, these two concepts are important for counselors to take into consideration in their work with individuals and groups, and several examples of theories related to these concepts are presented.

Almost all of the developments in the field of applied psychology on which the field of counseling is based have concentrated on the individual and the individual's specific traits, states, aptitudes, and attitudes. Little attention has been paid to the environments in which individuals function. Certain behavioral settings have a very strong and often coercive influence on individuals, and it is necessary to pay particular attention to the perceived situations and environments that influence human behavior. The emphasis thus far has been an attempt to assess the environment and thereby help people to understand and organize their behavior in the social environments in which they find themselves, in order to behave more effectively. Several theories have been developed that emphasize the importance of the environment to the way that individuals think and behave. They emphasize the value that can often result from changes in the environment, as opposed to the more typical counseling approach of assisting the individual to adapt to the situation.

Person-environment interaction theories are usually based on the work of Kurt Lewin (1935) and his famous formula B = f(PE), in which behavior (B) is a function (f) of the interaction of the person (P) and the environment (E). Thus an individual's behavior is seen as a function of the interaction between the person and his or her environment. These theories give particular attention to the environment portion of this formula, emphasizing the important role that environments play in shaping behavior. Another theorist (Barker, 1968) maintained that individuals tend to behave in similar ways in similar environments even though, as individuals, they differ from each other in many important ways. He pointed out that human environments often have a coercive effect on behavior. Environmental or situational variables are seen as the primary influences on behavior, with individuals behaving in a variety ways depending on the social environments in which they find themselves.

Holland's theory of vocational choice was discussed in a previous chapter. In his theory, human behavior is a function of the interaction between personality and environment, and the choice of a vocation is in part an expression of personality. The ways people think about occupations and vocational stereotypes influence vocational preferences. People with particular personality types create the environments within these occupations, and thus the process is a circular one. People in each of Holland's six personality and environmental types create an atmosphere that reflects that type, and people search out and choose environments where their interests, attitudes, and personalities fit. Their behavior is thus determined by an interaction between their personality and their environment. Individuals choose environments because of their personalities and remain in these environments because of the reinforcements and satisfactions they obtain in these environments.

Several researchers have developed instruments to use in the assessment of different environments. Rudolph Moos (1974) studied social climates in such widely varying institutions as hospitals, military companies, nursing homes, school classrooms, and university student living units. He developed a series of inventories to assess the psychosocial dimensions of environment in these settings. His scales provide information about how those in a particular psychosocial environment perceive that environment. The inventories can be used to compare perceptions of different environments over time or to evaluate how individuals or groups of people differ in their perceptions of an environment.

One of Moos's findings was that the social environments in a variety of settings can be described by common sets of dimensions. These dimensions generally fall under three categories. The relationship dimension refers to the extent to which individuals are involved in the setting, the extent to which they generally support and help each other, and the extent to which they feel able to express themselves. The personal growth dimension includes the extent to which personal growth and self-enhancement occur within the basic functions of the setting. The third dimension is that of system maintenance or change and includes the extent to which the environment is structured and expectations are clear, the extent to which control is maintained in the setting, and how changes can occur.

Individuals are usually more satisfied and successful in those environments where positive social climates exist. For example, workers report greater job satisfaction in work settings, patients are more satisfied and less depressed in psychiatric settings, and students are more interested and engaged in their course materials in educational settings (Moos, 1976b).

Pace has developed an instrument designed to measure college environments called the College and University Environment Scale (CUES) (1969) composed of seven scales on which environments of colleges and universities differ from one another. They are:

1. Practicality—Environment emphasizes enterprise, organization, material benefits, and social activities.
2. Community—Describes a friendly, cohesive, group-oriented campus.
3. Awareness—Emphasizes concern about personal and political meanings, questioning and assent, creativity, and tolerance of nonconformity.
4. Propriety—Describes a polite, decorous, considerate atmosphere on the campus.
5. Scholarship—Campus environment emphasizes academic achievement and scholarship.
6. Campus Morale—Emphasizes acceptance of social norms, group cohesiveness, commitment to intellectual pursuits, and freedom of expression. (Items overlap with other scales.)
7. Quality of Teaching and Faculty-Student Relationships—Describes a scholarly faculty with high standards but adaptable and flexible. (Items overlap with other scales.)

PSYCHOSOCIAL THEORIES

Young people develop in psychosocial areas, and various psychosocial developmental theorists have presented ways to describe positions students achieve in the psychosocial areas and how these developmental changes occur.

These theorists have generally built upon the work of Erik Erikson (1968) and believe that an individual develops through a sequence of stages that define the life cycle. Each phase or stage is created by the convergence of a particular growth phase and certain developmental tasks. These include learning certain attitudes, formation of particular facets of the self, and learning specific skills that must be mastered if one is to successfully manage that particular life phase. In these theories, the development follows a chronological sequence; at certain times of life a particular facet of the personality emerges as a central concern that must be addressed. The particular timing and methods by which the concerns are addressed are influenced by the individual's society and culture. Psychosocial theorists examine these particular concerns or personal preoccupations that occur at various points in the life cycle. The adolescent is likely to be preoccupied with the concerns of "Who am I?" or "What am I to believe?" The young mother has the question "What type of parent shall I try to be?" and the older worker "What type of identity will I have when I retire from my professional position?"

Analogous to the moral and cognitive theories in chapter 6 advanced by Kohlberg and Perry, Arthur Chickering (1969) developed a theory of college student development that is an elaboration of Erikson's stages of identity and intimacy. Chickering focused on the particular developmental concerns of students that are relevant to the social situation in which they find themselves during their years at the university. He attempted to construct a framework of the developmental changes occurring in young adulthood in a more detailed way than did the psychosocial theorists such as Erikson. This framework has been presented in a form that draws on and gives coherence to the wealth of empirical data on college student change reported by a variety of researchers who have studied college students.

He has postulated seven vectors or dimensions of development, rather than the developmental tasks or developmental stages used by other theorists. The seven vectors along which development occurs in young adulthood are as follows: Achieving Competency, Managing Emotions, Developing Autonomy, Establishing Identity, Freeing of Interpersonal Relationships, Developing Purpose, and Developing Integrity.

Two sets of inventories have been developed to assess status on these developmental vectors. They include the Student Developmental Task and Lifestyle Inventory (Winston & Miller, 1987) and the Iowa Student Development Inventories (Hood, 1986). These inventories are designed to assess status on these vectors and the changes on them that occur during the college years. Recommendations regarding activities students might undertake to help them develop on those vectors on which they feel they would like to grow might be made from an individual's scores on these instruments. At this point, however, they do not represent instruments on which reliance can be placed in regard to differential diagnoses or selection.

SUMMARY

This chapter included a description of three projective instruments along with two personality theories useful to counselors and human development professionals.

1. For a number of both practical and psychometric reasons, projective instruments such as the Rorschach Ink Blot Test and the Thematic Apperception Test (TAT) are seldom used by counselors.

2. A condensed version of the TAT is sometimes used by counselors as a rapport-building technique that may also yield insight into the client's personality.

3. Person-environment theories and inventories emphasize situational variables that often have been overlooked by counselors and human development professionals who have traditionally placed more emphasis on the assessment and treatment of individuals.

4. Psychosocial developmental theories offer useful concepts when counselors and human development specialists use assessment techniques to assess individuals with particular concerns that occur at various points in the life cycle.

CHAPTER 13

Assessment of Interpersonal Relationships

Counselors and human development professionals who deal with educational-vocational issues often make extensive use of interest and aptitude tests, and those who deal with personal adjustment problems often make use of personality tests. When working with clients on marriage or relationship issues, psychological tests are infrequently a part of the counseling process. When tests are used in marriage counseling, they are often those commonly used in other types of counseling, such as the Minnesota Multiphasic Personality Inventory or the Myers-Briggs Type Indicator. There are a number of instruments designed specifically for marriage and relationship counseling, some of which are routinely used by some counselors and receive occasional use by others. Several of the more commonly used instruments of this type are briefly discussed in this chapter. There are also a large number of instruments that have been developed but do not receive much use. Most of these lack substantial amounts of normative and validity data. In addition, there are a number of additional marriage, family, and relationship instruments that can be considered experimental at this point but are often the assessment instruments used in research studies in this field.

INVENTORIES FOR MARRIAGE, COUPLES, AND FAMILY COUNSELING

The Marital Satisfaction Inventory

The Marital Satisfaction Inventory (MSI) (Snyder, 1981) is a self-report inventory designed to assess marital interaction and the extent of marital distress. Scores are obtained on 11 different scales with titles such as Affective Communication, Problem-Solving Communication, Disagreement about Finances, Sexual Dissatisfaction, Conflict Over Child-Rearing, and a Global Distress Scale, which measures general unhappiness and uncertain commitment in the marriage. A social desirability scale (conventionalization) is included as a check on the response set of the test taker. The scales contain 15 to 43 items per scale and have reliability coefficients ranging from .80 to .95. It takes approximately 30 minutes to complete.

The MSI is intended to be used in couples counseling, with both the husband and wife taking the scale and the results being displayed on a single profile that indicates areas of agreement and disagreement. It is typically administered during the initial contact with the counselor or agency so that results are available for the ensuing counseling sessions. The MSI provides useful information for counselors by providing a picture of the couple's overall marital distress, the general quality of their communication, and the differences between their perceptions of aspects of their relationship. Validity studies of the MSI scales generally show reasonable correlations with other measures of marital satisfaction. The MSI significantly differentiates between various criterion groups experiencing marital dissatisfaction. The manual for the MSI reports internal consistency coefficients and test-retest reliability coefficients in the .80 to .95 range.

The Derogatis Sexual Functioning Inventory

The Derogatis Sexual Functioning Inventory (DSFI) (Derogatis, 1979) yields 12 scores consisting of 10 scales with titles such as Information, Experience, Psychological Symptoms, Gender Role Definition, and Sexual Satisfaction. A total score and the subject's evaluation of current functioning are also included. The Information subscale consists of 26 true-false items measuring the amount of a subject's accurate sexual information. The Experience subscale lists 24 sexual behaviors ranging from kissing on the lips to oral-genital sex. The Sexual Drive subscale measures the frequency of various sexual behaviors, and the Attitude subscale measures the diversity of liberal and conservative attitudes.

The entire inventory can be expected to take 45 minutes to an hour to complete and was designed to assess individual rather than couple sexual functioning. The DSFI is designed to assess current functioning, although the Sexual Experience and the Sexual Fantasy subscales ask the subject to report lifetime experiences. Because the DSFI is one of the most thoroughly studied instruments in sexual research, several different types of norms are available for the instrument. Certain of the subscales, such as sexual information, sexual desire, and gender roles, have relatively low reliability coefficients of below .70. Others tend to be more adequate, falling in the .80 to .92 range. The instrument can provide counselors with considerable information regarding sexual functioning.

Taylor-Johnson Temperament Analysis

The Taylor-Johnson Temperament Analysis (TJTA) (Taylor, Morrison, & Nash, 1985) is designed for use in individual, premarital, and marital counseling. It consists of 180 items equally divided among nine scales measuring traits such as Nervous-Composed, Depressive-Lighthearted, Responsive-Inhibited, Dominant-Submissive, and Self-Disciplined-Impulsive. Norms are based on large samples, and a separate set of norms based on high school students is also provided. An additional edition is available for use with populations whose vocabulary and reading comprehension are below the eighth-grade level.

A unique feature of this instrument is the "criss-cross" procedure in which one person records his or her impressions of another person. This use can be valuable in family counseling involving parent-adolescent interaction, in sibling conflict, or in premarital or marital counseling.

Stuart Couples' Precounseling Inventory

The Stuart Couples' Precounseling Inventory (Stuart & Stuart, 1975) is a revision of the former Marital Precounseling Inventory. Norms are now based on a small representative sample (60 couples) that includes nonmarried heterosexual and homosexual couples. The purpose of the instrument is for use in planning and evaluating relationship therapy based on a social learning model. Scores are obtained in 13 different areas with such titles as Communication Assessment, Conflict Management, Sexual Interaction, Child Management, Relationship Change Goals, General Happiness with the Relationship, and Goals of Counseling. In taking the instrument, couples describe current interaction patterns rather than personality characteristics. Items tend to emphasize positive characteristics, and, if taken with some seriousness by the couple, the instrument can be educational and therapeutic.

Family Environment Scale

The Family Environment Scale is one of a number of social climate scales developed by Moos and his associates (Moos, 1976a). This 90-item inventory yields 10 scores with titles such as Cohesion, Intellectual-Cultural Orientation, Active Recreational Orientation, Moral-Religious Emphasis, Expressiveness, and Control. In addition, a "family incongruence score" can be obtained by summing the differences in subscale scores for various pairs of family members. Standard deviations and standard scores are provided for each of the 10 subscales and for the family incongruence score.

The 10 subscales are grouped into three underlying domains: the relationship domain, the personal growth domain, and the system maintenance domain. The assumption behind all of the social climate scales is that environments, and in this case families, have unique personalities that can be measured in the same way as individual personalities. Norms are based on a group of approximately 1,000 normal and 500 distressed families. The items on the Family Environment Scale are statements about family environments originally obtained through structured interviews with family members. Validity evidence is based primarily on the difference in mean scores between normal and distressed families.

Myers-Briggs Type Indicator

The MBTI (Myers & McCaulley, 1985) (see chapter 11) is also often used in counseling with couples and families. Here its use is to help couples understand their differences in the four dimensions measured by the MBTI and therefore to help them use these differences constructively rather than destructively. Data accumulated by the Center for Applications of Psychological Type (CAPT) indicate that people are only slightly more likely to marry individuals of similar than of opposite types. The proportion of couples alike in three or all four dimensions is only slightly higher than would be expected from a random assortment of types. The MBTI thus can be used to assist couples in understanding their differences and similarities.

When couples differ on the thinking-feeling dimension, feeling spouses may find their partner cold, unemotional, and insensitive, whereas the thinking spouse can become irritated with the seeming lack of logic of feeling types. Counselors can help thinking types to improve relationships by openly showing appreciation and by refraining from comments that sound like personal criticism. They can encourage feeling types to state wishes clearly, so the thinking partner does not have to guess their wishes. One spouse may be an extrovert needing considerable external stimulation, whereas the other, an introvert, needs sufficient time alone. This becomes a problem when the husband is introverted, expends a good deal of energy in extroverted work all day, and has little energy left for sociability in the evening. His wife, on the other hand, as an extrovert who works in a more solitary setting, may look forward to his providing stimulation and sociability on their return home in the evening. Problems arising from judging-perceiving differences can be found when planning, order, and organization are important to the judging partner whereas freedom and spontaneity are important to the perceptive partner, who also has a great deal more tolerance for ambiguity.

In using the MBTI with couples, couples are sometimes asked to guess the types of their partners after having the types briefly described. It is also possible to have each partner answer the MBTI twice, once for themselves and once as they believe their partner will respond. In either case the accuracy of type descriptions of partners can be discussed, and these differences can be useful to them as they see how they affect their relationship.

The MBTI can also be useful in family counseling in discussing difficulties in communication and differences in child-rearing styles and in attitudes toward other family members. For example, a counselor can help an orderly, practical, sensing-judging parent to see that it is easier for him or her to raise a sensing-judging child, who desires structure and organization, than it is for that parent to raise an independent, intuitive-perceptive child, who rebels against structure and order.

GENOGRAMS

A genogram is a map that provides a graphic representation of a family structure. It involves the collection of information about three generations of a family and organizes the information into a kind of family tree. It contains the names and ages of all family members along with information

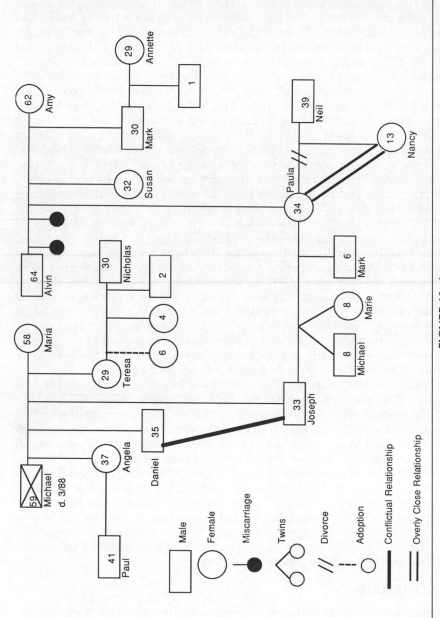

FIGURE 13–1
Genogram of Joseph and Paula

about major events such as births, deaths, marriages, divorces, adoptions, and conflicts. As the information is collected in this way, it allows family relationship problems to be seen in the context of the developmental cycle for the whole family in addition to that of the individual who is presenting the problem.

By examining the relational structure, including family composition, sibling constellations, and unusual family configurations, the counselor can hypothesize certain roles or relationships that can then be checked out by eliciting further information. Repetitive patterns of functioning and relationships often occur across generations, and by recognizing these patterns, counselors can help family members to alter them.

In drawing a genogram, some counselors obtain the basic information to structure the genogram and then go back and ask about each individual on it and their relationships with other family members, both within and across generations. Others obtain this information as each individual is placed on the genogram. Some counselors obtain only a basic genogram illustrating the general family structure, and others, through the use of figures, abbreviations, and symbols, develop a genogram that contains a great deal of organized data about the generations of a family system (McGoldrick & Gerson, 1985). A sample genogram is shown in Figure 13–1.

The construction of a genogram is a cooperative task between the counselor and the client. Clients readily become very interested and involved in the construction of a genogram; they enjoy the process and usually reveal a great deal of information about various relatives and their relationships with them. Counselors often find that genogram construction provides much insight into both the family constellation and the individual's interpersonal relationships within the family system. Even from reticent clients, both the quantity and the emotional depth of the data produced are often superior to that obtained through the typical interview process, and are more easily obtained as well. The construction of genograms in marriage and relationship counseling as well as in other types of counseling has thus been enthusiastically embraced by many counselors and has become an increasingly commonly used assessment technique.

SUMMARY

1. Personality inventories such as the Minnesota Multiphasic Personality Inventory, the California Psychological Inventory, and especially the Myers-Briggs Type Indicator, commonly used in other types of counseling, are most likely to be used by counselors with clients concerned with marriage or relationship issues.

2. There are instruments specifically developed to assess marital satisfaction, sexual functioning, communication issues, and family environments with which counselors can assist clients to understand and deal with relationship problems.

3. Through the cooperative construction of a multigeneration graphic family structure—the genogram—insight into family constellations and interpersonal relationships within the family can be revealed to both the counselor and the client.

CHAPTER 14

Mental Health Assessment: Interview Procedures

In the course of helping people solve problems, counselors and human development specialists will work with a number of clients who could be diagnosed as mentally ill. In a recent epidemiological study conducted by the National Institute of Mental Health (NIMH), researchers found that 15% of adults suffered from mental disorder within a 1-month period (Regier et al., 1988). Anxiety disorders, including phobias, panic, and obsessive-compulsive disorders, were most common (7.3%). Mood disorders, including depression, manic-depression, and dysthymia, were next most common (5.1%). According to a related NIMH study, nearly one third of adults in the United States will meet the psychiatric diagnostic criteria for a mental disorder sometime in their lifetime (Robins et al., 1984).

Other research also shows that a significant proportion of the clients at university counseling centers or mental health centers are psychopathologically disturbed. In one study, approximately 30% of the students at a university mental health clinic met the medical criteria for mental illness (Hersh, Nazario, & Backus, 1983). In another study, at least one fourth to one third of the clients at a university counseling service showed signs of a psychiatric disorder (Johnson, Ellison, & Heikkinen, 1989).

These studies indicate the need for counselors to be familiar with procedures for assessing mental illness. Many of their clients will exhibit symptoms of mental illness, especially depression and anxiety. Many of the people in the population that they serve will also show signs of mental illness even though they do not seek treatment. Counselors must be able to recognize the symptoms of mental illness and to provide at least a preliminary assessment of the client's mental state. They must be able to determine when services such as crisis intervention, psychiatric consultation, and long-term treatment may be necessary. Interview procedures to aid counselors in this endeavor are presented in this chapter. The use of standardized inventories for this purpose will be discussed in the next chapter.

DIAGNOSTIC AND STATISTICAL MANUAL OF MENTAL DISORDERS, THIRD EDITION, REVISED (DSM-III-R)

The DSM-III-R provides a means of classifying psychiatric and psychological disorders for treatment and research purposes (American Psychiatric Association, 1987). In contrast with earlier editions, the third edition assumes an atheoretical position. Classification of disorders depends strictly on descriptive, not etiological, factors. The diagnostic categories used by the DSM-III-R serve as the official means of classifying mental disorders in most medical and psychological settings in the United States.

The DSM-III-R employs a multiaxial classification system as indicated below:

Axis I: Clinical Syndromes
Axis II: Personality and Developmental Disorders
Axis III: Physical Disorders and Conditions
Axis IV: Severity of Psychosocial Stressors
Axis V: Global Assessment of Functioning

The clinical syndromes on Axis I encompass all mental disorders except personality disorders and developmental disorders. Each disorder is defined in terms of specific criteria. For example, the diagnostic criteria for bulimia nervosa (DSM-III-R code number 307.51), an eating disorder, include the following symptoms (American Psychiatric Association, 1987, pp. 68–69):

1. Recurrent episodes of binge eating (rapid consumption of a large amount of food in a discrete period of time).
2. A feeling of lack of control over eating behavior during the eating binges.
3. The person regularly engages in either self-induced vomiting, use of laxatives or diuretics, strict dieting or fasting, or vigorous exercise in order to prevent weight gain.
4. A minimum average of two binge eating episodes a week for at least three months.
5. Persistent overconcern with body shape and weight.

Note that the criteria describe the frequency, duration, and severity of the symptomatic behaviors. A person must display each of these behaviors to be classified as an individual suffering from bulimia nervosa.

Axis II differs from Axis I in focusing on developmental disorders and personality disorders that may underlie the presenting problem. In contrast with Axis I disorders, Axis II disorders generally begin in childhood or adolescence and persist in a relatively stable form into adult life. Developmental disorders pertain to delays or disturbances in the acquisition of cognitive, language, motor, or social skills. Such disorders include mental retardation, autism, learning disabilities, and speech disorders.

Personality disorders refer to lifelong maladaptive behavior patterns that are often triggered by specific events in the person's life (Othmer & Othmer, 1989). DSM-III-R defines a total of 13 personality disorders grouped in four categories as indicated below.

Cluster A: *Emotional withdrawal and odd behavior* includes paranoid, schizoid, and schizotypal personality disorders.

Cluster B: *Exaggerated, dramatic emotionality* includes antisocial, borderline, histrionic, and narcissistic disorders.

Cluster C: *Anxious, restive submissiveness* includes avoidant, dependent, obsessive-compulsive, and passive-aggressive disorders.

Cluster D: *Destructiveness* includes sadistic and self-defeating disorders.

Personality disorders represent extreme forms of personality traits, enduring and pervasive patterns of behavior, that have become dysfunctional for the person. The trait is expressed in such a rigid or inappropriate manner that it interferes with the person's adjustment.

People with personality disorders usually lack insight into the source of their difficulties. Clients do not usually seek counseling because of a personality disorder itself, but because of difficulties associated with the disorder. For example, a person with a dependent personality disorder might seek counseling because of loneliness or indecisiveness, but not for dependency. The counselor needs to look beyond the symptoms to find the personality disorder.

The third axis of DSM-III-R lists any current physical illness or condition of the individual. In some cases, a physical illness may mask itself as a psychiatric ailment. The counselor needs to be aware of physical disorders that might be influencing a client's mental state.

The first three axes provide the official classification of psychiatric patients for most purposes; however, information provided by the last two axes allows the counselor to gain a more complete picture of the person. The fourth axis measures the severity of psychosocial stressors faced by the client. The fifth axis rates the client's general level of functioning both at the time of treatment and during the previous year. The five axes together offer an integrated view of a client's problems from the standpoint of a biopsychosocial model of human functioning.

Use of DSM-III-R in Counseling

The following points should be considered in using the DSM-III-R in counseling:

1. Consider using the DSM-III-R with clients who seem to be suffering from a psychiatric disorder. Use of the DSM-III-R classification system improves the reliability and validity of the assessment process.

2. Learn to use the DSM-III-R system by applying it to actual cases. The computer-based tutorial program distributed by Psychoeducational Software Systems (Hayden & Furlong, 1988) provides 33 case vignettes that counselors can use to practice assigning DSM-III-R codes. Use the decision-tree approach described in the back of the manual to help make differential diagnoses (American Psychiatric Association, 1987, Appendix B).

3. Become familiar with techniques for determining DSM-III-R classifications through interviewing as outlined by Othmer and Othmer (1989). They distinguish between symptom-oriented interviewing and insight-ori-

ented interviewing. The first yields descriptions of the client's behavior, which is necessary for DSM-III-R classifications. The second provides possible explanations for the client's behavior. Both types of interviewing need to be pursued in counseling.

4. Be careful to use the DSM-III-R categories to classify a client's condition, not to label the client. For example, a client should be viewed as a person with schizophrenia, not as a schizophrenic. Labeling can lead to stereotyping and self-fulfilling prophecies.

5. Consult the books *Treatment of Mental Disorders* (Greist, Jefferson, & Spitzer, 1982) or *Selecting Effective Treatments* (Seligman, 1990) for treatment suggestions for the different types of mental disorders listed in the DSM-III-R.

6. Use the DSM-III-R classification system to form diagnostic impressions of clients in communicating with mental health referral sources. Many agencies require that clients or patients be assigned a DSM-III-R code for third-party payments.

7. Be cautious when using the DSM-III-R to make diagnoses for people from different ethnic or cultural groups. The DSM-III-R was not specifically designed for people reared in minority cultures or in non-Western countries.

SUICIDE RISK ASSESSMENT

Counselors must always be ready to evaluate the risk of suicide among the clients they see. As indicated in chapter 4, it is a good practice to routinely ask clients about any recent thoughts of suicide. Approximately 30% of the clients (474 of 1,589) seen at one university counseling service during a 1-year period indicated that they had experienced "thoughts of ending their life" during the week prior to their first counseling session (Johnson, Heikkinen, & Ellison, 1988). Counselors need to respond to this issue by undertaking a systematic assessment of suicidal risk. The counselor should be careful to establish rapport with the client so that the assessment can be as complete and as accurate as possible.

Clients should be asked directly about their suicidal thoughts if there is any hint of suicidal thinking. The counselor can usually approach this with a series of graded questions. For example, the counselor might ask, "How have you been feeling lately?" "How bad does it get?" "Has it ever been so bad that you wished you were dead?" "Have you had thoughts of suicide?" If the client has had thoughts of suicide, the counselor needs to inquire about the extent of these thoughts.

Some counselors are apprehensive about bringing up the topic of suicide with a client for fear that this will encourage the client to think about suicide as an option. In reality, clients who have had suicidal thoughts need the opportunity to talk about these thoughts. In this respect, assessment is part of the treatment. Talking about suicidal thoughts helps to validate the client's experience. It provides a sense of relief and communicates hope to the client that the problem can be addressed. In contrast, clients who have not had suicidal thoughts will usually reassure the counselor that this is not a concern. In fact, it is sometimes a relief for such clients to see their problems from this perspective: Even though they are struggling with a problem, things are not so bad that they think of suicide.

In making a suicidal risk assessment, counselors should be both calm and direct. Calmness indicates that it is acceptable for clients to talk about the things they find to be most troubling. The counselor helps clients to look at problems in depth and from different points of view. Counselors should make a point of using the words "suicide" or "kill yourself" while conducting the suicide risk assessment. The enormity of the act should be faced directly. It should not be romanticized.

Virtually all clients who discuss killing themselves with a counselor have ambivalent thoughts about suicide. Suicidal clients have a wish to live at the same time that they have a wish to die. The client would not seek counseling if there were not some underlying desire to live. Counselors need to identify and to align themselves with the part of the client that wishes to live. Counselors provide support to clients at the same time they enable them to see situations from alternative points of view.

Significant Factors in Suicide Risk Assessment

The assessment of suicide risk is basic to the formulation of a treatment or intervention plan. As indicated by Cesnik and Nixon (1977), the assessment should involve a consideration of six significant factors.

1. *Self-reported risk*. After clients have acknowledged suicidal ideation, they will usually tell the counselor of their perception of their risk level when asked. Questions such as "How likely do you think it is that you will act on your thoughts of suicide?" or "How long can you continue to tolerate the situation as it is?" will often generate responses that will be helpful in the assessment process. A self-report of high risk must always be taken seriously.

2. *Suicide plan*. If the client does express thoughts of suicide, the counselor should ask if the client has considered a plan. Information about the plan is critical in helping to assess a client's suicide potential. The counselor should evaluate the plan in terms of (a) its lethality, (b) the availability of the means, and (c) the specificity of the details.

First, some plans are much more lethal, or likely to succeed, than others. Guns, jumping, and hanging are highly lethal. Holding one's breath until one dies or starving oneself to death are much less likely to succeed.

Second, does the client have access to the means of killing him- or herself? Is a gun available? Has ammunition been purchased? The counselor needs to get clear answers to these specific questions. At times, it may be necessary to interview friends or family members to obtain this information.

Finally, how detailed are the client's plans? The risk of suicide increases as plans become more detailed and specific. For example, has the client made plans to give away possessions? Has the client considered what he or she might write in a note? Where would the suicide take place? When would it take place? Clients who have worked out a detailed suicide plan with a high likelihood of success demand immediate attention. Even more alarming are clients who have started to act on their plans, for example, those who have written a suicide note or given a pet animal to a friend. Provisions for further psychological or psychiatric assessment and treatment must be undertaken at once in such cases.

3. *Suicide history*. One quarter to one half of the people who commit suicide have made previous attempts (Patel, 1974). Their second try is more likely to be successful than their first try. If a person has attempted or seriously thought about suicide at some earlier time, the risk of suicide for that person is significantly increased.

The counselor should also check on the history of suicide in the family and among friends. Have family members or friends committed suicide or made suicide threats or attempts? If so, what was the nature of the relationship between that person and the client? Did the person represent a model for the client? What does the client feel about these situations? When did the suicide or suicide attempt take place? Anniversary dates can sometimes provide the impetus for a suicide attempt.

Try to determine the significance of any suicidal behavior in the client's history. In general, the risk of suicide for clients increases if they have been exposed to suicide as part of their history. One must keep in mind, however, that people with no history also commit suicide.

4. *Psychological symptoms*. Clients who are suffering from mental disorders or psychological distress are much more likely to commit suicide than those who are not (Miles, 1977). All client symptoms should be reviewed. The SCL-90-R (discussed in chapter 4), if used as part of the intake procedure, could be used for this purpose.

Look for symptoms of depression—feelings of helpnessness and hopelessness, profound sadness, withdrawal from others, diminished effectiveness, misdirected anger, rapid mood swings, difficulty in sleeping (either too little or too much sleep), significant weight loss or weight gain, lack of concentration, loss of interest in sex, and inability to enjoy any part of life. Counselors should be particularly concerned about feelings of hopelessness. According to experts on the topic (Wetzel, 1976; Beck, Kovacs, & Weissman, 1979), hopelessness seems to be the crucial feature of depression that predicts suicidal behavior. Restlessness or agitation associated with any of these symptoms increases the risk for suicide.

Sometimes signs of improvement can increase the risk of suicide. Clients may become more actively suicidal as they begin to come out of a deep depression, that is, when they acquire enough energy to act on their suicidal thoughts. In a similar fashion, clients sometimes will give an appearance of improvement when they have resolved their ambivalence by deciding to commit suicide.

Symptoms that suggest severe mental illness such as schizophrenia, bipolar disorder, or other psychotic disorders demand prompt attention. Has the client lost contact with reality? Does the client hear voice commands (auditory hallucinations) telling him or her what to do? All psychotic persons with thoughts of suicide should be hospitalized immediately to provide protection and relief from their psychosis. Many people who kill themselves are people with severe and persistent mental illness.

Alcohol or other drug abuse also increases the risk of suicide for a client. Approximately 15% of alcoholics eventually commit suicide (Miles, 1977). Medications can also be associated with suicide. The side effects of many medications include depression. The counselor should be sure to note if the client is taking any medications, including any recent change in medications. Medications are also frequently used as a means of suicide. As a safety precaution, antidepressant medications prescribed for highly suicidal persons should be controlled by others.

5. *Environmental stress.* Stressful situations are often the precipitating cause of suicidal ideation. What is the nature of the client's environment? Why is the client feeling suicidal at this particular time? What are the precipitating factors? How would the client benefit from suicide? Clients who wish to commit suicide to escape from stressful situations represent a greater risk than do clients who see suicide as a means of manipulating the environment.

To what degree can the client cope with the stress that he or she may be encountering? For example, can the client identify a solvable problem? Can the client distinguish between wanting to die and wanting to be rid of a problem? Can the client see more than one solution to a problem? Some clients experience "tunnel vision" so that they cannot conceive of options other than suicide for dealing with their stress. Does the client benefit from the counselor's attempts to provide assistance? Positive answers to these questions help to reduce the risk of suicide for the client.

Has the client encountered significant changes in his or her life, such as divorce, death of a family member, sickness, loss of a job, academic failure, or an overwhelming work assignment? Any change, even one that is positive, such as a job promotion or the end of an unhappy relationship, can be preceived as stressful. Change involves loss. Losses that pose the greatest threat include loss of a relationship, loss of a significant role, loss of a dream, or a large financial loss. Sometimes anticipating a loss can be more stressful than the actual loss. Loss can be particularly stressful if the client accepts most of the blame for the loss. Client stress can be evaluated more thoroughly by means of the Life Events Scale (Sarason, Johnson, & Siegel, 1978).

Sometimes stress can relate to events that may have happened years earlier if these events have not been addressed. Such events include sexual abuse, physical abuse, the suicide of a parent or sibling, and other traumatic events. Ask clients if there are things from their past that they find very difficult to talk about. If so, help them to begin to look at these issues in a supportive atmosphere. Recognize the need for long-term treatment for many of these issues.

6. *Available resources.* Counselors need to determine what resources are available for the client. Three levels of resources should be considered: (a) internal, (b) family, close friends, neighbors, coworkers, and others who may have contact with the client, and (c) professionals.

First of all, what are the client's internal resources? In trying to assess these resources, ask what has helped the client in the past in similar situations. What is keeping the client from commiting suicide? How is the client responding to your interactions with him or her? Does the client have plans for the future?

Second, find out what type of support system the client has. If nobody seems to be involved with the client at the present time, ask who used to care. Does the client have regular contact with anyone else? Does the client have any confidants? Would the client be willing to share his or her concerns with family members or close friends? In some respects, suicide can be looked upon more as a social than as a psychiatric phenomenon. Evaluation of the client's social support system is critical from this point of view.

What community resources are available for the client? Possibilities include a 24-hour crisis phoneline, emergency treatment center, or mental health specialist with whom the client has good rapport. Would the client make use of these resources in case of a crisis? Will the client sign a contract that he or she will contact the counselor or another mental health professional before attempting to commit suicide?

Not all of these points need to be covered with all clients. Move from the general to the specific. Ask for more detail in the areas in which you detect a problem. A review of each of the factors listed above should help you to evaluate the risk of suicide for your client. It also helps to give the client a sense of reassurance that you are taking his or her concern seriously. In many cases, talking about suicide can serve as a substitute for attempting suicide. The client needs to be taken seriously. Suicide can be looked on as a desparate means of communication. Honestly confronting this level of desperation in counseling can provide great relief for the client.

If you are having difficulty in making a suicide risk assessment, be sure to consult with another mental health professional. Clients who are at risk for suicide often need to be referred for psychiatric evaluation. Psychiatrists can evaluate the client's need for medication, hospitalization, or long-term treatment. The assessment and treatment of suicidal clients frequently requires a team approach.

SAD PERSONS Scale

The SAD PERSONS scale provides a convenient acronym for 10 basic points to keep in mind when assessing a client for suicidal risk (Patterson, Dohn, Bird, & Patterson, 1983). The 10 points are listed in Table 14–1. The demographic characteristics of sex and age are included in these points because of their relationship with suicide (Patterson et al.). Even though women make more suicide attempts than do men, three times as many men as women actually kill themselves. People are also more likely to attempt suicide when they are under 25 or over 45 than they are in midlife. The other eight points have been discussed above.

Guidelines for interpreting scores based on the SAD PERSONS scale are shown in Table 14–1. These guidelines are not meant to substitute for clinical judgment. The counselor will need to weigh all aspects of the situation in making a decision. Some points may deserve greater weight than others depending on the particular situation.

TABLE 14–1
The SAD PERSONS Scale for Assessing the Risk of Suicide

Items from the SAD PERSONS Scale

Sex	Previous attempt
Age	Ethanol abuse
Depression	Rational thinking loss
	Social support loss
	Organized plan
	No spouse
	Sickness

One point is scored for each factor deemed present. The total score thus ranges from 0 (very low risk) to 10 (very high risk).

Guidelines for Interpreting Scores from SAD PERSONS Scale

Total points	Proposed clinical action
0–2	Send home with follow-up
3–4	Consider hospitalization
5–6	Strongly consider hospitalization, depending on confidence in follow-up arrangements
7–10	Hospitalize or commit

Note. From "Evaluation of Suicidal Patients: The SAD PERSONS Scale" by W. M. Patterson, H. H. Dohn, J. Bird, and G. A. Patterson, 1983, *Psychosomatics, 24*, pp. 343–349. Copyright 1983 by American Psychiatric Association. Reprinted by permission.

Students who have been taught how to use the SAD PERSONS scale make judgments similar to those of experienced psychiatrists (Patterson et al., 1983). Trainees who do not know how to use the SAD PERSONS scale tend to overestimate the suicide risk of the people they evaluate.

ASSESSMENT OF ALCOHOL USE

A section on the assessment of alcohol use is included in this chapter because of the prevalence of abusive drinking and alcohol-related problems in our culture. According to the NIMH epidemiological study of mental disorders, 13% of the people in this country will meet the DSM-III-R criteria for alcohol abuse or dependence sometime in their lifetime (Christie et al., 1988). Counselors need to be sensitive to alcohol and other substance abuse among their clients. Because denial is a central issue in the abuse of alcohol or other drugs, counselors may not learn of the problem if they do not systematically review this matter with clients.

A variety of assessment procedures may be used to evaluate alcohol use. In most cases, the interview will probably be used to determine the nature and the gravity of drinking problems. The interview can be supplemented by self-monitoring methods and physiological indices such as blood alcohol concentration (BAC) levels. Standardized measures (to be discussed in the next chapter) may also be used as part of the assessment process. In addition to individual assessment, the counselor will often need to assess the environment in which the drinking takes place.

Diagnostic Criteria for Alcohol Dependence or Abuse

Although this chapter focuses on assessment of alcohol use, the DSM-III-R employs the same diagnostic criteria to determine dependence or abuse for all psychoactive substances. Psychoactive drugs include all drugs that alter one's mood or thought processes by their effect on the central nervous system. DSM-III-R recognizes 10 classes of psychoactive drugs (alcohol, amphetamines, cannabis, nicotine, cocaine, PCP or phencyclidine, inhalants, hallucinogens, opioids, and sedatives). The drugs show some differences in respect to tolerance and withdrawal symptoms; however, the same criteria suffice for all classes.

The specific criteria used to determine alcohol (or other substance) *dependence* are listed below (American Psychiatric Association, 1987, pp. 167–168):

1. Substance often taken in larger amounts or over a longer period than the person intended;
2. Persistent desire or one or more unsuccessful efforts to cut down or control substance use;
3. A great deal of time spent in activities necessary to get the substance (e.g., theft), taking the substance, or recovering from its effects;
4. Frequent intoxication or withdrawal symptoms when expected to fulfill major role obligations at work, school, or home (e.g., does not go to work because hung over, goes to school or work "high," intoxicated while taking care of his or her children), or when substance use is physically hazardous (e.g., drives when intoxicated);
5. Important social, occupational, or recreational activities given up or reduced because of substance use;
6. Continued substance use despite knowledge of having a persistent or recurrent social, psychological, or physical problem that is caused or exacerbated by the use of the substance (e.g., keeps using alcohol despite family arguments about it, alcohol-induced depression, or having an ulcer made worse by drinking);
7. Marked tolerance; need for markedly increased amounts of the substance (i.e., at least a 50% increase) in order to achieve intoxication or desired effect, or markedly diminished effect with continued use of the same amount;
8. Characteristic withdrawal symptoms, depending on the particular substance. Symptoms of alcohol withdrawal include coarse tremor of hands, tongue, or eyelids, and at least one of the following: nausea or vomiting, malaise or weakness, autonomic hyperactivity such as rapid heartbeat or sweating, anxiety, depressed mood or irritability, transient hallucinations or illusions, headache, or insomnia; and
9. Substance often taken to relieve or avoid withdrawal symptoms.

Of the nine criteria listed, three must be satisfied for a person to be diagnosed as alcohol-dependent. Some symptoms of the disturbance must have persisted for at least 1 month, or must have occurred repeatedly over a longer time period. In general, counselors should assess the client's ability to control his or her use of alcohol and the degree to which alcohol usage causes problems in the person's life. The severity of the problem can be noted by indicating level (mild, moderate, or severe) of the dependency.

Alcohol *abuse* refers to problematic drinking that does not fulfill the criteria for alcohol dependence. People who suffer from this condition continue to drink despite problems or to drink in dangerous situations (e.g., driving while intoxicated). Problems associated with drinking occur in all spheres of life: occupational, social, psychological, and physical. Counselors will often see clients because of the problems produced by the drinking, such as deterioration in work performance, conflicts with others, depression, or poor health. The counselor will need to be careful to assess for drinking (or other substance) abuse that may have caused the problem.

Interview Schedules

A number of interview schedules have been developed to aid in the assessment of alcohol use (Miller, 1976). The CAGE Questionnaire (named for the key words in each of four questions) can be readily used to screen clients for problems related to alcohol use (Ewing, 1984). It consists of the four questions listed below, each of which significantly differentiates between patients who are alcoholic and those who are not:

- Felt need to *Cut down* drinking?
- Ever felt *Annoyed* by criticism of drinking?
- Had *Guilty* feelings about drinking?
- Ever take morning *Eye-opener*?

If clients respond "Yes" to any of these questions, additional inquiry should be undertaken.

Two extensive schedules that may be particularly valuable for counselors are the Comprehensive Drinking Profile (CDP) and the Time-Line Follow-Back (TLFB). The CDP is a structured intake interview procedure requiring 1 to 2 hours for completion (Marlatt & Miller, 1984). It provides detailed information regarding the history and current status of an individual's drinking problems and related matters. It assesses both consumption and problematic behaviors. A short form of the CDP, the Brief Drinker Profile, is also available, as well as the Follow-up Drinker Profile (a measure of client progress) and the Collateral Interview Form (an instrument for obtaining information from other people who are close to the client).

The TLFB enables the client and the counselor to reconstruct the client's drinking behavior for the past year (Sobell et al., 1980). It analyzes the patterns (e.g., daily, weekly, sporadically) and the intensity (light, heavy) of drinking behavior. Connections between drinking episodes and significant events ("anchor points") in the person's life are studied. Research indicates that the TLFB is highly reliable and relatively accurate. TLFB reports obtained from the client agree reasonably well with those obtained from the client's spouse or partner. This procedure yields information that is highly informative to the client as well as to the counselor (Vuchinich, Tucker, & Harllee, 1988).

Self-Monitoring Methods

Self-monitoring can enhance assessments made by means of interview procedures in a number of ways. Because self-monitoring is based on planned observations, data obtained in this manner should be more accurate and more complete than data based on recall. Self-monitoring has the added advantage of helping clients to see more clearly the relationship between certain events and their drinking behavior. Finally, self-monitoring provides a means of plotting the client's progress in controlling drinking behavior.

Self-monitoring charts typically include the amount of alcohol consumed in a given period of time, the situation in which the alcohol was consumed, and presence of other people (Vuchinich et al., 1988). The thoughts or feelings of the person at the time may also be recorded. Temptations to drink, as well as actual drinking behavior, may be tracked.

Situational Factors

Besides assessing individual factors, counselors should help clients look at environmental factors that may encourage abusive drinking. Miller and Munoz (1982, p. 75) provided a checklist of 10 such situations:

- Drinking after work, especially after hard days
- Drinking after a stressful or emotional experience
- Drinking beer from barrels, kegs, or pitchers
- Drinking from the bottle (except beer)
- Drinking during automatic or boring activities
- Drinking during or with rewarding activities
- Drinking with heavy drinkers
- Drinking when thirsty or hungry
- Drinking with those who pressure you to drink faster or more
- Drinking "the usual" in the usual place.

In a survey conducted by Ziemelis (1988), approximately 60% of college students reported that they often found themselves in situations in which they were encouraged to drink more than they wished.

Use of Alcohol Assessment Procedures in Counseling

Guidelines concerning the assessment of problems related to alcohol or other substance use are listed below:

1. Be sure to ask about the use of alcohol or other drugs as part of the initial contact procedure.

2. Inquire about problems related to drinking. Abusive drinking may be most evident in the problems it produces. Ask if other people have been concerned about the client's drinking behavior. Inquire about "blackouts" (loss of memory while intoxicated) and "the shakes" (withdrawal symptoms), signs of a significant drinking problem. Use the CAGE questions as part of the screening process.

3. Keep the DSM-III-R criteria in mind in assessing alcohol dependence or abuse. Determine frequency, duration, and severity of pertinent symptoms. Remember that these same criteria can be used in assessing other types of psychoactive substance dependence or abuse.

4. If alcohol or other drug problems are detected, use a more thorough assessment procedure to gain a better understanding of the problem or refer the client to specialists for this purpose. Interview schedules such as the CDP or TLFB (briefly discussed above) or the Alcohol Use Inventory (briefly discussed in the next chapter) could be used for a more extended assessment.

5. Engage the client in self-assessment. Self-monitoring of drinking behavior can be helpful both in defining the problem and in gauging the success of treatment efforts.

6. Help clients to become aware of those situations that may trigger drinking behavior for them. Also help them to identify problems associated with drinking. Use of checklists can be helpful for this purpose. For example, "Alcohol and Other Drugs: A Self Test" includes 51 items that can be used to stimulate greater self-awareness (Wisconsin Clearinghouse, 1987).

7. Teach the use of Blood Alcohol Concentration (BAC) tables to clients with drinking problems so that they can assess the influence of alcohol consumption on their judgment and reaction time. Help them to use these tables to set alcohol consumption limits.

8. For clients who do not accept the fact that they have a problem of control of their drinking behavior (an essential feature of dependency), ask them to try to limit their drinking to a certain amount (e.g., no more than three drinks) on any one ocassion for a period of 3 months. This has sometimes been referred to as the "acid test" of one's ability to control drinking behavior.

9. If denial seems to be a problem, obtain permission from the client to speak with other family members as a means of gaining information about his or her drinking behaviors. Interview these people with the client present in the room.

10. Refer clients with persistent drinking problems to specialists for assessment and treatment. Inpatient or intensive outpatient treatment in a multidisciplinary setting may be necessary.

SUMMARY

1. Mental illnesses, particularly anxiety and mood disorders, occur frequently in the United States. Counselors and human development professionals need to be able to detect psychopathology among clients within their caseload.

2. The DSM-III-R offers a clear and comprehensive means of diagnosing possible mental disorders among clients.

3. All counselors should be able to undertake suicide risk assessments and substance abuse assessments within the counseling session.

4. If counselors are concerned about a client's suicide risk, they should ask about suicide intentions, specific suicide plans, previous suicide attempts, psychological symptoms, environmental stress, and available resources.

5. Alcohol assessment should focus on the client's ability to control his or her drinking and the problems in the client's life associated with drinking. The DSM-III-R criteria can be used to diagnose alcohol dependence or abuse.

CHAPTER 15

Mental Health Assessment: Standardized Inventories

Standardized measures of mental health are presented in this chapter. General-purpose measures contain a variety of scales that can be used to assess different aspects of psychopathology. Specific-purpose measures, on the other hand, focus upon a particular type of psychological problem, such as depression, anxiety, alcohol abuse, or eating disorders, that counselors are likely to confront.

GENERAL-PURPOSE MEASURES

The two most frequently used general-purpose standardized inventories of psychopathology are the Minnesota Multiphasic Personality Inventory-2 and the Millon Multiaxial Clinical Inventory-II. Both measures are reviewed in this section.

Minnesota Multiphasic Personality Inventory-2 (MMPI-2)

The MMPI-2 replaces the MMPI, which was first constructed 50 years ago (Butcher, Dahlstrom, Graham, Tellegen, & Kaemmer, 1989). In a recent survey, psychologists reported that they used the MMPI more frequently than they did any other psychological test (Lubin, Larsen, & Matarazzo, 1984). The MMPI has also generated more research than any other psychological test (Mitchell, 1985). Counselors need to be informed about the MMPI and its successor because of its wide use and because of the information it can convey regarding a client's personality characteristics and psychological difficulties.

The MMPI-2, which requires an eighth-grade reading level, may be used with clients beginning at age 18. A new version of the MMPI for adolescents will be released in the near future (Williams, 1989).

The original MMPI, as developed by Starke Hathaway and J. Charnley

TABLE 15–1
Description of Standard Scales on Minnesota Multiphasic Personality Inventory

Scale	Original Name and Abbreviation	Behaviors Associated With Elevated Scores
	Validity scales	
?	Cannot say (?)	Indecisiveness, rebelliousness, defensiveness
L	Lie (L)	Faking good, naivete, scrupulosity
F	Frequency (F)	Faking bad, unusual behavior, confusion while taking test
K	Correction (K)	Faking good, defensiveness, self-reliance
	Clinical scales	
1	Hypochondriasis (Hs)	Bodily complaints, fatigue, weakness
2	Depression (D)	Dejection, dissatisfaction, tendency to give up
3	Hysteria (Hy)	Denial of problems, desire for social acceptance, psychosomatic symptoms
4	Psychopathic deviate (Pd)	Impulsivity, acting out, not bound by rules
5	Masculinity-femininity (Mf)	Men: Cultural-aesthetic interests, passivity, academic achievement
		Women: Outdoor-mechanical interests, dominating, competitive
6	Paranoia (Pa)	Sensitive, suspicious, preoccupied with rights and privileges
7	Psychasthenia (Pt)	Anxious, obsessive, compulsive
8	Schizophrenia (Sc)	Unusual thoughts or behavior, detached, introspective
9	Hypomania (Ma)	High energy level, restless, distractible
0	Social introversion-extroversion (Si)	Introverted, reserved, reticent

McKinley, contained a total of 4 validity scales and 10 clinical scales that formed the standard MMPI profile (see Table 15–1). The validity scales enable the counselor to assess the client's attitude toward the testing process. Most of the clinical scales consist of items that significantly differentiate between people in a particular psychiatric diagnostic category (e.g., depression) and people in the the general reference group (often referred to as "the Minnesota normals"). For example, the Depression scale (Scale 2) contains 60 items that depressed people endorsed significantly more (or less) often than did the Minnesota normals.

Subsequent research has indicated that the MMPI scales cannot be used to classify individuals into psychiatric categories with a high degree of accuracy. Instead, the scales are most useful in providing descriptions of personality and as a source of inference regarding a person's behavior. Because of the large amount of research that has been conducted with the MMPI, the scales convey a wealth of information about an individual's personality that transcends the original purpose of the scale. For this reason, the original names for the MMPI scales have been replaced by the scale numbers for most purposes (e.g., scale 7 instead of *Pt* or Psychasthenia).

The MMPI-2 authors have corrected problems with the original normative sample and have brought the instrument up to date (Butcher et al., 1989). The total number of items (567) remains about the same. Ineffective, offensive, and repeated items have been eliminated. Sexist or dated items have been reworded. New items tap areas not well represented in the original MMPI item pool, including family relationships, eating disorders, and drug abuse.

The authors of MMPI-2 have left the standard MMPI scales virtually intact. None of these scales lost more than four items. Scores obtained on MMPI-2 standard scales correlate highly (.66 to .92) with scores obtained on similar scales from the original MMPI (Ben-Porath & Butcher, 1989). The order of the items has been changed so that all of the standard scales can be scored by having a client complete the first 370 items in the MMPI-2 booklet.

In contrast with the original standardization procedures, members of the new normative sample (1,462 women and 1,138 men) were selected so that they would be representative of the adult U.S. population in terms of age, marital status, ethnicity, and geography. Some questions about the success of the revision have been raised in regard to the educational level of the normative sample (Adler, 1990). The percentage of college graduates in the new normative sample is much higher than that found in the original sample or reported by the U.S. Census Bureau. According to Butcher (1990), the change in the educational level of the normative sample should have a minimal impact on the interpretation of the MMPI-2 scores.

With the new norms, the cut-off score used to detect psychological problems has dropped from 70 on the MMPI to 65 on MMPI-2. Research indicates that a *T*-score of 65 provides optimal separation between clinical groups and the standardization sample (Butcher et al., 1989). The scores on MMPI-2 have also been adjusted so that the distribution of the profile scores will be the same for the eight clinical scales (all but scales 5 and 0) used to assess psychopathology. For example, a *T*-score of 65 equals the 92nd percentile (based on the restandardization sample) for each of these scales.

The MMPI scales should be interpreted in conjunction with the other scales on the profile, not in isolation. Common MMPI patterns are listed in MMPI sourcebooks (e.g., Dahlstrom, Welch, & Dahlstrom, 1972–1975; Duckworth & Anderson, 1986; Graham, 1990; Greene, 1989). Counselors should be acquainted with the vast literature pertaining to the MMPI if they work with mentally disturbed clients; however, they cannot expect to become proficient in its use without specialized training and extensive clinical experience.

Counselors should note critical items that the client has checked as well as scale scores. For example, if the client marked "True" to item 506, "I have recently considered killing myself," or item 524, "No one knows it but I have tried to kill myself," the counselor should review these items with the client. Clients might not bring these topics up on their own. They may assume that the counselor already knows this information from their responses to these items on the MMPI-2.

Several critical item lists have been developed. Most of these items consistently separate normal from psychiatric samples. Lachar and Wrobel (1979) identified 111 items that suggest psychopathology in 13 different areas. All but 4 of these items have been retained in the MMPI-2. A revised version of the Koss-Butcher critical item set has been prepared for the MMPI-2 (Butcher et al., 1989). This list contains 78 items related to six crisis areas. Most computer-based MMPI scoring programs will flag critical items checked by clients (see Butcher, 1989a, 1989b). This information can also be obtained by means of hand-scoring. The critical item lists provide a simple and straightforward means for counselors to discuss MMPI results with clients and to determine which topics should be pursued in counseling.

A number of additional scales have been created for the MMPI that can be used to help interpret the clinical scales. Most of the clinical scales have been divided into subscales that can help clarify the meaning of scores on the scales (Harris & Lingoes, 1968, cited by Graham, 1990). For example, the Depression scale has been divided into the following subscales: Subjective Depression, Psychomotor Retardation, Physical Malfunctioning, Mental Dullness, and Brooding.

Besides the subscales, 15 content scales devised by Butcher, Graham, Williams, and Ben-Porath (1989) can also be used to clarify the meaning of the MMPI-2 profile scores. In contrast with the clinical scales, which were developed by empirical means, the content scales were constructed by logical analysis of the item content on MMPI-2. The scales were refined by statistical procedures to ensure homogeneity of item content. Scales developed in this fashion are easier to interpret than empirical scales. The content scales also assess aspects of personality not measured by the standard scales, including type A behavior, work interference, family problems, and negative treatment indicators.

In addition to the scales discussed thus far, many other scales have been constructed from the MMPI item pool for various purposes. Popular supplementary scales include *A* (Anxiety), *R* (Repression), and *Es* (Ego strength). *A* and *R* represent the two main factors derived from factor analyses of the clinical scales. As such, they offer a quick summary, or overview, of the MMPI-2 results. Scale *A* provides a measure of anxiety or general maladjustment; Scale *R* shows the client's tendency to repress or deny psychological difficulties. The *Es* scale is based on items that differentiated between clients with psychological problems who responded to therapy and those who did not. In contrast with most of the scores on the MMPI-2, high scores on *Es* should be interpreted favorably.

When the MMPI is computer-scored, counselors can easily obtain scores on all of the scales listed above in addition to the standard scales. A variety of computer-based scoring services are available for the MMPI-2.

Case Example

Janet, a 19-year-old college sophomore, requested counseling because of low self-esteem, relationship difficulties, family conflict, and eating concerns. She marked "5" (Very much) to the following items on the Inventory of Common Problems:

- Feeling irritable, tense, or nervous
- Feeling fearful
- Feeling lonely or isolated
- Eating, appetite, or weight problems

She also completed the Beck Depression Inventory as part of the initial contact session, for which she received a raw score of 32, indicating "severe depression." The counselor asked the client to complete the MMPI-2 during her next visit to the counseling center to assess more thoroughly the nature and the level of her psychological problems. She obtained the profile shown in Figure 15–1.

The scores on the three validity scales—L,F, and K—indicate self-criticism and a possible plea for help. Her low L and K scores indicate that she is describing herself in a negative fashion. The elevated F score suggests self-criticism together with moderately severe psychopathology. Among the clinical scales, she obtained elevated scores on scales 2, 6, 7, and 0. Her highest two scores are scales 7 and 2. According to Graham (1990, p. 94), individuals with this type of profile configuration "tend to be anxious, nervous, tense, high-strung, and jumpy. They worry excessively, and they are vulnerable to real and imagined threat. They tend to anticipate problems before they occur and to overreact to minor stress. Somatic complaints are common." He goes on to state that individuals with this profile respond well to psychotherapy. They are most likely to receive a psychiatric diagnosis of anxiety disorder, depressive disorder, or obsessive-compulsive disorder.

Janet's elevated scores on scales 6 and 0 both indicate possible difficulties in interpersonal relationships. According to the MMPI-2 Manual (Butcher et al., 1989, p. 39) scores between 66 and 75 on scale 6 can possibly be interpreted as follows: Angry and resentful, displaces blame and criticisms, hostile and suspicious, rigid and stubborn, and misinterprets social situations. Similarly, scores between 66 and 75 on scale 0 suggest behavior that is introverted, shy and timid, lacking self-confidence, moody, submissive, and rigid (Butcher et al., p. 43).

The counselor provided counseling to Janet to help her deal with her immediate siutation. At the same time, she made arrangements to refer Janet to a psychiatrist for a more complete assessment of some of the psychological problems suggested by the MMPI-2.

Millon Clinical Multiaxial Inventory-II (MCMI-II)

The MCMI-II provides an alternative to the MMPI-2 for diagnosing psychopathology. It is considerably shorter than the MMPI-2, containing 175 items compared with 567 items on MMPI-2. Most people can complete the MCMI-II in 20 to 30 minutes. It is also more closely tied in with the

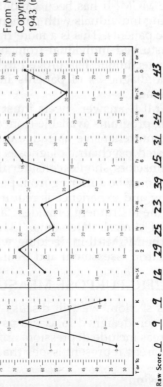

FIGURE 15-1

MMPI-2 Profile for Counseling Center Client

From Minnesota Multiphasic Personality Inventory-2 (MMPI-2).
Copyright © by the Regents of the University of Minnesota, 1942,
1943 (renewed 1970), 1989. This profile form 1989.

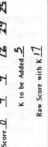

DSM-III-R than is the MMPI-2, so that psychiatric classifications can be made more easily. The MCMI is also more closely related to psychological theory than is the MMPI (Millon, 1969, 1981).

The MCMI-II provides two broad sets of scores that correspond with Axis I (clinical syndromes) and Axis II (personality disorders) on the DSM-III-R. The scales are scored in terms of base rates so that the percentage of people classified by means of the MCMI-II as suffering from a particular psychological problem correspond with the actual percentages found in society. Because of the scoring procedure, it is important that the MCMI-II be used only with people who fit the normative population, that is, people suspected to be suffering from a mental disorder. The MCMI-II will overpathologize for people who do not fit this population. Clients should be screened by other criteria such as an interview, the Beck Depression Inventory, or the Inventory of Common Problems before they are assigned the MCMI-II.

The MCMI-II differs from the MCMI by the addition of two new personality scales, several new validity measures, and other statistical refinements. Forty-five of the 175 items have been rewritten or replaced with new items.

The MCMI-II has been validated in terms of its effectiveness in differentiating individuals with particular psychiatric diagnoses from other psychiatric patients. This is a more rigorous criterion than simply differentiating the disturbed individual from nondisturbed individuals in general. The former technique has proved to be more accurate in identifying the psychiatric diagnoses of patients in subsequent studies than has the latter technique.

MCMI-II answer sheets must be scored by means of computer-based scoring programs available from the publisher. The scoring programs provide comprehensive narrative interpretations of the scores, together with suggested psychiatric diagnoses and treatment possibilities.

Counselors should consider the use of the MCMI-II with clients they believe may be suffering from psychiatric disorder; however, considerable training and experience is required for its use. As noted by Millon (1987, p. 8), the instrument provides "a series of tentative judgments rather than a set of clinical statements." The counselor can use information gained from the MCMI-II in deciding whether the client needs to be referred for psychiatric assessment and treatment.

SPECIFIC-PURPOSE MEASURES

In this section, we will discuss the use of standardized inventories that have been designed to assess psychopathology in specific areas. The specific areas include depression, anxiety, alcohol abuse, and eating disorders. These areas represent issues that can become life-threatening for clients.

Depression

A large number of self-rating scales have been devised to assess depression. Ponterotto, Pace, and Kavan (1989) identified 73 different self-report mea-

BECK DEPRESSION INVENTORY

On this questionnaire are groups of statements. Please read each group of statements carefully. Then pick out the one statement in each group that best describes the way you have been feeling the PAST WEEK, INCLUDING TODAY. Check the box beside the statement you picked. If several statements in the group seem to apply equally well, check the box for each one. *Be sure to read all the statements in each group before making your choice.*

☐ I do not feel sad.
☐ I feel sad.
☐ I am sad all the time and I can't snap out of it.
☐ I am so sad or unhappy that I can't stand it.

☐ I don't have any thoughts of killing myself.
☐ I have thoughts of killing myself, but I would not carry them out.
☐ I would like to kill myself.
☐ I would kill myself if I had the chance.

FIGURE 15–2
Instructions and Sample Items From Beck Depression Inventory

sures for depression used by mental health professionals for research or counseling purposes. Among these instruments, the Beck Depression Inventory (BDI) was used 10 times as often as the next most popular measure.

Beck Depression Inventory (BDI)

Ponterotto et al. (1989) rated the BDI higher in terms of its overall effectiveness than any other self-report measure of depression. They gave it the highest possible rating for utility, that is, ease of use by counselor and client. They also rated it highly (4 on a 5-point scale) for both reliability and validity. Based on their analysis, counselors should give first consideration to the BDI when attempting to assess depression in a client.

Sample items from the most recent version of the BDI can be seen in Figure 15–2. The complete BDI lists 21 items that describe various components of depression (affective, cognitive, behavioral, and physiological). Each item shows four levels of intensity. Clients mark the level of intensity for each item that best describes how they have been feeling "during the past week."

Most clients complete the BDI within 10 to 15 minutes. Scoring, which involves tallying answers for 21 items, takes just a few minutes. For this reason, it can easily be administered, scored, and interpreted as part of a regularly scheduled counseling interview.

Burns and Beck (1978) recommended that BDI scores be interpreted by means of the following classification system:

 0– 9 = No depression or minimal depression
10–14 = Borderline depression
15–20 = Mild depression
21–30 = Moderate depression
31–40 = Severe depression
41–63 = Very severe depression

The cutoff scores shown above should be looked upon as general guidelines. The counselor will need to obtain more information to judge the severity of a client's depression. The duration of the symptoms and the possible cause of the symptoms (e.g., loss of a loved one) need to be considered. If the symptoms are of short duration (less than 2 weeks) or if they can be attributed to a grief reaction, they are less likely to indicate psychopathology.

As a general rule, if the score exceeds 25 the counselor should consider referring the client for psychiatric evaluation. As noted by Ponterotto et al. (1989), the symptoms measured by items 16 through 21, all of which are physiological in nature, can be used together with the rest of the information from the BDI to help determine if a depression may be endogenous in nature. Endogenous depressions, persistent depressions not attributable to outside forces, are more likely to need long-term psychotherapy or medication.

The item content of the BDI can be easily reviewed with clients to obtain more information about a symptom. It usually helps to ask clients which items they are most concerned about. Counselors should pay particular attention to item number 9, which inquires about suicidal thoughts. If this item is marked "1" or higher, the counselor should be sure to consider this matter with the client.

Scores on the BDI are internally consistent, but subject to change over time. The BDI was designed to be highly sensitive to changes in mood over short time periods. If people experience significant changes in their lives, or if they are responding positively to a counseling program, their BDI score should reflect these events.

Hammen (1980) noted that BDI scores for college students often dropped upon retesting even without treatment. Depression for these students may be caused by situational factors, such as impending exams or relationship conflicts, which could change rather quickly. Such factors must be taken into account. For this reason, it is a good idea to readminister the BDI during the course of counseling to help monitor changes that may occur. Information obtained from readministrations of the BDI can often be helpful in trying to decide if a client should be referred for additional assessment or treatment or if he or she can be successfully discharged from counseling.

Anxiety

Anxiety can be defined as "a pervasive feeling of dread, apprehension, and impending disaster" (Goldenson, 1984, p. 53). The nature of the anxiety can be either *general* or *specific*. In the case of general anxiety, the source of the danger remains unknown or vague. In the case of specific anxiety (or fear), on the other hand, the cause of the anxiety, such as snakes or crowded places, can be clearly identified. Counselors should be prepared to help clients to assess both general and specific anxieties.

The State-Trait Anxiety Inventory (STAI), the most popular and well researched of all anxiety measures, includes scales for both general and specific anxiety (Spielberger, Gorsuch, Lushene, Vagg, & Jacobs, 1983). The Trait scale measures general, or persistent, anxiety, whereas the State scale assesses specific, or transitory, anxiety. Both scales consist of 20 items marked on a 4-point scale. Instructions for the Trait scale ask clients to rate how they "generally feel"; instructions for the State scale ask clients to indicate how they feel "at this moment." Differences between the two scores can be used to help determine whether anxiety is associated with a particular event, such as an upcoming exam, or with the process of living in general. Katkin (1978, p. 283) has described the STAI as "an easy-to-administer, easy-to-score, reliable, and valid index" of both general and specific anxiety.

Standardized inventories of specific anxiety of interest to counselors include the Test Anxiety Scale (Sarason, 1980), Mathematics Anxiety Rating Scale-Revised (Plake & Parker, 1982), Achievement Anxiety Scale (Alpert & Haber, 1960), and Fear Questionnaire (Marks & Mathews, 1978). The Achievement Anxiety Inventory contains scales that distinguish between "facilitating" (or motivating) anxiety and "debilitating" (or interfering) anxiety in regard to academic achievement. The Fear Questionnaire measures the extent to which a client may be suffering from a particular type of phobia (agoraphobia, blood-injury phobia, and social phobia).

Alcohol Abuse

No single personality type represents all alcoholics. Graham and Strenger (1988) identified six different personality types for alcoholics, but none of these were unique to alcoholics. The authors emphasized the individual differences among the alcoholic patients they studied.

Michigan Alcoholism Screening Test (MAST)

The MAST was designed to be administered orally by the counselor, but it can also be completed directly by the client (Selzer, 1971). It is a brief instrument that can be answered by the client within a few minutes. The items describe symptoms of excessive drinking, problems (social, family, work, legal, and health) that one may have encountered as a result of drinking, concerns expressed by others about one's drinking, and efforts that one may have made to control drinking or to obtain treatment for excessive drinking. The instrument and the scoring weights for each item are shown in Figure 15–3. Scores of 5 or more indicate alcoholism, scores of 4 suggest the possibility of alcoholism, and scores of 3 or less indicate the absence of alcoholism.

Research indicates that the MAST has been highly successful in distinguishing between alcoholics and nonalcoholics (Selzer, 1971). The MAST

MICHIGAN ALCOHOLISM SCREENING TEST (MAST)

Instructions: Please answer each question "Yes" or "No" as it pertains to you.

(2) *1. Do you feel you are a normal drinker?

(2)   2. Have you ever awakened the morning after some drinking the night before and found that you could not remember a part of the evening before?

(1)   3. Does your spouse (or do your parents) ever worry or complain about your drinking?

(2) *4. Can you stop drinking without a struggle after one or two drinks?

(1)   5. Do you ever feel bad about your drinking?

(2) *6. Do friends or relatives think you are a normal drinker?

(0)   7. Do you ever try to limit your drinking to certain times of the day or to certain places?

(2) *8. Are you always able to stop drinking when you want to?

(5)   9. Have you ever attended a meeting of Alcoholics Anonymous (AA)?

(1) 10. Have you gotten into fights when drinking?

(2) 11. Has drinking ever created problems with you and your spouse?

(2) 12. Has your spouse (or other family member) ever gone to anyone for help about your drinking?

(2) 13. Have you ever lost friends or girlfriends/boyfriends because of drinking?

(2) 14. Have you ever gotten into trouble at work because of drinking?

(2) 15. Have you ever lost a job because of drinking?

(2) 16. Have you ever neglected your obligations, your family, or your work for two or more days in a row because you were drinking?

(1) 17. Do you ever drink before noon?

(2) 18. Have you ever been told you have liver trouble? Cirrhosis?

(5) 19. Have you ever had delirium tremens (DTs), severe shaking, heard voices, or seen things that weren't there after heavy drinking?

(5) 20. Have you ever gone to anyone for help about your drinking?

(5) 21. Have you ever been in a hospital because of drinking?

(2) 22. Have you ever been a patient in a psychiatric hospital or on a psychiatric ward of a general hospital where drinking was part of the problem?

(2) 23. Have you ever been seen at a psychiatric or mental health clinic, or gone to a doctor, social worker, or clergyperson for help with an emotional problem in which drinking had played a part?

(2) 24. Have you ever been arrested, even for a few hours, because of drunk behavior?

(2) 25. Have you ever been arrested for drunk driving or driving after drinking?

*Negative responses to these items indicate alcoholism; for all other items, positive responses indicate alcoholism.

Note. From "The Michigan Alcoholism Screening Test: The Quest for a New Diagnostic Instrument" by M. L. Selzer, 1971, *American Journal of Psychiatry, 127*, p. 1655. Copyright 1971 by the American Psychiatric Association. Reprinted by permission.

FIGURE 15-3
Items and Scoring Weights (Shown in Parentheses) for Michigan Alcoholism Screening Test

results should be confirmed by means of other assessment procedures. The MAST can be used with all clients in an agency to detect possible alcohol problems that otherwise might be missed. According to one study, 22% of new clients at a university counseling center scored high enough on MAST to suggest possible alcoholism (Hay, 1988).

Case Example

Sally, a client at a community counseling service, received a score of 16 on MAST. She answered items 1, 2, 5, 6, 8, 10, 11, 12, and 23 in the scored direction. Sally had been brought to the counseling agency by friends because of problems related to her drinking. The score of 16 far surpasses the cutoff score of 5 used on MAST to signal alcoholism.

The MAST contributed to counseling by emphasizing the importance of her drinking problem. Information obtained from MAST was confirmed by other information related to Sally's drinking habits. Her alcoholic consumption (13 drinks per week) surpassed that of more than 82% of American adults who drink (Miller & Munoz, 1982). Counseling with Sally revealed that she came from a broken home. She frequently fought with her mother while she lived at home. Sally suffered from low self-esteem and a perfectionistic nature. She was demanding and dependent in her relationships. Testing with the California Psychological Inventory revealed that she was highly critical of herself (low Good Impression score; T = 34), undercontrolled (low Self-Control score; T = 39), and lacking in confidence (low Capacity for Status; T = 39). Her personality type was "Gamma" (externally oriented and norm-questioning) at the midpoint (level 4 of 7 levels) of self-realization.

The counselor worked with her on family issues and relationship matters. Sally became more self-sufficient during the course of counseling and more confident in her relationships with others. She began to deal with some of the personal issues represented by her drinking problem. By addressing unresolved problems, and by the use of self-monitoring techniques, Sally was able to reduce the amount of her drinking during the course of counseling.

Alcohol Use Inventory (AUI)

The AUI is a self-report inventory that "identifies distinct patterns of behavior, attitudes, and symptoms associated with the use and abuse of alcohol" (Horn, Wanberg, & Foster, 1986). Most people complete the AUI, which requires a sixth-grade reading level, within 35 to 60 minutes. It contains 24 scales based on 228 items organized at three levels: 17 primary scales, 6 second-order scales, and 1 general alcohol use scale. The scales evaluate alcohol usage in terms of benefits, styles, consequences, and concerns. It is most appropriate for individuals who enter a treatment program as a result of alcohol dependence or abuse. It can be used to establish a treatment plan for a person with alcohol-related issues.

Eating Disorders

The number of people, particularly women, with eating disorders or problems has increased dramatically in recent years (Garner & Garfinkel, 1985;

Mintz & Betz, 1988). The major eating disorders include anorexia nervosa (self-induced starvation), bulimia (binge-purge syndrome), and bulimarexia (a combination of the two). The DSM-III-R does not list obesity as an eating disorder because it is not usually associated with a specific psychological syndrome.

According to the DSM-III-R, the essential features of anorexia nervosa include refusal to maintain body weight (e.g., the person weighs less than 85% of expected body weight), intense fear of gaining weight, a disturbed body image, and loss of menstrual cycle for women. Anorexia nervosa, which means nervous loss of appetite, is a misnomer; the person resists eating, but actual loss of appetite is rare. Bulimia nervosa, on the other hand, is characterized by binge eating (rapid consumption of food in a short period of time), a feeling of lack of control of one's eating behavior while binge eating, drastic attempts to prevent weight gain (e.g., self-induced vomiting, use of laxatives or diuretics, strict dieting or fasting, or vigorous exercise), and persistent overconcern with body shape and weight (American Psychiatric Association, 1987). Some individuals, who can be classified as bulimarexics, share the symptoms of both disorders.

Individuals suspected of meeting the DSM-III-R criteria for an eating disorder should be referred to an eating disorders clinic or health service with a multidisciplinary team including a physician, nurse, dietitian, and mental health professional. The person may require a complete medical examination, nutritional assessment, and psychological assessment. Treatment also entails cooperation among the different disciplines to help clients address medical complications, alter eating habits, and alleviate psychological problems by such means as improving social skills and self-image.

Individuals with eating disorders typically wait several years from the onset of the disorder before entering treatment. Early assessment of a person's eating problems can reduce the length of this time period. Counselors can help determine the need for referral of a client to an eating disorders clinic by the use of the standardized tests discussed below. The Eating Attitudes Test and the Eating Disorders Inventory are the two most widely used standardized measures available for evaluating eating problems (Rosen, Silberg, & Gross, 1988).

Eating Attitudes Test (EAT)

The EAT contains 40 items that measure the symptoms and behaviors associated with anorexia nervosa and other eating problems (Garner & Garfinkel, 1979). Total scores on the EAT have clearly differentiated between patients diagnosed as anorexic and control groups of "normals" in research investigations. The scores are sensitive to treatment, so that recovered anorectics obtain scores similar to normals.

The EAT can be scored in terms of three subscales—Dieting, Bulimia, and Oral Control—to help determine the nature of the eating problems. Rosen et al. (1988) found that scores on each of the three subscales correlated significantly with scores on the Restraint Scale (a measure of restrained eating) and self-reported diet behavior (skipping meals, fasting, using diet pills, vomiting, and taking laxatives).

Case Example

Joan's counselor asked her to take the EAT as a means of reviewing her eating habits and assessing the need for a referral to the eating disorders clinic at the local hospital. Joan had come to the community mental health service for assistance with relationship issues, family conflicts, and eating problems. She "binged" on bakery goods and sweets about once a week, then used laxatives to purge the extra food.

Joan obtained a score of 36 on the EAT, which placed her almost two standard deviations above the mean (98th percentile) compared with adult women. Scores above 30 suggest serious eating concerns. She marked Always or Very often to items such as "Am terrified about being overweight," "Am preoccupied with a desire to be thinner," and "Feel that food controls my life." Her score indicated that she could probably profit from a referral to an eating disorders clinic with a multidisciplinary staff for a more thorough assessment of her eating and nutritional habits as well as her physiological and psychological well-being. After discussing the matter with her, her counselor made arrangements for such a referral.

Eating Disorders Inventory (EDI)

The EDI consists of 64 items that assess the psychological and behavioral characteristics that underlie anorexia nervosa and bulimia (Garner, Olmsted, & Polivy, 1983). It differs from EAT by the inclusion of personality items as well as behavioral and symptomatic items. Of the eight scales on the EDI, five measure psychological traits—Ineffectiveness, Perfectionism, Interpersonal Distrust, Interoceptive Awareness, and Maturity Fears—and three measure behavioral or attitudinal factors—Drive for Thinness, Bulimia, and Body Dissatisfaction.

Separate norms for EDI for male and female adolescents have been developed by Rosen et al. (1988). They found that girls obtained higher scores than boys on all of the scales except Perfectionism, Interpersonal Distrust, and Maturity Fears. No sex differences existed for the latter three scales. Girls scored particularly high on two of the three scales that directly pertain to eating disorder symptoms (Drive for Thinness and Body Dissatisfaction). Although separate-sex norms are necessary, separate norms based on age, socioeconomic class differences, and race do not seem to be warranted.

Studies by the authors show that the scales produce reliable (internally consistent) results for people with eating disorders. Validity studies indicate that EDI scores correlate highly with clinician ratings. Scores on the EDI also differentiate eating disorder patients from both nonpatients and recovered patients (Garner et al., 1983).

SUMMARY

1. The MMPI-2 provides a more comprehensive assessment of a client's mental health than any other personality inventory. The MMPI has generated more research than any other assessment instrument since its introduction in the 1940s.

2. The MCMI-II represents a viable alternative to the MMPI for assessment of client psychopathology. It is shorter and more closely related to theory and to the DSM-III-R categories than is the MMPI-2.

3. The Beck Depression Inventory serves as a quick, yet relatively thorough, measure of a client's state of depression. It is particularly helpful for monitoring changes in depression over time.

4. The State-Trait Anxiety Inventory provides valid and reliable measures of both specific (transitory) and general (enduring) anxiety.

5. Problems related to alcohol use can be detected by the Michigan Alcohol Screening Test (MAST). Individuals with problems can be further evaluated by means of the Alcohol Use Inventory.

6. Both the Eating Disorders Inventory and the Eating Attitudes Test can be used to screen clients for possible eating disorders.

Section V

Professional Practices and Considerations

CHAPTER 16

Assessment of Ethnic and Special Populations

Controversy has surrounded psychological tests almost from their beginnings. The development of the Army Alpha for testing World War I recruits caused much debate (Haney, 1981), particularly when differences between socioeconomic and ethnic groups became known. Since then controversy has continued, especially regarding multiple-choice aptitude tests used for selection procedures (Gross, 1962).

CULTURAL BIAS IN TESTING

There are three commonly considered ways in which tests may be biased against a person or groups of persons. They may contain items that favor one group over another. For example an item on a verbal analogies test that includes the word "toboggan" might tend to favor persons from northern states over those from southern states. Many sociocultural factors—ethnicity, socioeconomic class, region, and situation—contribute to mismatches between the language of test takers and that of test makers. Thus, tests may be biased because the language of the test taker varies from the language that he or she is presumed to have by the examiner. An example of this type of bias is a test that includes the language or values typical to White middle-class people but that are less familiar to Blacks, Hispanics, or other distinct cultural groups (Lonner & Sundberg, 1987).

The second source of bias comes from test-related factors such as the motivation, anxiety, or test sophistication of those taking the test—sources of bias that are external to the test itself. Extreme forms of test anxiety, self-esteem, and achievement motivation have been found to be related to test performance, but there has been little evidence that there are substantial differences in these areas between races, sexes, or social classes.

A third possible source of bias comes from the use of test results in selection for employment or college admissions—if the model used for selection and prediction varies greatly among different groups.

In discussing the problem of test bias or group differences, it is important to distinguish between test results and innate aptitude. The statement that men as a group achieve higher levels of competence in mathematics than women is a statement regarding past achievement on a given test. This does not imply that men possess a greater aptitude for mathematics than women—a statement that suggests innateness or biological or genetic determinism. Almost no one these days believes that intellectual functioning, no matter how measured—by tests or academic achievement—is exclusively a function of either one's heredity or one's environment, it is a complex function of both.

In using standardized tests in counseling with a person from another culture, it is probably a general rule that the less the counselor knows of the client's culture, the more errors the counselor is likely to make. It is important to be knowledgeable regarding the culture of the person being assessed and develop skills for dealing with culture-related behavior patterns. On the other hand, it is important not to "over culturalize." Culture is important in understanding an individual, but it is not the only variable influencing human behavior. There are many factors that all people experience that lead them to seek to counseling, and these are all important in assessing a person (Lonner & Sundberg, 1987). With increased interest in counseling individuals from different cultural backgrounds, counselors need to be aware of various problems associated with the cross-cultural use of psychological tests. These problems include the difficulty in establishing equivalence across cultures, the difficulty of not possessing appropriate norms, differences in response sets across different cultures, the nature of the test items, and the differing attitudes toward psychological testing across cultures.

APTITUDE AND COGNITIVE ASSESSMENT

A basic assumption of standardized testing is that it is perfectly appropriate for the test taker to be willing to provide obvious information and to give a performance for a total stranger—the examiner. These basic social assumptions may be in conflict with the interactional rules for individuals in some cultures. For example, it might be hypothesized that Black working class children or Native American children are less oriented to public performance for unfamiliar adults than are White middle-class children. It might even be argued that child-rearing practices of many White middle-class parents, which encourage public verbal performance for strangers, program their children for eventual success on standardized tests.

Black Americans

Although tests could be biased against any minority, the most serious controversy exists over the fact that, as a group, Black Americans score approximately one standard deviation below White Americans on most standardized tests of cognitive ability. Even more aggravating is the fact that the magnitude of this difference persists from preschool children through college applicants. There is, of course, a great deal of overlap between the two distributions, with almost 20% of Blacks scoring above the mean for

Whites and 20% of Whites scoring below the mean for Blacks. In addition, of course, some Blacks score as high as the highest Whites and some Whites score as low as the lowest Blacks. Because counselors usually deal with individuals rather than total populations, these differences are of less importance. The counselor is concerned only with the particular ability of a particular individual, whether Black or White. The counselor is not concerned with overall mean differences among populations but with the question of whether a particular aptitude test score has equal validity; that is, does it predict equally well for Black as for White Americans.

Because Blacks as a group have experienced great racial discrimination in the past and this discrimination has had an impact on their socioeconomic status, their opportunities, and their home environments, it is not surprising that this would have an effect upon test results. Much of the controversy centers on the cause of the differences. There are those who attribute the differences to the disadvantages that Black Americans suffer in their economic status and their educational and occupational opportunities. There are others who attribute much of the difference to genetic factors.

A frequently offered argument is that intelligence tests and other measures of cognitive aptitude are constructed by and for White middle-class individuals and therefore are biased against Blacks and others who are not members of the majority culture. Some of this cultural bias could be found in the items on which suburban children might have more familiarity than ghetto children. Ghetto children, brought up using a Black dialect, might be less able to comprehend the language used on such instruments. Test developers have now become extremely sensitive to this issue and have established panels of experts that include representatives from many cultural groups. Most of this content bias has therefore been eliminated from many of the current forms of these tests, although such changes have been shown to have little if any effect on the scores obtained by minority individuals.

If the validity of cognitive aptitude tests is different for majority and minority groups, and if counselors encourage or discourage clients about pursuing different levels of education or types of jobs based on these test results, then this type of bias could affect counseling outcomes. Numerous studies have been conducted predicting various criteria both for education and job performance for Black and White groups. In general, results have shown that ability tests are equally valid for both minority and majority groups. These studies have used IQ tests to predict school achievement, scholastic aptitude tests to predict college grades, and job-related aptitude tests to predict job success. Both correlations and regression lines tend to be similar for both groups, and in the cases where minor differences have occurred, there has been a slight tendency for the test to slightly overpredict the achievement of Black students—contrary to what might be expected if the tests were significantly racially biased (Messick, 1980; Cleary, Humphreys, Kendricks, & Wesman, 1975).

In attempts to demonstrate the unfairness of achievement and intelligence tests for Blacks, two different tests were developed on which they might be expected to score higher than Whites, because the knowledge about the culture being tested was that of Black Americans rather than of middle-class Whites. Dove's Counterbalance General Intelligence Test (known as the Chitling Test) (Samuda, 1975) and Williams's Black Intelligence Test of Cultural Homogeneity (known as the BITCH Test) (Williams, 1972) are vocabulary tests based on Black American slang common in Black ghettos. On each of these tests Black students significantly outperform White students. If this type of test measures the ability to acquire knowledge about one's culture or the possession of good reasoning skills, then the results should predict performance on other important criteria. Thus far, that has not been shown. To the extent that these instruments merely measure knowledge of ghetto slang, they are unlikely to predict useful performance, as such knowledge is not an important factor in most educational or work settings.

Hispanics

Although Spanish-speaking individuals often share the poor economic conditions of Black Americans, their difficulties do not lie solely in their poverty. The Spanish-speaking student meets difficulties in communication and understanding from whatever social background. A student from another cultural background who scores low on a standardized test in English may actually have obtained a remarkably good score if the student has been learning English for only a short period. The counselor must consider individual differences and circumstances in interpreting the test results of non-native-English-speaking clients.

In the case of Hispanic individuals, a Spanish edition of an assessment instrument may be appropriate, and Spanish language editions have been developed for several popular tests, including the Strong Interest Inventory, the Myers-Briggs Type Indicator, the Wechsler intelligence scales, the Self-Directed Search, the 16 PF, and Cattell's Culture-Fair Intelligence Test.

Native Americans

In counseling Native American individuals, caution must be used in interpreting the results of various assessment procedures. There is a wide range of differences with regard to culture among various Native American tribes, and because of such large differences few generalizations are possible. In norming samples of tests, very small numbers of Native Americans are likely to have been included in the sample, and even those are likely to represent only a few of the many different cultures from which Native Americans may come.

In testing situations, Native Americans may underestimate the seriousness of tests, lack test-taking skills, or lack motivation to perform on tests. For some, tribal beliefs may discourage the type of competitive behavior often present in test-taking situations. They may also have learned English as a second language, and learned their first language as a nonwritten language—factors that can easily affect English reading skills (Brescio &

Fortune, 1989). Thus, they may have similar handicaps on tests as do individuals from other cultural backgrounds. In addition, because they often come from isolated, rural, or impoverished settings, they may lack the type of knowledge and experience expected on certain test instruments.

Asian-Americans

Test results and the interpretations of these results vary greatly for different Asian-American clients. They come from widely divergent cultural backgrounds and range all the way from fourth and fifth generation Asian-Americans to the more recent Filipino and Vietnamese immigrants.

The later generations of Japanese and Chinese Americans come from backgrounds in which the mean income level equals or surpasses that of Whites, and they hold many similar attitudes and values. There are aspects of their cultures, however, that influence them to place increased emphasis on the results of achievement and aptitude tests and less on other types of performance. In addition, education, especially higher education, is much valued and supported, with particular value placed on attending prestigious institutions of higher education. Thus there is considerable pressure to attain high enough scores on academic aptitude tests to gain entrance to these types of colleges and universities.

Test results for recent Southeast Asian immigrants have much less validity because these individuals are affected by all of the language problems, vast cultural differences, and economic difficulties common to newly arrived immigrants.

Culture-Fair Tests

The typical intelligence test administered in the United States assumes a relatively common cultural background found in contemporary society along with English as a native language. For tests above the lower elementary levels, literacy in reading English is also necessary to obtain valid results on most of the group-administered tests. To provide valid assessment devices useful in other cultures or for use with subcultures or minority cultures in this country, attempts have been made to develop culture-fair tests that function independently of a specific culture, primarily by eliminating, or at least greatly reducing, language and cultural content.

Cattell's Culture-Fair Intelligence Test

The Culture-Fair Intelligence Test (Cattell, 1973) is a paper-and-pencil test that has no verbal content and is designed to reduce the effects of educational background and cultural influences. The test consists of four parts in multiple choice formats: (1) series—a figure must be chosen to complete the series, (2) classification—the object is to choose the figure that is different from the series, (3) matrices—the pattern of change occurring in the figures must be completed, and (4) conditions—the alternative with similar conditions to the example figure must be chosen. The test is available in two parallel forms and for three different age or ability levels: (1) children aged 4 through 8 and retarded adults, (2) children aged 8 through 14 and average adults, and (3) college students and adults with above-average intelligence. Within particular age levels the raw scores can be converted to normalized deviation IQ scores that have a mean of 100 and standard deviation of 16.

Raven's Progressive Matrices

Raven's Progressive Matrices (Raven, Court, & Raven, 1978) is a widely used culture-fair test that requires the subject to solve problems involving abstract figures and designs by indicating which of various multiple-choice alternatives complete a given matrix. Progressive changes occur in the vertical dimension, horizontal dimension, or both dimensions of a matrix and the space in the lower right-hand corner is blank. The examinee must determine the principle by which the matrices are progressively changing and select the correct alternative from the six that are provided. It is available in two forms, a black and white version for grade 8 through adulthood and the Coloured Progressive Matrices for children aged 5 to 11 years and for retarded adults. Developed in England, Raven's Progressive Matrices has been used in a large number of cross-cultural studies in many countries. Results of certain of these studies suggest that although this test is one of the best such tests available, it might better be described as culturally reduced rather than culture-fair or culture-free. Norms are based on samples of English children and adults, and one drawback for its use in this country is lack of normative data in the United States.

Raven's Progressive Matrices and other attempts to develop culture-fair tests not only represent attempts to increase the fairness of intelligence tests but also provide interesting ways of studying this type of ability and for assessing mental ability in widely differing cultures. Most studies in this country have found that children in lower socioeconomic groups score substantially lower than middle-class White groups on these tests, as well as on the more common culturally loaded intelligence tests. In addition, culture-fair tests typically do less well in predicting academic achievement or job performance than do the standard culturally loaded tests. This is not surprising, because academic achievement and often job performance include much culturally important content.

Cultural Differences

Test results based on norms of typical middle-class students cannot be appropriately applied to other ethnic minorities. In schools in which the counselor has considerable influence in determining guidance and testing procedures for these students, he or she can influence the adoption of appropriate programs and policies to prevent the misuse of test results.

The melting pot philosophy of cultural assimilation of all minorities into the Anglo-American culture has been generally rejected in favor of a multiethnic culture. Counselors who hold positive attitudes toward cultural differences are better able to accommodate the cultural predispositions of students from other ethnic backgrounds. The positive attitudes of counselors are more valuable than specific techniques or special materials. As students are accepted by counselors, they accept themselves and their abilities, as well as their limitations.

CAREER ASSESSMENT

A major question with regard to the use of vocational interest inventories is whether minority students are sufficiently familiar with the vocabulary, the examples, the occupational terms, and the problems that are used in these tests. Because many minority students bring to counseling differences from average middle-class White students with regard to experiences, orientations, and values (even though the minority students' aspirations may equal or exceed those of the middle-class student) their view of available occupations may be restricted. Students from disadvantaged backgrounds are likely to be less aware of the great variety of occupations and the skills required for certain occupations. They may also view potential occupations in quite different ways than is implied in occupational literature. Minority students tend to enter narrower ranges of fields of study.

Within minority communities there is often a lack of continuity and values between the school and the family and a lack of diversity in the representation of occupations that exist as models for children from these backgrounds. On various interest inventories minority students often achieve lower scores on the different scales than did the population on which norms were based, because such students indicate liking fewer occupational titles or interests than did those in the norm group.

Studies have shown that despite these differences, interest measures have similar validities among various minority groups in this country. Interest inventories can therefore be used with minority clients with the same amount of confidence as with Whites, with the possible exception of those coming from particularly disadvantaged backgrounds. Studies have also shown that interest measures predict college majors similarly for students from various minority backgrounds. Differences have been found on interest measures among different minorities, but these differences have equal predictive value (Lamb, 1974). For example, Blacks tend to score higher on social interests and in fact are more likely to enter social occupations, whereas Oriental students obtain higher scores on biological and physical science interests and lower scores on social and sales interests and are more likely to pursue occupations in line with these interests. Counselors should also be aware that some of the female-male differences found among Whites are similar but more extreme for Hispanic women.

There is a tendency among Asian-Americans to choose vocations only in business, science, mathematics, or engineering fields to the exclusion of humanities, social sciences, or law. When interpreting the results of interest inventories in educational and vocational counseling, this tendency to consider only a narrow range of possible career goals should be kept in mind. Expanding the range of occupations being considered may well be one of the goals of such counseling.

For minority students, the development of appropriate attitudes and behaviors can be enhanced by using representative minority models and pointing out their accomplishments in various fields. In this way counselors and human development professionals can assist minority students in understanding and appreciating the contributions that have been made and continue to be made by members of their own group.

Counselors must evaluate the testing and appraisal instruments to determine whether they meet criteria for nondiscrimination. Are data provided that assist in making sound occupational choices? What is the racial and socioeconomic makeup of the population on which the test is based?

Several interest inventories have been translated into a number of other languages. A question that needs to be asked in administering such a version of the inventory is whether the person taking the test is from a culture that has similar expectations and social customs as that for the culture in which the test was devised. Unfamiliarity with the nature and purpose of tests could be a problem, as could different ways of responding. Clients from a culture in which the emphasis is on agreeing with nearly everything (because it is considered impolite to disagree) may obtain test results that lack validity.

PERSONALITY ASSESSMENT

Although racial bias has seldom been a major issue in personality measurement, there is some evidence that various minority groups obtain scores on personality inventories that differ from those typically obtained in a White majority population. If personality measures such as the MMPI are to be used for selection purposes, such as in selecting airline pilots or graduate students in clinical psychology, then it is possible that some minority group members could be unfairly discriminated against in such selection procedures and this could happen if the instruments were used inappropriately. Differences on personality tests among minority groups and those from other cultures are to be expected and should be taken into consideration by counselors in their interpretations of personality test results. The scales of various personality inventories, however, usually indicate the same types of behavioral and personality characteristics of both minority and majority group members and therefore with caution can be appropriately used in counseling and psychiatric situations.

In general, test results obtained from Black clients on the MMPI should be interpreted with care. Greene (1987), in reviewing a large number of studies examining differences between Black and White Americans on the MMPI, reported no consistent pattern to such differences on any of the standard validity and clinical scales. Although Blacks frequently score higher on the F scale and scales 8 and 9 than White Americans, differences usually disappeared if the groups were matched on education and severity of psychopathology. There is a tendency for Black Americans to score higher on scale 8 and scale 9, but whether these scores reflecting higher levels of nonconformity, alienation, or impulsivity are due merely to different types of values and perceptions rather than higher levels of maladjustment is a question that has not been resolved (Groth-Marnat, 1984). There have been suggestions that the importance of scales 1, 8, and 9 should be decreased in importance when interpreting a Black person's profile.

No consistent differences were found in comparing Hispanics and White Americans on these scales. A number of other variables such as socioeconomic status, education, and intelligence seem to be more important determinants of MMPI performance than ethnic status.

There is some evidence that normal Native Americans tend to score higher on the clinical scales on the MMPI than do Whites, but similar differences do not appear on the validity scales (Greene, 1987).

Asian-Americans tend to underutilize counseling and mental health services and less often share experiences and emotions with those outside the family. They are more likely to express concerns in an indirect manner such as in physical symptoms. Thus more somatic complaints are likely to be found on an instrument such as the MMPI (Sue & Sue, 1974). There have been very few studies of the scores on personality inventories of Asian students as compared with Whites, but there is some suggestion that Asian-Americans may score higher on scale 2 of the MMPI (Greene, 1987).

Projective techniques are personality assessment instruments that undoubtedly have less value as assessment tools for minority clients. This is probably true for lower socioeconomic groups in general, as interpretations of protocols of persons from different cultures or lower socioeconomic classes tend to result in diagnoses of more severe illness.

ASSESSMENT OF CLIENTS WITH DISABILITIES

Assessment in rehabilitation settings may involve three different approaches to vocational evaluation. One approach is that of psychological testing, a second involves the use of work activities or work samples, and the third is evaluation of actual on-the-job activities (Berven, 1980).

For some disabled clients, psychological testing that provides relatively objective and reliable measures of individual abilities and interests can yield sufficient data to assist in decisions regarding vocational choice, training, and job placement while avoiding the great additional amount of time and expense involved in the other types of evaluation. For others, employability can better be explored through work samples and on-the-job evaluations. The employer becomes directly involved with the problems of the disabled, client characteristics can be ascertained, particularly in relation to the ultimate objective of more independent living, and a functional appraisal of job-related characteristics can be provided. Disadvantages include dependence on the good will of potential employers, insurance and wage laws, and regulations that make cooperation by employers difficult. Considerable evaluation information about clients must be obtained in advance if job tryouts are to be successful. For certain clients the characteristics of satisfactoriness and satisfaction associated with work adjustment become particularly important (Lofquist & Dawis, 1969).

Personality measures, interest inventories, general intelligence tests, measures of specific aptitudes, and tests of achievement or current skills have potential for use with various types of special populations. In using such instruments, however, results must be viewed with caution; for example, the inclusion of items related to general health and physical symptoms on a personality test may be answered in a "deviant" direction by persons who are physically ill or disabled and therefore yield scores that are difficult to interpret or are easily misinterpreted.

Section 504 of the 1973 Rehabilitation Act requires that testing be adapted for disabled students so that it measures what it is designed to measure while allowing for the student's disability. For disabled students, academic standards should be maintained while appropriate accommodations in test administration are made. Considerable information regarding the assessment and testing of persons with physical disabilities is found in a monograph published by Technical Education Research Centers (1977). Included in this monograph are lists of assessment instruments appropriate for particular types of disabilities, with recommendations for modifications where necessary.

The national testing programs such as ACT and the College Board provide special test forms and special testing arrangements for examinees with disabilities who are unable to take the test under standard testing conditions. These options include audiocassettes, braille and large-type editions, use of a reader, use of an amanuensis to mark responses, or extended time for testing. In general, predictions of college grades obtained from the special testing situations are less accurate, and more emphasis should be placed on other data (Laing & Farmer, 1984).

A number of the widely used school achievement tests are available in braille, large type, or both. The verbal scales on the WISC-R and the WAIS-R are widely used with blind and partially sighted persons. Certain of the comprehension items need rephrasing to be appropriate, and attention should be paid to the possibility that lower scores on certain subtests may result from experiential deprivation. The performance scales have less validity if visual impairment is more than minimal. For the hearing-impaired, on the other hand, the performance scale is one of the most accurate instruments for such assessment, whereas a number of tests that make up the verbal scale are not appropriate. Interest inventories such as the Strong or Kuder inventories are frequently used with visually impaired persons by reading items aloud or by tape recording.

The Peabody Picture Vocabulary Test and the Raven Progressive Matrices are two intelligence tests that require only a pointing response and are useful for the assessment of persons with cerebral palsy and other physical handicaps. Verbal scales of the Wechsler tests can also be used for the severely motor impaired. Certain of the performance subtests are not easily adapted because they require both adequate vision and some arm and hand use.

SUMMARY

1. Care must be taken in using tests with individuals or groups from different cultures because the instruments may be biased in their language, in their construction, and in their use or misuse. This care is particularly important when tests are used with minority individuals for whom different cultures, socioeconomic backgrounds, or language problems often significantly influence their test results.

2. Cultural factors influence not only aptitude test results but scores on interest and personality inventories as well.

3. With different types of accommodations, psychological test data can provide useful information in counseling handicapped individuals, but results obtained under atypical testing conditions must be viewed with caution.

CHAPTER 17

Communication of Test Results

One of the most important aspects of the assessment process is the communication of the results of such assessment. Counselors and human development professionals are constantly required to interpret assessment results both to clients and to others—parents, agencies, and other professionals. This chapter contains three sets of guidelines for such communications. The first lists some general guidelines regarding the communication of assessment procedures and the results. The second pertains to the actual interpretation of tests in the interview with the client. In the final section, the format and content of a typical written report on an assessment procedure are outlined.

The counselor's theoretical orientation usually determines how the test scores are interpreted to the client. Counselors whose orientation is client-centered are likely to present clients with key scores or percentiles and encourage the clients to join in the process of interpretation. They pay particular attention to how clients feel about the test results and the interpretations. More directive counselors typically review the purpose of testing, present the scores, clarify what they mean, and discuss their implications. Both types should consider assisting clients to make their own interpretations. The advantage of helping clients to interpret and react to test results assists the counselor in obtaining more insight about the client. Also, clients may become accepting of the results more readily by participating in the discussion and may be more likely to make use of the information in making decisions. Client participation in the interpretations, of course, usually takes more time on the part of both the counselor and the client, and this must be weighed when determining the type of approach to be used.

It is necessary to have a thorough understanding of tests, particularly of their theoretical foundations, if a counselor is to function as a professional interpreting the test rather than as a technician using a simple cookbook approach. Tests are used to diagnose and predict; interpretations must lead to the desired understanding and results. It must be remembered that a huge number of factors are involved in producing a particular test score.

These include clients' inherited abilities; their educational, cultural, family, and other experiences; their experiences with other tests, particularly psychological tests; their motivation; their text anxiety; the physical and psychological conditions under which they took the test; and the random variation in the test itself.

It is in the interpretation of the test that the various types of validity become extremely important. In every kind of test interpretation there is the assumption that there is a definite relationship between the person's score or result on a test and what it is being related to in the interpretation. It is therefore important to understand the construction and development of the test as well as its validity as determined by its relationship to that aspect or construct to which it is being related. Often this relationship is expressed in statistical terms. These include correlation coefficients, descriptive and comparative statistics, or expectancy tables. These statistics can often be presented to clients through profiles and other graphic means.

GENERAL GUIDELINES FOR COMMUNICATING TEST RESULTS

1. The first step in interpreting a test is to know and understand the test manual. In this way the validity of a test can be related to the purpose for which the test was used. The manual is also likely to contain information regarding the limits to which the test can be used and suggestions for interpreting the results.

2. In interpreting test results it is important to review the purposes for which the client took the test and the strengths and limitations of the test.

3. In interpreting results, the procedure by which the test is scored should be explained, along with an explanation of percentile ranks or standard scores if they are to be included in the interpretation.

4. Where possible, the results should be presented in terms of probabilities rather than certainties or specific predictions.

5. The emphasis should be on increasing client understanding and, where appropriate, encouraging clients to make their own interpretations.

6. The test results should be presented as they relate to other available information about the client.

7. The counselor should ensure that the interpretation of the test information is understood by the client and that clients are encouraged to express their reactions to the information.

8. Any relevant information or background characteristics, such as gender or handicapping conditions, should be examined, along with any apparent discrepancies or inconsistencies that appear.

9. Both strengths and weaknesses revealed by the tests results should be discussed objectively.

Some of the more difficult tests to interpret are those in which a pattern or profile of scores is provided and one on which the client's pattern is a flat profile with no particularly high or low scores. In educational and vocational counseling, flat profiles on interest inventories are often encountered by the counselor because it is the client's indecision that both brings the client into counseling and yields a flat profile. In other circumstances the individual's response set when taking the test may be a factor. The client makes little differentiation among the responses—all are high, neutral, or low. Validity indices and response patterns should therefore be examined before results are interpreted. With some inventories on which some scale scores are either slightly higher or slightly lower, there may be patterns that can be pointed out and discussed. Other relevant information such as past experiences, values, life-style goals, and previous work activities can be investigated.

On aptitude and achievement tests, flat profiles indicate a general level of performance in all areas that may be average, above average, or below average. Again, results from other types of tests and relevant past experiences may be taken into consideration in assisting with decision making.

GUIDELINES FOR THE TEST INTERPRETATION INTERVIEW

1. Show confidence in the client's ability to understand and make use of the test information. Emphasize the importance of adding the test data to other information that clients have about themselves. Emphasize the importance of clients themselves using the test information to help to assist them in making the decisions they are facing.

2. Ask clients to tell how they feel about the particular tests they took before beginning the interpretation process. This may yield information about their attitudes toward the particular tests and provide information about the usefulness or validity of some of the test results. An understanding of how the client perceives the test is often useful in the interpretation process. Stress the ideas that they can ask questions, that you, as a counselor, are particularly interested in their reactions to the interpretation, and that you want to know their thoughts about the results.

3. Do not begin discussing the results of any test without reminding clients which test is being discussed. Refresh their memory about it, for example, "Remember the test where you checked whether the two sets of names and numbers were exactly the same or were different? That was a test designed to measure clerical aptitude or ability. . ."

4. Try to make sure that the client is involved in the interpretation process. Do not merely state the results. Ask clients to estimate their scores before disclosing the results of a particular measure. After refreshing the client's memory about an instrument, ask "What were your reactions to that test? How do you think you did on it?"

5. Be prepared with a brief, clear description of what the instrument measures, including what the results mean and what the results do not mean. Be sure to clarify the differences between interests and aptitudes or abilities and personality characteristics. For example, "These are some of the activities which you indicated you liked and these are some that you said you did not like. Your interests seem to be more like those of people

in social service fields and unlike those of most people in mechanical and technical occupations."

6. Emphasize the usefulness of the tests for the clients' decision making rather than for information it provides to the counselor. Thus, "With this set of scores you can see how you compare with other college-bound students regarding your ability to learn academic subject matter." Rather than, "These results confirm my belief that you have the ability to do well in most colleges."

7. Discuss the test results in the context of other information the client has, particularly relating the test results to past, present, and future behavior. Past information and current test results should be related to current decisions and to future longer range plans rather than treating each of these subjects separately.

8. Present the purpose of a test in useful and understandable terms, trying to stay away from psychological jargon. Adjust the pace of the instructions and interpretations to the client's ability and understanding. Have clients summarize often in order to make sure the results are being understood. If necessary, additional information or alternative methods of interpretation can be used.

9. Where possible, use a graphic representation of the results in addition to a verbal explanation. Remember to turn test profiles so that the client can read them directly. If anyone is going to have to read the profile upside-down, it should be the counselor, who is familiar with profile sheets, rather than the client. It is probably better to position chairs so that counselor and client can go over the results together from similar angles. Complicated profile sheets should be grouped and summarized; this way a number of scores can be more easily assimilated by the client. It should not be assumed that most clients have the ability to do this on their own. The results should be explained simply, without the use of elaborate statistics.

10. Avoid overidentifying with the client's test results. Discuss a client's rejection of low test scores. The primary concern is what the results mean to the client, not what they mean to the counselor. Low performance scores should be expressed honestly but with perspective. They should not be ignored or attributed to inadequate measures or chance.

11. Make alternative plans sound respectable without imposing the biases of the typical middle-class counselor. Encourage clients to make their own plans rather than simply agreeing with the counselor's suggestions.

12. Be certain that both the counselor and the client relate the test information to other experiences of the client. For example, scholastic aptitude scores should be related to school grades. It should be remembered that the usual purpose of a scholastic aptitude test is to predict academic course grades. When such grades are available, emphasis should be placed on actual grades rather than on test results that merely predict those grades.

13. Whenever possible use the types of norms that are most relevant to the client. When such norms are not directly appropriate, information about this should be presented to the client and the interpretation of the results should make certain that this is clear.

14. Use only tests that you, the counselor, have personally taken, scored, and interpreted for yourself. Know the reasons a particular test was administered, what was expected from its interpretation, and the validity of the test for the purpose for which it was used. In addition, be aware that psychological tests should not be used to provide information that can be easily gathered in other ways. Tests should not be overused.

15. Toward the end of the interview, have the client summarize the results of the entire interview rather than attempting to do this for the client. Allow enough time to discuss this summarization and to discuss discrepancies or misunderstandings. Attempt to end on a positive note even though some portions of the interview have not yielded information that the client has been happy to receive. If the client has received discouraging information about educational, vocational, or other types of plans, try to broaden the scope of alternatives that might be considered. Emphasis should not only be placed on narrowing the focus of future plans, but also on broadening them.

16. Remember that in counseling there is almost always an implicit future orientation. Even though the immediate goal is to help clients to make a particular decision or to understand themselves better, there is also the belief that it is important for people to know themselves better but that ultimately the self-knowledge gained in counseling and testing will enable them to have more effective and satisfying lives and to make wiser and more realistic plans.

REPORT WRITING

In writing a report it is important to have some conceptualization of what is necessary to include in the report and a conceptualization of the client or person about whom you are writing the report. In writing a test report, the focus of the report and the way it is to be used are the first considerations in determining its content. The reasons for referral testing and the general purposes of the tests used provide the decisions about whether the report will be primarily oriented toward an objective summary of test results or an overall description of the individual being examined. Often there is a large amount of information available, and the report writer must decide what information should be included and what excluded (Drummond, 1988).

The first decision is determining the principal idea that should be communicated and what other types of information play an auxiliary role. One of the ways of emphasizing material is by the order in which it is presented, with the most important information first. Another way is through the adjectives and adverbs used in describing the person and his or her behavior. It can also be done through illustrations, using the most vivid example that points out the information that you wish to emphasize. Another mode is through repetition. Obviously repetition needs to be handled skillfully to avoid repeating the same material more often than necessary. Repeating information in the summary or conclusion is another way of adding emphasis.

Problems that should be avoided include (a) poor organization, in which the results are not integrated as a whole, (b) use of psychological jargon that will not be understood, (c) the use of terms that do not have clearly understood definitions, or (d) lack of integration between the test results and other information and recommendations related to the individual based on observation or other data.

What Gets Included in a Case Report

The following is an outline of a typical case report.

1. *Brief Description of Client.* Including some of the demographic information, a description might begin by saying "This is a 32-year-old man of medium build, with wrinkled and soiled clothes, who was extremely verbal and articulate in the interview." This beginning gives a bit of an impression and may include some identifying information such as age, race, and perhaps occupation or year in school.

2. *Reason for Counseling or Referral.* The next piece of information is the reason that the person is seeking counseling, the problem they present, or the reason they were referred for testing. A brief description of a client along with a brief description of the nature of the problem and the reason for undertaking the evaluation give a general focus for the report.

3. *Relevant Background Information.* Next to be included might be some additional demographic data and some of the information available from the referral source. The background information should be relevant to the purpose of the testing, should be related to the overall purpose of the report, and should be as succinct as possible. It is certainly likely to include the client's educational background, occupation, family background, health status, and current life situation. It should also include other aspects of personal history that are related to the reason for testing and help to place the problem or reason for testing in its proper context.

4. *Evaluation Procedures.* Evaluation procedures can be briefly described giving the rationale for testing, the names of the tests used, and why the particular tests were selected.

5. *Behavioral Observations.* Specific behaviors that were observed during the interviews and during the tests can be included in the next section. The way the client approached the test, any problems that arose, and any other factors that might bring into question the validity of any of the tests used should be mentioned. Only relevant observations should be included. This section is likely to be very brief if the behavior was normal and much more lengthy if behaviors were unusual.

6. *Test Results and Their Interpretation.* Next is a report of the test results, an overall interpretation, and diagnostic impressions. The description of the test results does not necessarily need to include the actual test scores, but they should be included if the report is for other professionals who are knowledgeable about testing. The most important part of this section is the interpretation of the results. Here all of the test data are integrated, along with the behavioral observations and relevant background information. A discussion of the client's strengths and weaknesses is included.

A statement regarding the client's future prospects in relation to the reason for the testing often needs to be included. These would include both favorable and unfavorable predictions.

7. *Recommendations.* The primary reason for testing and the subsequent case report is usually to gain recommendations. Particularly if the case is a referral, recommendations can include further testing or activities that the client or others should undertake in relation to the problem. Recommendations should relate to the problem and to the general purpose of the testing and report. They should be as practical and specific as possible.

8. *Brief Concluding Summary.* A summary paragraph should succinctly restate the most important findings and conclusions (Maloney & Ward, 1976).

Writing Style

Writing a report is often much easier if an overall case conceptualization is developed first. Reports often include the general theoretical framework that is followed by the counselor. When psychoanalytic theory was the primary theory followed by counselors, a great deal of emphasis was placed on early childhood experiences. Those who follow Rogerian theory probably pay particular attention to the person's self-concept. The Gestalt theorist looks specifically at current relationships, and the behavioral counselor will be interested in things that reinforce particular behaviors. Counselors may not feel they have a particular theory of behavior, but in the case report their general theory of personality often emerges because it influences what they perceive from the interviews and test results and therefore what they report.

In reporting test results it is a good idea to stay away from testing jargon. It is also important in writing a report to avoid the extremes of focusing either too much or too little on the test results themselves. It is possible to report extensive test results without relating them to the individual and the individual's situation and future plans, and thus not offer much in the way of conclusions or practical suggestions. It is also possible to depart too much from the test results and downplay them, particularly if the test information does not come out as expected or if it is not likely to be seen in positive terms by the client.

It should also be remembered that it is better to get to a report immediately after counseling and testing rather than letting a considerable period of time go by. Counselors enjoy working with people much more than writing reports, so it is easy to put these aside. Timeliness becomes particularly important when a number of clients are seen each day. It is important to at least write down the information that will be needed to write a report, even if it is not possible to write the final report immediately. In writing a report it is necessary to come out and say what needs to be said, making clear statements and clear recommendations. On the other hand, where results must be considered inconclusive, this also needs to be said.

SUMMARY

The influence of the counselor's theoretical orientation and the importance of case conceptualization are related both to the interpretation of the test results and the content of a report of the results of an assessment. Nine general guidelines for communicating test results were presented in this chapter, along with 16 counselor behaviors useful in the test interpretation interview. A sample outline provided eight topics typically included in a written case report.

CHAPTER 18

Ethical and Social Issues in Testing

ETHICAL STANDARDS

There are a number of situations when psychological tests are used in counseling and placement in which ethical principles are called into question. In this chapter important ethical issues related to tests are discussed, along with the accompanying ethical principles that need to be considered. The second portion of this chapter includes several social issues related to testing that have not been included in previous chapters.

Because of the number of cases that have arisen in the past regarding the ethical use of psychological tests, each of the different professional organizations whose members make use of tests have developed, among their codes of ethics, principles that deal specifically with psychological testing. The American Association of Counseling and Development's *Ethical Standards* (AACD, 1988) and the American Psychological Association's *Ethical Principles of Psychologists* (APA, 1990) each contains a section related to educational and psychological testing. In addition, the AACD statement *The Responsibilities of Test Users* (the RUST statement revised) (AACD, 1989) and the joint committee *Standards for Educational and Psychological Testing* (AERA, APA, NCME, 1985), which were discussed in chapter 2, also contain statements of test user responsibilities and ethical standards. Excerpts from these two statements most relevant to test use in the counseling process are presented in appendices A and B.

Ethical Standards for Test Quality

A portion of *Standards for Educational and Psychological Testing* deals with the technical quality of tests and test materials and standards to be followed by test developers and by test publishers before distributing the test. Test publishers and authors make money from the royalties on tests that are sold, and there is an obvious temptation to exaggerate the usefulness or the validity of such tests. This is an area in which the committee that developed the standards placed considerable emphasis in order to put pressure on publishers to maintain "truth in advertising" in test publishing.

These standards include providing evidence of reliability and validity, information regarding the method of estimating reliability and the population on which it was measured, and types of validity evidence, including validity relevant to the intended purpose of the test.

Certain of the standards are designed to prevent the premature sale of tests for general use and to specify when the test is to be released for research purposes only. The standards emphasize that the test manual should not be designed to sell the test but should include adequate information about the administration, scoring, norms, and other technical data to permit the potential user to adequately evaluate the test itself, its potential use, and provide information important in interpreting its results.

Counselor Competence in Testing

An important ethical issue lies with competence of the counselor or human development professional to use the various available assessment instruments. The issue is whether those who use various tests have sufficient knowledge and understanding to select tests intelligently, and to interpret their results (*Responsibilities*, III, *Standards*, 6.6). Because different tests demand different levels of competence for their use, users must recognize the limits of their competence and make use only of instruments for which they have adequate preparation and training. The administration and interpretation of individual intelligence tests such as the Stanford-Binet or the Wechsler tests, certain personality tests such as the Minnesota Multiphasic Personality Inventory, or projective personality tests such as the Rorschach or the Thematic Apperception Test require advanced training and practice to obtain the necessary background and skill for their appropriate use.

In an attempt to deal with this problem, a number of publishers will sell tests only to those who are qualified, and require a statement of qualifications from purchasers of psychological tests. In cooperation with the Test User Qualifications Working Group (see chapter 2), publishers have produced forms that must be completed by those purchasing the tests regarding their educational background and experience. Tests are graded in regard to the amount of background and experience required and are sold only to those who meet the standards required for particular tests. These statements of qualifications are usually included in the test publishers' sales catalogs, and purchasers complete the information regarding their qualifications. Typically a master's degree and a course in psychological assessment are the minimum qualifications required to purchase many of the tests commonly used by counselors. Graduate students who need to purchase particular tests for training or research purposes must have the order signed by the graduate instructor, who takes on responsibility for seeing that the tests are properly used.

The major responsibility for the proper use of tests, however, is that of the professional who makes use of them. Is the test appropriate for the person who is being tested? How are the results going to be used? Is the test reliable enough? Does it have enough validity to be used for the purpose for which it is planned? Counselors who are well trained select tests that are appropriate both for the person to whom they are administered and for the specific purpose for which the person is being tested. They are also sensitive to the many conditions that affect test performance. They are knowledgeable enough about individual differences and human behavior not to make unwarranted interpretations of test results. The ethical statements of the different associations have sections dealing with test selection (e.g., *Responsibilities*, IV; *Standards*, 9.1–9.6).

CLIENT WELFARE ISSUES

Occasionally an ethical issue arises regarding the welfare of the client in the testing process. Is the welfare of the client being taken into consideration in the choice and use of tests (*Standards*, 6.4–6.7)? Except in such cases as court referrals or custody determinations, this is seldom an issue in counseling because tests are usually used to help the client and not for other purposes.

Another client welfare issue deals with the questions of privacy and confidentiality (*Responsibilities*, VIII). In counseling situations, clients are typically willing to reveal aspects about themselves to obtain help with their problems; thus the invasion of privacy issue, often a concern in psychological testing elsewhere, is seldom a concern in counseling. Clients obviously would not wish this information to be disclosed to others. Test data, along with other records of the counseling relationship, must be considered professional information for use in counseling and must not be revealed to others without the expressed consent of the client. Certain types of test results, such as those assessing intelligence or aptitude and those that ask for or reveal emotional or personality or attitudinal traits, often may deal with sensitive aspects of personal lives or limitations that an individual would prefer to conceal and certainly not have disclosed to others.

Problems of confidentiality often arise when the counselor is employed by an institution or organization, which results in conflicting loyalties. In these circumstances counselors should tell clients in advance how the test results will be used and make clear the limits of confidentiality. In general, ethical principles state that the test results are confidential unless the client gives his or her consent for the test results to be provided to someone else. The limits of confidentiality and the circumstances under which it can be broken (such as clear and present danger or court subpoena), must be communicated to and understood by the client.

In addition, the Family Education Rights and Privacy Act of 1974 requires that educational institutions release test result information to parents of minor students and to those students 18 years of age or older. In reporting results to others who have a reason and need to make use of the results, counselors must ensure that the results of the assessment and their interpretations are not misused by others. Is the person receiving the information qualified to understand and interpret the results? It is incumbent on the counselor to interpret the results in a way that they can be intelligently understood by those receiving them, and this can include teachers and parents (*Responsibilities*, VII, VIII). In addition, the counselor has an obligation to point out the limitations of the results and any other important information about reliability or validity, as well as a description of the norms used and their appropriateness.

Clients, of course, have the right to know the results of tests, with interpretations of the results communicated to them in a language they can clearly understand. They must be interpreted to clients in such a way that clients understand what the tests mean and also what they do not mean. It is important that clients not reach unwarranted conclusions from the interpretation that they receive (*Responsibilities*, VII). An additional problem is related to the communication of the test results to others.

Results should usually be communicated descriptively rather than with particular numbers, and especially avoiding labels that can be misinterpreted or actually damaging. Labeling someone as schizophrenic or with a low IQ can stigmatize a person even when such terms are appropriate. They not only suggest a lack of any chance to grow or change, but may also become self-fulfilling prophecies. Instead, interpretations should be presented in terms of likely levels of academic achievement or formulations of interventions to assist the individual in behaving more effectively.

An additional consideration regarding confidentiality requires that the test results be kept in a place where they are accessible only to authorized individuals and should be kept in records only so long as they serve a useful purpose. With the advent of computerized record keeping, the problem of keeping test results secure and inaccessible to all but authorized users has increased. Effective measures for protecting the security of individual records must be maintained.

Tests must be administered in a standardized fashion if the results are to be adequately interpreted. One problem in the area of test administration involves test security. It is obvious that test results will not be valid if people can obtain the tests for study in advance. For tests such as the College Boards or the Medical College Admission Test, elaborate procedures are established to ensure that there is adequate security for these tests on which important decisions will be based. In addition, tests need to be accurately scored and accurately profiled if the results are to have valid meaning.

Another ethical issue, probably a minor one for counselors, is in regard to what might be called impersonal service in using tests. It is possible for a counselor or a psychologist to use tests in which test booklets are sent to clients, returned, scored, and an interpretation sent back to each client. A fee is charged for this service but the counselor does not meet the client face to face. Considerable money in fees could be generated for this service. Without knowing why the person is requesting the tests, the purposes for which test results are to be used, or the interpretation that clients could give to the results, such a practice would constitute a misuse of testing. Therefore this practice, along with other types of impersonal psychological services, is considered unethical. The opportunity for such practices has increased with the use of computer interpretations. It is now possible for a person to take a test and then receive a very elaborate interpretation of the results. The client may either have taken the test itself on a computer or had the test scored and interpreted by a computer. These computer interpretations are, of course, based on norms, which are not necessarily appropriate for a particular individual. The misuse of such computer-generated test interpretations has become an issue of increased concern to the counseling and psychological professions.

A final issue deals with the ethical use of psychological tests in research. When tests are given for research purposes, the first principle to be employed is that of informed consent—having had the procedures explained to them, individuals must have the opportunity to choose not to participate. Minors should also be informed, to the extent of their comprehension, and parental consent is often necessary as well. A particular problem arises in testing research when knowledge regarding the specific objectives of a test has a substantial effect on the attitude of the person taking it, therefore yielding invalid research results. In research studies there are also the ethical issues of privacy and confidentiality.

In general, counselors have had fewer ethical problems in the use of tests than have various other professionals, because counselors typically use tests in their activities on behalf of the client—to assist the client in regard to decision making or to provide additional information for treatment. They do not usually use tests for institutional purposes such as selection or placement.

ISSUES OF GENDER BIAS IN TESTING

During the past several decades, testing has been a controversial subject that has become involved with a number of social issues. In particular, testing has been attacked for its discrimination against minority groups (see chapter 16). Tests are designed to measure differences among individuals, but when they reveal differences among ethnic or gender groups they are considered to be biased.

These issues have led to much disenchantment with psychological tests—particularly intelligence and academic aptitude tests. Much of the controversy has resulted when test scores have shown group differences. There is less controversy when the discussion is restricted to individual differences, and it is individual differences with which counselors are typically concerned.

Gender Bias in Aptitude Testing

Intelligence tests have not been shown to produce significant differences between men and women. Mean scores for both sexes are essentially the same. On specific aptitudes, however, women tend to score higher than men on tests of verbal ability whereas men obtain higher scores on numerical and spatial aptitudes. Women tend to achieve higher grades in elementary school, high school, and in college, although the difference in college disappears when controlled for types of majors and types of courses. The question regarding lower scores on mathematical ability is a controversial one at the present time; some argue that the difference is an inherent sex-related difference, whereas others argue that it is due to stereotypical attitudes on the part of parents and teachers, which result in the two sexes being differentially encouraged to learn mathematics. Again, this mean difference is of less consequence to counselors as they work with individual students of either sex, who may obtain scores anywhere throughout the entire range.

A recent development dealing with the gender bias of tests is related to the awarding of scholarships to the top 1% or 2% on the basis of scores on a scholastic aptitude test. In the case of awarding certain scholarships, this has resulted in a higher proportion of men receiving scholarships than women. The underlying cause of this problem may very well be the differences in variance between the two sexes (Benbow, 1988). On many psychological variables, as well as on numerous other factors, men vary over a greater range than do women. Thus more men than women are likely to be found at both extremes. Just as the top 1% on many factors contains more men than women, so does the bottom 1%. There is pressure to develop tests to qualify for scholarships that eliminate this type of bias, but if the variance hypothesis holds, this will be a difficult task. In the case of the National Merit Testing Program, different cut-off scores are already used for different states, so that the top 1% of the students in each state qualify. If this practice were extended to the sexes, then qualifying scores could be established to ensure that the top 1% of both men and women would qualify.

Gender Bias in Personality Measurement

Although most of the controversy regarding bias in tests has centered around aptitude or intelligence tests, certain of the tests used in counseling, such as interest and personality measures, have not been entirely free of bias. Most personality measures are scored on norms developed for each sex, and thus a particular score on a particular personality trait achieved by a man or a woman is scored on the respective male or female norms; thus the bias that would result if men and women tended to score particularly differently on a personality characteristic is eliminated. Counselors using particular tests, such as the MMPI, should be aware that certain behavior patterns likely to be attributed to certain profile types often differ for men and women.

Gender Bias in Interest Measurement

During the decades of the 1960s and 1970s, charges of gender bias were leveled against vocational interest inventories and their use in the vocational and educational counseling of women. Several of the interest inventories used only male pronouns and male-oriented occupational names and listed primarily stereotypical occupations for each sex. Earlier versions of both the male and female forms of the Strong Interest Inventories were particularly criticized for this bias. The bias that existed has been examined by several national committees, with resulting recommendations to eliminate both the sexually stereotypic language that exists among the inventories and also to eliminate the tendency of test results to channel students on the basis of gender, and limit their consideration of certain careers.

There are several methods by which publishers have attempted to eliminate, or at least reduce, gender bias on interest inventories. One is by using single-sex norms. In the case of the Strong Interest Inventory and the Kuder Occupational Interest Survey, the occupational scales are based on separate criterion groups for each sex. All clients receive scores on both the male and female scores. Thus individuals can compare their interests with those of both sexes in a wide variety of occupations. On basic interest scales, profiles now show scores for both male and female norm groups; thus gender bias is eliminated by use of the inclusion of norms for both sexes. In the case of the earlier forms of these instruments, many more occupations were shown for men than for women, which has the tendency to limit the number of careers considered by women. In recent years test authors have attempted to develop the same number and type of scales for both men and women. The only exceptions are occupations where it is very difficult to find a norm group of one sex, such as male home economics teachers or female pilots. Virtually all inventories have eliminated sexist language, replacing "policeman" with "police officer" and "mailman" with "postal worker."

Another method by which publishers of interest inventories have attempted to make them free of gender bias has been to include only interest items that are equally attractive to both sexes. For example, on an interest inventory containing items related to the six Holland themes, many more men than women respond to a realistic item such as "repairing an automobile," and many more women to a social item such as "taking care of very small children." Through the elimination of items that are stereotypically masculine or stereotypically feminine, such differences can be largely avoided. For example, realistic items such as "refinishing furniture" or "operating a lawn mower" or a social item such as "teaching in high school" tend to receive approximately equal responses by both men and women (Rayman, 1976). An interest inventory such as the UNIACT (Hanson, Prediger, & Schussel, 1977), published by the American College Testing Program, is a sex-balanced inventory, increasing the probability that men will obtain higher scores on the social scale and women on the realistic scale, and thus that each sex would be more likely to give consideration to occupations in a full range of fields.

Holland has resisted constructing sex-balanced scales on his Self-Directed Search, believing that the use of sex-balanced scales destroys much of the predictive validity of the instrument. An inventory that predicts that equal numbers of men and women will become automobile mechanics or become elementary school teachers is going to have reduced predictive validity given the male and female socialization and occupational patterns found in today's society. When such inventories are used primarily for vocational exploration, however, an instrument that "channels" interests into stereotypical male and female fields can be criticized for containing this gender bias.

By including scores on all occupational scales for both sexes, including norms for both sexes on interest scales, by eliminating stereotypical language and, for some instruments, developing sex-balanced items, gender bias in interest testing has been greatly reduced. It must be remembered, however, that gender-based restrictions in interest preferences and career choices will continue as long as societal influences limit the experiences men and women are exposed to or are able to explore (Walsh & Betz, 1990).

COUNSELING PROCESS ISSUES

It is probably to be expected that tests used for selection into desirable programs and occupations will be criticized, particularly by those not selected. The use of tests in counseling situations, however, has been much less controversial. Counselors and human development professionals typically use tests for problem-solving purposes to assist the individual. Personality inventories can reveal information useful in the counseling process, and interest and aptitude test results can assist in educational and vocational planning. Diagnostic tests in academic areas such as reading or arithmetic skills can help to identify those who need special instruction in particular areas and to plan future educational programs. Because of criticisms leveled against psychological tests when used in selection procedures (and perhaps in part due to some counselors' own experiences with scholastic aptitude tests used for selection purposes), counselors occasionally develop a bias against psychological tests. They refuse to use them in individual counseling programs where they can often be particularly valuable.

Much of the criticism of psychological testing and assessment and attacks on their use in educational institutions and employment situations has resulted mainly in constructive effects. Increased awareness of the utility and limitations of testing has resulted in the need for more carefully trained users of test results as the personal and social consequences of testing have become increasingly apparent. Consistent with these needs, the primary objective of this book has been to improve the knowledge and understanding of counselors and human development professionals who administer and interpret the results of these assessment procedures.

Counselors should not blame the tests themselves when tests have been used inappropriately. Obviously tests are often misused and occasionally misused by counselors and other human development professionals, but that does not mean the tests are at fault. When pliers are used on a bolt where an adjustable wrench is called for, it is not the pair of pliers nor its manufacturer that is criticized.

One of the earlier criticisms of psychological tests was that they were dominating the counseling process. With the development of many new counseling theories and techniques, there are few if any strict practitioners of what used to be known as trait-and-factor counseling, for whom psychological tests totally dominate their counseling practices.

In using tests in counseling, it is important that the counselor attempt to understand the frame of reference of the client. If the counselor is knowledgeable about tests, the counselor can then better help the client understand the information that tests can provide. In interpreting test results, the counselor must help clients to understand their implications and their limitations, to help clients integrate the test information into their self-perceptions and decision-making strategies.

It has been suggested (and even mandated by legislative action) that tests should not be used because certain disadvantaged groups make poor showings on them. In these situations, the test results are often indicative of symptoms of a societal ailment, analogous to a fever thermometer that indicates an illness. When the tests reveal that the disadvantaged have not had the opportunity to learn certain concepts, there should be an attempt to provide these opportunities, not to dispose of the instruments that reveal such symptoms.

Another criticism of using tests in counseling is the point that validity coefficients are based on groups of persons, and it is not possible to discern the validity of any test score for any one individual. It is in the counseling process that the counselor attempts to help clients determine the validity of that test score for that individual. To use tests properly in counseling, the counselor must know as much about the client and the client's environment as possible. Counselors must also be well informed about tests and have a basic familiarity with them. Although they do not need to have a great deal of understanding regarding the technical aspects of test development and standardization, they do need to have a clear understanding of the general purposes of the particular tests they use, the uses to which they can be put, and the role these tests can play in the counseling process.

In the information age, test results will continue to provide important data needed for many decisions. In addition to individual personal and career decisions, there will be increased reliance on tests to determine minimum skills and competencies for educational institutions, licensing and certification, and personnel selection.

The increasing automation of psychological assessment will make the administration and scoring of tests, as well as the interpretation of their results, more efficient, more extensive, and more complex. Already many tests commonly administered by counselors are available for administration, scoring, and interpretation with a microcomputer (e.g., CPI, DAT, Millon, MMPI, MBTI, 16 PF, Strong, and Wechsler tests). Standardized interview data may also be obtained through interaction with a computer.

FINAL STATEMENT

Psychological tests are used by personnel staff to select employees, by school psychologists to track pupils, by clinical psychologists to diagnose patients, by college admissions staffs to admit students, and by forensic psychologists to determine sanity. In the counseling setting, however, psychological tests are used to help clients to understand themselves. With the prevalence of negative attitudes toward psychological tests, counselors may be reluctant to make adequate use of them in assisting clients, but they should remember that the use of tests in counseling differs from other test use. Counselors use tests primarily to assist individuals in developing their potentialities to the fullest and to their own satisfaction. Test results are designed to be used by the clients themselves, and only in the ways in which they decide to make or not to make use of them. In counseling, tests are not used by others to make decisions for or against a client.

The concept of individual differences is a basic tenet of counseling. Assessment procedures enable counselors to measure and compare the different characteristics of clients and their environments. Tests and assessment data can provide important behavior samples useful in the counseling process to assist counselors to understand their clients better and clients to understand themselves.

The purpose of this text has been to help current and future counselors and human development professionals, as well as others in the helping professions, to become better consumers and interpreters of psychological and educational tests and assessment procedures. We have attempted to cover some of the philosophical and ethical principles related to the use of tests, basic knowledge about certain of the tests, when they should be used, and how to interpret and report test and assessment results.

By using tests ethically, appropriately, and intelligently counselors and human development professionals can make use of tests in assisting their clients to understand their problems, make use of their potentialities, function more effectively, make more effective decisions, and live more satisfying lives.

Permissions

We are grateful to the following authors and publishers for permission to reproduce sample items from the assessment instruments named below:

SCL-90-R by L. R. Derogatis, PhD, professor and director of Division of Clinical Psychology, Hahnemann University Medical Center. Published by Clinical Psychometric Research, Towson, MD. Copyright 1983.

My Vocational Situation by J. L. Holland, D. C. Daiger, and P. G. Power. Reproduced by special permission of the publisher, Consulting Psychologists Press, Inc., Palo Alto, CA 94306. Further reproduction is prohibited without the publisher's consent. Copyright 1980.

Values Scale by D. E. Super and D. D. Nevill. Reproduced by special permission of the publisher, Consulting Psychologists Press, Inc., Palo Alto, CA 94306. Further reproduction is prohibited without the publisher's consent. Copyright 1985.

Strong Interest Inventory, Form T325 of the Strong Vocational Interest Blanks® by Edward K. Strong, Jr. Copyright 1985 by the Board of Trustees of the Leland Stanford Junior University. Reproduced by special permission of the agent, Consulting Psychologists Press, Inc., Palo Alto, CA 94306, with the permission of the publishers, Stanford University Press.

Kuder General Interest Inventory, Form E. Copyright 1963, 1985 by G. Frederic Kuder. Reprinted by permission of CTB, 2500 Garden Road, Monterey, CA 93940.

Career Assessment Inventory by C. B. Johansson. Copyright 1973, 1976, 1980, 1982, 1984, 1985, 1986 by National Computer Systems, Inc. All rights reserved. Reproduced by permission of National Computer Systems, Inc.

ACT Career Planning Program by American College Testing Program. Published by American College Testing Program. Copyright 1983.

USES Interest Inventory by United States Employment Service. Published by U.S. Department of Labor. Copyright 1981. Reproduced with permission of the U.S. Employment Service, U.S. Department of Labor.

Section VI

Appendices

APPENDIX A

Excerpts From The Responsibilities of Test Users (The RUST Statement Revised)

by
The Association for Measurement and Evaluation in Counseling and Development (AMECD)
and
The American Association for Counseling and Development (AACD)

March 1989

EXCERPTS FROM RESPONSIBILITIES OF TEST USERS (AACD/AMECD POLICY STATEMENT)

II. *TEST DECISIONS*: Decisions should be based on data. In general, test data improve the quality of decisions. However, deciding whether or not to test creates the possibility of three kinds of errors. First, a decision not to test can result in misjudgments that stem from inadequate or subjective data. Second, tests may produce data which could improve accuracy in decisions affecting the client, but which are not used in counseling. Third, tests may be misused. The responsible practitioner will determine, in advance, the purpose for administering a given test, considering protections and benefits for the client, practitioner, and agency.

A. Define purposes for testing by developing specific objectives and limits for the use of test data in relation to the particular assessment purpose:
   1. Placement: If the purpose is selection or placement, the test user should understand the programs or institutions into which the client may be placed and be able to judge the consequences of inclusion or exclusion decisions for the client.
   2. Prediction: If the purpose is prediction, the test user should understand the need for predictive data as well as possible negative consequences (e.g., stereotyping).
   3. Description: If the purpose is diagnosis or description, the test user should understand the general domain being measured and be able to identify those aspects which are adequately measured and those which are not.
   4. Growth: If the purpose is to examine growth or change, the test user should understand the practical and theoretical difficulties associated with such measurement.
   5. Program Evaluation: If the purpose of assessment is the evaluation of an agency's programs, the test user should be aware of the various information needs for the evaluation and of the limitation of each instrument used to assess those needs, as well as how the evaluation will be used.
B. Determine Information Needs and Assessment Needs:
   1. Determine whether testing is intended to assess individuals, groups, or both.
   2. Identify the particular individual and/or group to be tested with regard to the agency's purposes and capabilities.
   3. Determine the limitations to testing created by an individual's age; racial, sexual, ethnic, and cultural background; or other characteristics.
   4. Avoid unnecessary testing by identifying decisions which can be made with existing information.
   5. Assess the consequences for clients of deciding either to test or not to test.
   6. Limit data gathering to the variables that are needed for the particular purpose.
   7. Cross-validate test data using other available information whenever possible.

III.   *QUALIFICATIONS OF TEST USERS*: While all professional counselors and personnel workers should have formal training in psychological and educational measurement and testing, this training does not necessarily make one an expert and even an expert does not have all the knowledge and skills appropriate to some particular situations or instruments. Questions of user qualifications should always be addressed when testing is being considered.
      Lack of proper qualifications can lead to errors and subsequent harm to clients. Each professional is responsible for making judg-

ments on this in each situation and cannot leave that responsibility either to client or to others in authority. It is incumbent upon the individual test user to obtain appropriate training or arrange for proper supervision and assistance when engaged in testing.

Qualifications for test users depend on four factors:
A. Purposes of Testing: Technically proper testing for ill-understood purposes may constitute misuse. Because the purposes of testing dictate how the results are used, qualifications of test users are needed beyond general testing competencies to interpret and apply data.
B. Characteristics of Tests: Understanding the nature and limitations of each instrument used is needed by test users.
C. Settings and Conditions of Test Use: Assessment of the quality and relevance of test user knowledge and skill to the situation is needed before deciding to test or to participate in a testing program.
D. Roles of Test Selectors, Administrators, Scorers and Interpretors: test users must be engaged in only those testing activities for which their training and experience qualify them.

IV. *TEST SELECTION*: The selection of tests should be guided by information obtained from a careful analysis of the characteristics of the population to be tested; the knowledge, skills, abilities or attitudes to be assessed; the purposes for teaching; and the eventual use and interpretation of the test scores. Use of tests should also be guided by criteria for technical quality recommended by measurement professionals (i.e., the APA/AERA/NCME "Standards for Educational and Psychological Tests" and the APA/AERA/NCME/AACD/ASHA "Code of Fair Testing Practices in Education").
A. Relate Validity to Usage.
B. Use Appropriate Tests.
C. Consider Technical Characteristics.
D. Employ User Participation in Test Selection: Actively involve everyone who will be using the assessments (administering, scoring, summarizing, interpreting, making decisions) as appropriate in the selection of tests so that they are congruent with local purposes, conditions, and uses.

VI. *TEST SCORING*: Accurate measurement of human performance necessitates adequate procedures for scoring the responses of examinees. These procedures must be audited as necessary to ensure consistency and accuracy of application.
A. Consider Accuracy and Interpretability: Select a test scoring process that maximizes accuracy and interpretability.
B. Rescore Samples: Routinely rescore samples of examinee responses to monitor the accuracy of the scoring process.
C. Screen Test Results: Screen reports of test results using personnel competent to recognize unreasonable or impossible scores.

D. Verify Scores and Norms: Verify the accuracy of computation of raw scores and conversion to normative scales prior to release of such information to examinees or users of test results.

E. Communicate Deviations: Report as part of the official record any deviation from normal conditions and examinee behaviors.

F. Label Results: Clearly label the date of test administration along with the scores.

VII. *TEST INTERPRETATION*: Test interpretation encompasses all the ways that meaning is assigned to the scores. Proper interpretation requires knowledge about the test which can be obtained by studying its manual and other materials along with current research literature with respect to its use; no one should undertake the interpretation of scores on any test without such study.

A. Consider Reliability: Reliability is important because it is a prerequisite to validity and because the degree to which a score may vary due to measurement error is an important factor in its interpretation.

  1. Estimate test stability using a reliability (or other appropriate) coefficient.

  2. Use the standard error of measurement to estimate the amount of variation due to random error in individual scores and to evaluate the precision of cut-scores in selection decisions.

  3. Consider, in relationship to the uses being made of the scores, variance components attributed to error in the reliability index.

  4. Evaluate reliability estimates with regard to factors that may have artificially raised or lowered them (e.g., test speededness, biases in population sampling).

  5. Distinguish indices of objectivity (i.e., scorer reliability) from test reliability.

B. Consider Validity: Proper test interpretation requires knowledge of the validity evidence available for the intended use of the test. Its validity for other uses is not relevant. Indeed, use of a measure for a purpose for which it was not designed may constitute misuse. The nature of the validity evidence required for a test depends upon its use.

  1. Use for Placement: Predictive validity is the usual basis for valid placement.

    a. Obtain adequate information about the programs or institutions in which the client may be placed to judge the consequences of such placement.

    b. Use all available evidence to infer the validity of an individual's score. A single test score should not be the sole basis for a placement or selection recommendation. Other items of information about an individual (e.g., teacher report, counselor opinion) frequently improve the likelihood that proper judgments and decisions will be made.

    c. Consider validity for each alternative (i.e., each placement option) when interpreting test scores and other evidence.

    d. Examine the possibility that a client's group membership (socioeconomic status, gender, subculture, etc.) may affect test performance and, consequently, validity.

    e. Examine the probability of favorable outcomes for each possible placement before making recommendations.

    f. Consider the possibility that outcomes favorable from an institutional point of view may differ from those that are favorable from the individual's point of view.

2. Use for Prediction: The relationship of the test scores to an independently developed criterion measure is the basis for predictive validity.

    a. Consider the reliability and validity of the criterion measure(s) used.

    b. Consider the validity of a measure in the context of other predictors available (i.e., does the test make a valid contribution to prediction beyond that provided by other measures).

    c. Use cross validation to judge the validity of prediction processes.

    d. Consider the effect of labeling, stereotyping, and prejudging people (e.g., self-fulfilling prophecies that may result from labeling are usually undesirable).

    e. If a statistically valid predictor lacks both construct and content validity, analyze the mechanism by which it operates to determine whether or not its predictive validity is spurious.

3. Use for Description: Comprehensiveness of information is fundamental to effective description, since no set of test scores completely describes an individual.

    a. Clearly identify the domain assessed by any measure and the adequacy of the content sampling procedures used in developing items.

    b. Clarify the dimensions being measured when multiple scores from a battery or inventory are used for description.

    c. Distinguish characteristics that can be validated only empirically and those for which content specifications exist.

4. Use for Assessment of Growth: Assessment of growth or change requires valid tests as well as valid procedure for combining them.

    a. Specifically evaluate the reliability of differences between scores as measures of change.

    b. Establish the validities of the measures used to establish change in relation to one another as well as individually.

    c. Consider comparability of intervals in scales used to assess change.

      d. Assess potential for undesirable correlations of difference scores with the measures entering into their calculations (e.g., regression toward the mean).

      e. Recognize the potential lack of comparability between norms for differences derived from norms and norms for differences derived from differences (i.e., mathematically derived norms for differences are not necessarily equivalent to norms based on distributions of actual differences).

   5. Use for Program Evaluation: Assessments of group differences (between groups or within groups over time) are based on research designs which to varying degrees admit competing interpretations of the results.

      a. Use procedures in the evaluation which ensure that no factors other than those being studied have major influence on the results (i.e., internal validity).

      b. Use statistical procedures which are appropriate and have all assumptions met by the data being analyzed.

      c. Evaluate the generalizability (external validity) of the results for different individuals, settings, tests, and variables.

C. Scores, Norms, and Related Technical Features: The result of scoring a test or subtest is usually a number called a raw score which by itself is not interpretable. Additional steps are needed to translate the number directly into either a verbal description (e.g., pass or fail) or a derived score (e.g., a standard score). Less than full understanding of these procedures is likely to produce errors in interpretation and ultimately in counseling or other uses.

   1. Examine appropriate test materials (e.g., manuals, handbooks, users' guides, and technical reports) to identify the descriptions or derived scores produced and their unique characteristics.

      a. Know the operational procedures for translating raw scores into descriptions or derived scores.

      b. Know specific psychological or educational concepts or theories before interpreting the scores of tests based on them.

      c. Consider differential validity along with equating error when different tests, different test forms, or scores on the same test administered at different times are compared.

   2. Clarify arbitrary standards used in interpretation (e.g., mastery or nonmastery for criterion-referenced tests).

      a. Recognize that when a score is interpreted based on a proportion score (e.g., percent correct), its elements are being given arbitrary weights.

      b. Recognize that the difficulty of a fixed standard (e.g., 80 percent right) varies widely and thus does not have the same meaning for different content areas and for different assessment methods.

      c. Report the number (or percentage) of items right in addition to the interpretation when it will help others understand the quality of the examinee's performance.

3. Employ derived scores based on norms which fit the needs of the current use of the test.
   a. Evaluate whether available norm groups are appropriate as part of the process of interpreting the scores of clients.
   b. Choose a score based on its intended use.
D. Administration and Scoring Variation: Stated criteria for score interpretation assume standard procedures for administering and scoring the test. Departures from standard conditions and procedures modify and often invalidate these criteria.
   1. Evaluate unusual circumstances peculiar to the administration and scoring of the test.
      a. Examine reports from administrators, proctors, and scorers concerning irregularities or unusual conditions (e.g., excessive anxiety) for possible effects on test performance.
      b. Consider potential effects of examiner-examinee differences in ethnic and cultural background, attitudes, and values based on available relevant research.
      c. Consider any reports of examinee behavior indicating the responses were made on some basis other than that intended.
      d. Consider differences among clients in their reaction to instructions about guessing and scoring.
   2. Evaluate scoring irregularities (e.g., machine scoring errors) and bias and judgment effects when subjective elements enter into scoring.

VIII. *COMMUNICATING TEST RESULTS*: The responsible counselor or other practitioner reports test data with a concern for the individual's need for information and the purposes of the information. There must also be protection of the right of the person tested to be informed about how the results will be used and what safeguards exist to prevent misuse (right to information) and about who will have access to the results (right to privacy).
   A. Decisions About Individuals: Where test data are used to enhance decisions about an individual, the practitioner's responsibilities include:
      1. Limitations on Communication:
         a. Inform the examinee of possible actions that may be taken by any person or agency who will be using the results.
         b. Limit access to users specifically authorized by the law or by the client.
         c. Obtain the consent of the examinee before using test results for any purpose other than those advanced prior to testing.
      2. Practitioner Communication Skills:
         a. Develop the ability to interpret test results accurately before attempting to communicate them.
         b. Develop appropriate communication skills, particularly with respect to concepts that are commonly misunderstood by

the intended audience, before attempting to explain test results to clients, the public, or other recipients of the information.

3. Communication of Limitations of the Assessment:
    a. Inform persons receiving test information that scores are not perfectly accurate and indicate the degree of inaccuracy in some way, such as by reporting score intervals.
    b. Inform persons receiving test information of any circumstances that could have affected the validity or reliability of the results.
    c. Inform persons receiving test information of any factors necessary to understand potential sources of bias for a given test result.
    d. Communicate clearly that test data represent just one source of information and should rarely, if ever, be used alone for decision making.

4. Communication of Client Rights:
    a. Provide test takers or their parents or guardians with information about any rights they may have to obtain test copies and/or their completed answer sheets, to retake tests, to have test rescored, or to cancel test scores.
    b. Inform test takers or their parents or guardians about how long the test scores will remain on file along with the persons to whom, and circumstances under which, they may be released.
    c. Describe the procedures test takers or their parents or guardians may use to register complaints or have problems resolved.

APPENDIX B

Excerpts From Standards for Educational and Psychological Testing

by
**Committee to Develop Standards for
Educational and Psychological Testing**

**American Educational Research Association (AERA)
American Psychological Association (APA)
National Council on Measurement in Education (NCME)**

1985

6. GENERAL PRINCIPLES OF TEST USE

Standard

6.1 Test users should evaluate the available written documentation on the validity and reliability of tests for the specific use intended.

6.2 When a test user makes a substantial change in test format, mode of administration, instructions, language, or content, the user should revalidate the use of the test for the changed conditions or have a rationale supporting the claim that additional validation is not necessary or possible.

6.3   When a test is to be used for a purpose for which it has not been previously validated, or for which there is not supported claim for validity, the user is responsible for providing evidence of validity.

6.4   Test users should accurately portray the relevance of a test to the assessment and decision-making process and should not use a test score to justify an evaluation, recommendation, or decision that has been largely on some other basis.

6.5   Test users should be alert to probable unintended consequences of test use and should attempt to avoid actions that have unintended negative consequences.

6.6   Responsibility for test use should be assumed by or delegated only to those individuals who have the training and experience necessary to handle this responsibility in a professional and technically adequate manner. Any special qualifications for test administration or interpretation noted in the manual should be met.

6.7   Test users should verify periodically that changes in populations of test takers, objectives of the testing process, or changes in available techniques have not made their current procedures inappropriate.

6.8   When test results are released to the news media, those responsible for releasing the results should provide information to help minimize the possibility of misinterpretation of the test results.

6.9   When a specific cut score is used to select, classify, or certify test takers, the method and rationale for setting that cut score, including any technical analyses, should be presented in a manual or report. When cut scores are based primarily on professional judgment, the qualifications of the judges also should be documented.

6.10   In educational, clinical, and counseling applications, test administrators and users should not attempt to evaluate test takers whose special characteristics—ages, handicapping conditions, or linguistic, generational, or cultural backgrounds—are outside the range of their academic training or supervised experience. A test user faced with a request to evaluate a test taker whose special characteristics are not within his or her range of professional experience should seek consultation regarding test selection, necessary modifications of testing procedures, and score interpretation from a professional who has had relevant experience.

9. TEST USE IN COUNSELING

Background   Uses of tests in counseling differ from most other test uses in that the test taker is viewed as the primary user of test results. Accumulated experience and research evidence have shown that standardized tests can be a valuable part of the counseling process. If used appropriately, tests can provide useful information to clients. However, because test takers do not typically have professional testing knowledge and skill, they need assistance and guidance from counselors and developers of interpretive materials, who have a unique role in facilitating the appropriate and effective use of tests.

Counselors are concerned with a range of assessment and guidance activities related to the life-span development and decision-making activities of individuals. Typical counseling concerns include the individual's personal and social skills, educational achievement, developed abilities, educational and vocational interests, occupational knowledge and preferences, occupational values, career development, study skills, coping and problem solving skills, and plans and values for other important roles in adult life, such as relationships with others, work, and parenting. These characteristics of the individual are assessed in counseling by a variety of formal and informal procedures—paper-and-pencil inventories, tests, work samples, interviews, card sorts, checklists, and so on. All such measures that yield classifications and raw or converted scores that result in suggestions for exploration or recommendations for action are considered tests and require evidence of reliability and validity.

Standard
9.1   Testing for counseling should have its primary goals the acquisition of relevant information and the reporting of that information with appropriate interpretations so that clients from diverse backgrounds can be assisted in making important educational, personal, and career decisions.

9.2   Counselors should review the interpretive materials provided to clients to evaluate accuracy, clarity, and usefulness of the materials. Manuals for tests or computer-based interpretations should be evaluated for evidence for the validity of specific interpretations made.

9.3   Counselors should review technical data and develop a rationale for the decision to use combined or separate norms for females and males in reports to test takers.

9.4 If a publisher packages tests that are to be used in combination for counseling, the counselor should review the manual for the rationale for the specific combination of tests used and the justification of the interpretive relationships among the scores.

9.5 Counselors should examine test manuals for any available information about how suggested or implied career options (i.e., the vocational program or occupation suggested by the highest scores on the test) are distributed for samples of the typical respondents of each gender and relevant racial or ethnic groups.

9.6 Counselors should review the test materials that are provided to the test takers to be sure that such materials properly caution the test taker not to rely on the test scores solely when making life-planning decisions. The counselor should encourage the test taker to consider other relevant information on personal and social skills, values, interests, accomplishments, experiences, and on other test scores and observations.

9.7 Counselors should encourage multiple valid assessments of an individual's abilities, social skills, and interests.

9.8 Counselors should review the interpretive materials for ability or interest measures and for other tests that are used with people who are reentering employment or education or changing work settings for their appropriateness for these clients. A counselor should consider the age, experience, and background of the client as they are compared with the characteristics of the norm groups on which the scores are based.

9.9 Counselors should review interpretive materials for tests to ensure that case studies and examples are not limited to illustrations of people in traditional roles.

Publishers or Distributors of Tests Commonly Used by Counselors, With Test Names and Acronyms

American College Testing Program
P.O. Box 168
Iowa City, IA 52243
(319) 337-1000
  Vocational Interest, Experience, and Skill Assessment (VIESA)
  Career Planning Program (CCP)
  Act Assesssment (ACT) [or Act]
  Preliminary ACT Assessment (P-ACT +) [pronounced "P-act-plus"]

American Guidance Service
P.O. Box 99
Circle Pines, MN 55014-1796
1-800-328-2560
  Harrington-O'Shea Career Decision-Making System
  Kaufman Assessment Battery for Children (K-ABC)
  Peabody Picture Vocabulary Test–Revised (PPVT-R)

Consulting Psychologists Press
577 College Avenue
Palo Alto, CA 94306-1490
(415) 857-1444
  Strong Interest Inventory (Strong)
  Myers-Briggs Type Indicator (MBTI) (or the Myers-Briggs)
  California Psychological Inventory–Revised (CPI-R)
  Career Development Inventory (CDI)
  Adjective Check List (ACL)
  FIRO Scales (FIRO) [Fie-Roe]

State-Trait Anxiety Inventory (STAI)
Wrenn Study Habits Inventory
Bem Sex-Role Inventory
Coopersmith Self-Esteem Inventories
Adult Career Concerns Inventory (ACCI)
Values Scale (VS)
Salience Inventory (SI)
Vocational Exploration and Insight Kit (VEIK)
My Vocational Situation (MVS)

CTB/McGraw-Hill
2500 Garden Road, Park
Monterey, CA 93940
1-800-538-9547
California Achievement Tests
Career Maturity Inventory
Kuder General Interest Survey (KGIS)
Kuder Occupational Interest Survey (KOIS)
School and College Ability Tests (SCAT)
Sequential Tests of Educational Progress (STEP)
Test of Cognitive Skills

Educational and Industrial Testing Service (EDITS)
P.O. Box 7234
San Diego, CA 92107
(619) 222-1666
Career Occupational Preference System (COPS)
Career Ability Placement Survey (CAPS) [Caps]
Career Orientation Placement and Evaluation Survey (COPES)
Eysenck Personality Questionnaire
Profile of Mood States (POMS)
Study Attitudes and Methods Survey (SAMS)

Educational Testing Service
Princeton, NJ 08541
(609) 921-9000
College Level Examination Program (CLEP) [Klep]
Scholastic Aptitude Test (SAT)
Preliminary Scholastic Aptitude Test (PSAT) [P-sat]
Graduate Record Examination (GRE)
College and University Environment Scales (CUES) [Kyues]

Institute for Personality and Ability Testing Incorporated (IPAT)
P.O. Box 188
Champaign, IL 61824-0188
1-800-225-4728
16 Personality Factor Questionnaire (16PF)
Culture Fair Intelligence Test

London House
1150 Northwest Highway
Park Ridge, IL 60068
1-800-221-8378
  Flanagan Aptitude Classification Tests (FACT)

National Computer Systems (NCS)
P.O. Box 1416
Minneapolis, MN 55440
1-800-NCS-7271
  Alcohol Use Inventory
  Guilford-Zimmerman Temperament Survey
  Millon Adolescent Personality Inventory (MAPI)
  Millon Clinical Multiaxial Inventory-II (MCMI-II)
  Minnesota Multiphasic Personality Inventory (MMPI)
  Career Assessment Inventory
  Temperament and Values Inventory (TVI)
  Vocational Information Profile
  Word and Number Assessment Inventory (WNAI)

Psychological Assessment Resources (PAR)
P.O. Box 998
Odessa, FL 33556-9901
1-800-331-TEST
  Career Decision Scale (CDS)
  Family Environment Scale (FES)
  Comprehensive Drinking Profile (CDP)
  Marital Satisfaction Inventory (MSI)
  Self-Directed Search (SDS)
  Eating Disorder Inventory (EDI)
  Vocational Preference Inventory (VPI)
  Occupational Stress Inventory (OSI)

The Psychological Corporation (Psych Corp)
555 Academic Court
San Antonio, TX 78204
1-800-228-0752
  Weschler Preschool and Primary Scale of Intelligence (WPPSI)
    [Whip-See]
  Weschler Intelligence Scale for Children–Revised (WISC-R) [Wisk-R]
  Weschler Adult Intelligence Scale–Revised (WAIS-R) [Ways-R]
  Differential Aptitude Tests (DAT)
  Ohio Vocational Interest Survey (OVIS)
  Rotter Incomplete Sentences Blank
  Beck Depression Inventory (BDI) [Beck]
  Survey of Study Habits and Attitudes (SSHA)
  Edwards Personal Preference Schedule (EPPS)
  Raven's Progressive Matrices and Vocabulary Scales

Rorschach Psychodiagnostic Plates (Rorschach)
Thematic Apperception Test (TAT)
Stanford Achievement Test
Metropolitan Achievement Test
Otis-Lennon School Ability Test (OLSAT)
Minnesota Clerical Test
Mooney Problem Checklists

Research Psychologists Press
1110 Military Street
P.O. Box 984
Port Huron, MI 48060-0984
1-800-265-1285
   Jackson Vocational Interest Survey (JVIS)
   Personality Research Form (PRF)
   Jackson Personality Inventory (JPI)
   Psychological Screening Inventory (PSI)
   Multidimensional Aptitude Battery (MAB)

Riverside Publishing Company
8420 Bryn Mawr Avenue
Chicago, IL 60631
1-800-323-9540
   Iowa Tests of Basic Skills (ITBS)
   Iowa Tests of Educational Development (ITED) or [I-Ted]
   Stanford-Binet Intelligence Scale (Stanford-Binet)
   Henmon-Nelson Test of Mental Ability (Henmon-Nelson Test)
   Cognitive Abilities Test (COGAT) [Co-gat]
   Work Values Inventory
   Allport-Vernon-Lindzey Study of Values (AVL)

Scholastic Testing Service Incorporated
480 Meyer Road
P.O. Box 1056
Bensenville, IL 60106
(312) 766-7150
   Torrance Test of Creative Thinking
   Kuhlman-Anderson Tests

U.S. Military Entrance Processing Command (USMEPCOM)
2500 Green Bay Road
North Chicago, IL 60064-3094
1-800-323-0513
   Armed Services Vocational Aptitude Battery (ASVAB) [As-Vab]

Western Psychological Services
12031 Wilshire Blvd.
Los Angeles, CA 90025
1-800-222-2670
  The Vocational Interest Inventory
  Assessment of Career Decision Making (ACDM)
  Wonderlic Personnel Test [Wonderlic]
  Tennessee Self-Concept Scale (TSCS)
  Taylor-Johnson Temperament Analysis

U.S. Department of Labor
Division of Testing
Employment and Testing Administration
200 Constitution Ave., N.W.
Washington, D.C. 20213
(202) 535-0157
  General Aptitude Test Battery (GATB) [Gat-bee]
  USES Interest Inventory
  USES Interest Check List

References

Adler, T. (1990, April). Does the "new" MMPI beat the "classic"? *APA Monitor*, pp. 18–19.

Alpert, R., & Haber, R. N. (1960). Anxiety in academic achievement situations. *Journal of Abnormal and Social Psychology, 61*, 207–215.

Allport, G. W. (1937). *Personality: A psychological interpretation*. New York: Holt.

Allport, G. W., Vernon, P. E., & Lindzey, G. (1960). *Manual for study of values* (3rd ed.). Boston: Houghton Mifflin.

American Association for Counseling and Development & Association for Measurement and Evaluation in Counseling and Development. (1989, May). The responsibilities of test users. *AACD Guidepost*, pp. 12–28.

American Association for Counseling and Development. (1988). *Ethical standards*. Alexandria, VA: Author.

American College Testing Program. (1983). *ACT Career Planning Program counselor's manual*. Iowa City, IA: Author.

American College Testing Program. (1988a). *Interim psychometric handbook for the 3rd edition ACT Career Planning Program*. Iowa City, IA: Author.

American College Testing Program. (1988b). *User's handbook for vocational interest, experience and skills assessment (levels 1 & 2)* (2nd ed.). Iowa City, IA: Author.

American College Testing Program. (1989a). *The enhanced ACT assessment*. Iowa City, IA: Author.

American College Testing Program. (1989b). *P-ACT plus program, technical manual*. Iowa City, IA: Author.

American Educational Research Association, American Psychological Association, & National Council on Measurement in Education. (1985). *Standards for educational and psychological testing*. Washington, DC: American Psychological Association.

American Psychiatric Association. (1987). *Diagnostic and statistical manual of mental disorders, third edition, revised*. Washington, DC: Author.

American Psychological Association. (1986). *Guidelines for computer-based tests and interpretations*. Washington, D.C.: Author.

American Psychological Association. (1990). *Ethical principles of psychologists*. Washington, DC: *American Psychologist, 45*, 390–395.

Anastasi, A. (1988). *Psychological testing* (6th ed.). New York: Macmillan.

Association of American Medical Colleges. (1977). *Medical College Admissions Test (MCAT) interpretive manual*. Washington, DC: Author.

Athelstan, G. T. (1966). *An exploratory investigation of response patterns associated with low profiles on the Strong Vocational Interest Blank for men*. Unpublished doctoral dissertation, University of Minnesota, Minneapolis.

Baker, R. W., & Siryk, B. (1984). Measuring adjustment to college. *Journal of Counseling Psychology, 31,* 179–189.

Barker, R. G. (1968). *Ecological psychology: Concepts and methods for studying the environment of human behavior.* Stanford, CA: Stanford University Press.

Barrios, B. A. (1988). On the changing nature of behavioral assessment. In A. S. Bellack & M. Hersen (Eds.), *Behavioral assessment: A practical handbook* (pp. 3–41). New York: Pergamon.

Barrons Educational Series. (1990). *Profiles of American colleges* (17th ed.). Hauppauge, NY: Author.

Bartling, H. C., & Hood, A. B. (1981). An 11-year follow-up of measured interest and vocational choice. *Journal of Counseling Psychology, 28,* 27–35.

Bauernfeind, R. H. (1987, February). CSCGI reports: Career Decision-Making System (CDM). *Association for Measurement and Evaluation in Counseling and Development Newsnotes,* pp. 2–3.

Bauernfeind, R. H. (1988, Fall). CSCGI reports: Armed Services Vocational Aptitude Battery (ASVAB). *Association for Measurement and Evaluation in Counseling and Development Newsnotes,* pp. 13–15.

Baxter-Magolda, M. B., & Porterfield, W. (1988). *Assessing intellectual development: A link between theory and practice.* Alexandria, VA: American College Personnel Association.

Beck, A. T., Kovacs, M., & Weissman, A. (1979). Assessment of suicidal intention: The Scale for Suicide Ideation. *Journal of Consulting and Clinical Psychology, 47,* 343–352.

Benbow, C. P. (1988). Sex differences in mathematical reasoning ability in intellectually talented preadolescents: Their nature, effects and probable causes. *Behavioral and Brain Sciences, 11,* 169–232.

Bennett, G. K., Seashore, H. G., & Wesman, A. G. (1977). *Counseling from profiles: Casebook for the DAT* (2nd ed.). San Antonio, TX: Psychological Corporation.

Bennett, G. K., Seashore, H. G., & Wesman, A. G. (1981). *Differential Aptitude Tests (Forms V and W).* San Antonio, TX: Psychological Corporation.

Benson, P. G. (1988). Review of the Minnesota Importance Questionnaire (MIQ). In J. T. Kapes & M. M. Mastie (Eds.), *A counselor's guide to career assessment instruments* (2nd ed.) (pp. 144–149). Alexandria, VA: National Career Development Association.

Ben-Porath, Y. S., & Butcher, J. N. (1989). The comparability of MMPI and MMPI-2 scales and profiles. *Psychological Assessment, 1,* 345–347.

Berven, N. L. (1980). Psychometric assessment in rehabilitation. In B. Bolton and D. W. Cook (Eds.), *Rehabilitation client assessment* (pp. 46–64). Baltimore, MD: University Park Press.

Blocher, D. H. (1989). *Career actualization and life planning.* Denver, CO: Love.

Block, J. (1961). *The Q-Sort method in personality assessment and psychiatric research.* Palo Alto, CA: Consulting Psychologists Press.

Bogatz, G. A., & Greb, A. (1980). *School and College Ability Tests (SCAT Series III) manual and technical report.* Monterey, CA: CTB/McGraw Hill.

Bolles, R. N. (1979). *The Quick Job-Hunting Map: A fast way to help* (Advanced version). Berkeley, CA: Ten Speed Press.

Bolles, R. N. (1989). *What color is your parachute? A practical manual for job-hunters and career-changers.* Berkeley, CA: Ten Speed Press.

Bolton, B. (1980). Second-order dimensions of the Work Values Inventory (WVI). *Journal of Vocational Behavior, 17,* 33–40.

Borgen, F. H. (1985). Predicting career choices of able college men from occupational and basic interest scales of the Strong Vocational Interest Blank. *Journal of Counseling Psychology, 19,* 202–211.

Borgen, F. H. (1988). Review of Strong-Campbell Interest Inventory. In J. T. Kapes & M. M. Mastie (Eds.), *A counselor's guide to career assessment instruments* (2nd ed.) (pp. 121–126). Washington, DC: National Career Development Association.

Borgen, F. H., Weiss, D. J., Tinsley, H. E. A., Dawis, R. V., & Lofquist, L. H. (1968). *Occupational Reinforcer Patterns: I (Minnesota Studies in Vocational Rehabilitation: XXIV)*. Minneapolis, MN: University of Minnesota, Industrial Relations Center.

Brandt, J. E., & Hood, A. B. (1968). Effect of personality adjustment on the predictive validity of the Strong Vocational Interest Blank. *Journal of Counseling Psychology, 15*, 547–551.

Brescio, W., & Fortune, J. C. (1989). Standardized testing of American Indian students. *The College Student Journal, 23*, 98–104.

Brickman, P., Rabinowitz, V. C., Karuza, J., Coates, D., Cohn, E., & Kidder, L. (1982). Models of helping and coping. *American Psychologist, 37*, 368–384.

Brown, W. F., & Holtzman, W. H. (1984). *Survey of Study Habits and Attitudes manual*. San Antonio, TX: Psychological Corporation.

Buck, J. N., & Daniels, M. H. (1985). *Assessment of Career Decision Making manual*. Los Angeles: Western Psychological Services.

Burns, D. D., & Beck, A. T. (1978). Modifications of mood disorders. In J. P. Foreyt & D. P. Rathjen (Eds.), *Cognitive behavior therapy* (pp. 109–134). New York: Plenum.

Butcher, J. N. (1989a). *User's guide for the Minnesota Report: Adult Clinical System*. Minneapolis: National Computer System.

Butcher, J. N. (1989b). *User's guide for the Minnesota Report: Personnel Selection System*. Minneapolis: National Computer System.

Butcher, J. N. (1990, August). Education level and MMPI-2 measured psychopathology: A case of negligible influence. *News and Profiles: A Newsletter of the MMPI-2 Workshops and Symposia*, p. 3.

Butcher, J. N., Dahlstrom, W. G., Graham, J. R., Tellegen, A., & Kaemmer, B. (1989). *Minnesota Multiphasic Personality Inventory-2: Manual for administration and scoring*. Minneapolis: University of Minnesota Press.

Butcher, J. N., Graham, J. R., Williams, C. L., & Ben-Porath, Y. (1989). *Development and use of the MMPI-2 content scales*. Minneapolis: University of Minnesota Press.

Campbell, D. P. (1972). *Handbook for the Strong Vocational Interest Blank*. Stanford, CA: Stanford University Press.

Campbell, D. P. (1977). *Manual for the Strong-Campbell Interest Inventory* (2nd ed.). Stanford, CA: Stanford University Press.

Campbell, D. P., & Hansen, J. C. (1981). *Manual for the SVIB-SCII* (3rd ed.). Stanford, CA: Stanford University Press.

Carney, C. G., & Wells, C. F. (1987). *Career planning: Skills to build your future* (2nd ed.). Monterey, CA: Brooks/Cole.

Cass, J., & Birnbaum, M. (1989). *The comparative guide to American colleges: For students, parents, and counselors* (14th ed.). New York: Harper & Row.

Cattell, R. B. (1973). *Measuring intelligence with the Culture Fair Test*. Champaign, IL: Institute of Personality and Ability Testing.

Cattell, R. B., Eber, H. W., & Tatsuoka, M. M. (1970). *Handbook for the 16 Personality Factor Questionnaire*. Champaign, IL: Institute for Personality and Ability Testing.

Cesnik, B. I., & Nixon, S. K. (1977). Counseling suicidal persons. In C. Zastrow & D. H. Chang (Eds.), *Personal problem solver* (pp. 275–289). Englewood Cliffs, NJ: Prentice-Hall.

Chickering, A. W. (1969). *Education and identity*. San Francisco: Jossey-Bass.

Christie, K. A., Burke, J. D., Regier, D. A., Rae, D. S., Boyd, J. H., & Locke, B. Z. (1988). Epidemiologic evidence for early onset of mental disorders and higher risk of drug abuse in young adults. *Americal Journal of Psychiatry, 145,* 971–975.

Clark, K. E. (1961). *The vocational interests of nonprofessional men.* Minneapolis: University of Minnesota Press.

Cleary, T. A., Humphreys, L. G., Kendrick, S. A., & Wesman A. (1975). Educational uses of tests with disadvantaged students. *American Psychologist, 30,* 15–41.

Cochran, L. (1983). Implicit versus explicit importance of career values in making a career decision. *Journal of Counseling Psychology, 30,* 188–193.

Code of Fair Testing Practices in Education. (1988). Washington, DC: Joint Committee on Testing Practices. (Mailing address: Joint Committee on Testing Practices, American Psychological Association, 1200 17th Street, N.W., Washington, DC 20036)

College Entrance Examination Board. (1978). *Implementing the Career Skills Assessment Program: A handbook for effective program use.* New York: Author.

College Entrance Examination Board. (1988). *Working with the PSAT/NMSQT: Preparation, administration, interpretation.* New York: Author.

College Entrance Examination Board. (1989). *The college handbook.* New York: Author.

Conoley, J. C., & Kramer, J. J. (Eds.). (1989). *Tenth Mental Measurements Yearbook.* Lincoln, NE: Buros Institute of Mental Measurements.

Coopersmith, S. (1981). *Self Esteem Inventories (SEI).* Palo Alto, CA: Consulting Psychologists Press.

Coopersmith, S., & Gilberts, R. (1982). *Professional manual: Behavioral Academic Self-Esteem (BASE), A rating scale.* Palo Alto, CA: Consulting Psychologists Press.

Corcoran, K., & Fischer, J. (1987). *Measures for clinical practice: A sourcebook.* New York: Free Press.

Crites, J. O. (1978). *Career Maturity Inventory: Theory and research handbook* (2nd ed.). Monterey, CA: CTB/McGraw-Hill.

Crites, J. O. (1984). Instruments for assessing career development. In N. C. Gysbers (Ed.), *Designing careers* (pp. 248–274). San Francisco, CA: Jossey-Bass.

Cronbach, L. J. (1979). The Armed Services Vocational Aptitude Battery—A test battery in transition. *Personnel and Guidance Journal, 57,* 232–237.

Cronbach, L. J. (1984). *Essentials of psychological testing* (4th ed.). New York: Harper & Row.

Cronbach, L. J., & Gleser, G. C. (1965). *Psychological tests and personnel decisions* (2nd ed.). Urbana: University of Illinois Press.

CTB/McGraw-Hill. (1981). *Test of Cognitive Skills test coordinator's handbook and guide to interpretation.* Monterey, CA: CTB/McGraw Hill.

Cyr, J. J., McKenna-Foley, J. M., & Peacock, E. (1985). Factor structure of the SCL-90-R: Is there one? *Journal of Personality Assessment, 49,* 571–577.

Dahlstrom, W. G., Welch, G. S., & Dahlstrom, L. (1972–1975). *An MMPI handbook (Vols. 1 & 2).* Minneapolis: University of Minnesota Press.

Dance, K. A., & Neufeld, R. W. (1988). Aptitude-treatment interaction research in the clinical setting: A review of attempts to dispel the "patient uniformity" myth. *Psychological Bulletin, 104,* 192–213.

Dawis, R. V., & Lofquist, L. H. (1984). *A psychological theory of work adjustment: An individual-differences model and its applications.* Minneapolis, MN: University of Minnesota Press.

Dawis, R. V., Lofquist, L. H., Henly, G. A., & Rounds, J. B., Jr. (1979). *Minnesota*

Occupational Classification System II. Minneapolis: University of Minnesota, Department of Psychology.

Derogatis, L. R. (1979). *Sexual Functioning Inventory manual.* Towson, MD: Clinical Psychometric Research.

Derogatis, L. R. (1983). *Administration, scoring, and procedures manual-II for the SCL-90-R.* Towson, MD: Clinical Psychometric Research.

Derogatis, L. R., Lipman, R. S., & Covi, L. (1973). An outpatient psychiatric rating scale: Preliminary report. *Psychopharmacology Bulletin, 9*(1), 13–27.

Derogatis, L. R., Lipman, R. S., Rickels, K., Uhlenhuth, E. H., & Covi, L. (1974). The Hopkins Symptom Checklist (HSCL): A self-report symptom inventory. *Behavioral Science, 19,* 1–15.

Derogatis, L. R., & Melisaratos, N. (1983). The Brief Symptom Inventory: An introductory report. *Psychological Medicine, 13,* 595–605.

Diamond, R. J. (1989). *Psychiatric presentations of medical illness: An introduction for non-medical mental health professionals.* Unpublished manuscript, University of Wisconsin-Madison, Department of Psychiatry, Madison, WI.

Division of Educational Measurements, Council on Dental Education. (1984). *Dental Admission Testing Program (DATP) overview.* Chicago, IL: American Dental Association.

Dolliver, R. H. (1982). Review of card sorts. In J. T. Kapes & M. M. Mastie (Eds.), *A counselor's guide to vocational guidance instruments* (pp. 147–160). Falls Church, VA: National Vocational Guidance Association.

Dolliver, R. H., Irvin, J. A., & Bigley, S. S. (1972). Twelve-year follow-up of the Strong Vocational Interest Blank. *Journal of Counseling Psychology, 19,* 212–217.

Dolliver, R. H., & Will, J. A. (1977). Ten-year follow-up of the Tyler Vocational Card Sort and the Strong Vocational Interest Blank. *Journal of Counseling Psychology, 24,* 48–54.

Dolliver, R. H., & Worthington, E. L., Jr. (1981). Concurrent validity of other-sex and same-sex twin Strong-Campbell Interest Inventory Occupational scales. *Journal of Counseling Psychology, 28,* 126–134.

Donlon, E. F. (Ed.). (1984). *The college board technical handbook for the Scholastic Aptitude Test and Achievement Test.* New York: College Entrance Examination Board.

Dorn, F. J. (1988). Utilizing social influence in career counseling: A case study. *Career Development Quarterly, 36,* 269–280.

Drasgow, J., & Carkhuff, R. R. (1964). Kuder neuropsychiatric keys before and after psychotherapy. *Journal of Counseling Psychology, 11,* 67–69.

Droege, R. C., & Hawk, J. (1977). Development of a U.S. Employment Service Interest Inventory. *Journal of Employment Counseling, 14,* 65–71.

Drumond, P. J. (1988). *Appraisal procedures for counselors and helping professionals.* Columbus, OH: Merrill.

Duckworth, J. (1990). The counseling approach to the use of testing. *The Counseling Psychologist, 18,* 198–204.

Duckworth, J. C., & Anderson, W. P. (1986). *MMPI interpretation manual for counselors and clinicians* (3rd ed.). Muncie, IN: Accelerated Development.

D'Zurilla, T. J., & Goldfried, M. R. (1971). Problem solving and behavior modification. *Journal of Abnormal Psychology, 78,* 107–126.

Educational Testing Service. (1983). *Guide to the use of Graduate Management Admission Test scores.* Princeton, NJ: Author.

Educational Testing Service. (1987). *Guide to the use of the Graduate Record Examination program.* Princeton, NJ: Author.

Edwards, A. L. (1959). *Edwards Personal Preference Schedule manual.* San Antonio, TX: Psychological Corporation.

Elizur, D., & Tziner, A. (1977). Vocational needs, job rewards, and satisfaction: A canonical analysis. *Journal of Vocational Behavior, 10,* 205–211.

Ellis, A. (1988). *How to stubbornly refuse to make yourself miserable about anything—yes, anything!* Secaucus, NJ: Lyle Stuart.

Engen, H. B., Lamb, R. R., & Prediger, D. J. (1982). Are secondary schools still using standardized tests? *Personnel and Guidance Journal, 60,* 287–290.

Epperson, D. L., Bushway, D. J., & Warman, R. E. (1983). Client self-terminations after one counseling session: Effects of problem recognition, counselor gender, and counselor experience. *Journal of Counseling Psychology, 30,* 307–315.

Epperson, D. L., & Hammond, D. C. (1981). Use of interest inventories with Native Americans: A case for local norms. *Journal of Counseling Psychology, 28,* 213–220.

Erikson, E. H. (1968). *Identity, youth and crisis.* New York: Norton.

Erwin, T. D. (1983). The Scale of Intellectual Development: Measuring Perry's scheme. *Journal of College Student Personnel, 24,* 6–12.

Ewing, J. A. (1984). Detecting alcoholism: The CAGE Questionnaire. *Journal of American Medical Association, 252,* 1905–1907.

Eyde, L. D., Moreland, K. L., Robertson, G. J., Primoff, E. S., & Most, R. B. (1988). *Executive Summary. Test user qualifications: A data-based approach to promoting good test use. Issues in Scientific Psychology.* Report of the Test User Qualifications Working Group of the Joint Committee on Testing Practices. Washington, DC: American Psychological Association.

Eysenck, H. J., & Eysenck, S. B. G. (1975). *Manual: Eysenck Personality Questionnaire (junior & adult).* San Diego, CA: Educational and Industrial Testing Service.

Feldt, L. S., Forsyth, R. A., & Alnot, S. D. (1989). *Teacher, administrator, and counselor manual, Iowa Tests of Educational Development.* Chicago, IL: Riverside.

Figler, H. E. (1979). *PATH: A career workbook for liberal arts students* (2nd ed.). Cranston, RI: Carroll Press.

Frary, R. B. (1988). Review of Career Maturity Inventory. In J. T. Kapes & M. M. Mastie (Eds.), *A counselor's guide to career assessment instruments* (2nd ed.) (pp. 180–185). Alexandria, VA: National Career Development Association.

French, J. W. (1962). Effective anxiety on verbal and mathematical examination scores. *Educational and Psychological Measurement, 22,* 553–564.

Gardner, E. F., Madden, R., Rudman, H. C., Kaulsen, B., Merwin, J. C., Callis, R., & Collins, C. S. (1985). *Stanford Achievement Tests (7th ed.): Guide for organizational planning.* San Antonio, TX: Psychological Corporation.

Garner, D. M., Olmstead, M. P., & Polivy, J. (1983). Development and validation of a multidimensional eating disorder inventory for anorexia nervosa and bulimia. *International Journal of Eating Disorders, 2*(2), 15–34.

Garner, D. M., & Garfinkel, P. E. (1979). The Eating Attitudes Test: An index of the symptoms of anorexia nervosa. *Psychological Medicine, 9,* 273–279.

Garner, D. M., & Garfinkel, P. E. (1985). *Handbook of psychotherapy for anorexia nervosa and bulimia.* New York: Brunner-Mazel.

Gelatt, H. B. (1989). Positive uncertainty: A new decision-making framework for counseling. *Journal of Counseling Psychology, 36,* 252–256.

Gellerman, S. W. (1963). Personnel testing: What the critics overlook. *Personnel, 40,* 18–26.

Goldenson, R. M. (Ed.). (1984). *Longman dictionary of psychology and psychiatry.* New York: Longman.

Goldfried, M. R., Stricker, G., & Weiner, I. R. (1971). *Rorschach handbook of clinical and research applications.* Englewood Cliffs, NJ: Prentice-Hall.

Goldman, L. (1971). *Using tests in counseling* (2nd ed.). New York: Appleton-Century-Crofts.

Goldman, L. (1972). Tests and counseling: The marriage that failed. *Measurement and Evaluation in Guidance, 4,* 197–205.

Goldman, L. (1990). Qualitative assessment. *The Counseling Psychologist, 18,* 205–213.

Goldman, R. D., Kaplan, R. M., & Platt, B. B. (1973). Sex differences in the relationship of attitudes toward technology to choice of field of study. *Journal of Counseling Psychology, 20,* 412–418.

Gottfredson, G. D., & Holland, J. L. (1989). *Dictionary of Holland Occupational Codes* (2nd ed.). Odessa, FL: Psychological Assessment Resources.

Gough, H. G. (1987). *California Psychological Inventory administrator's guide.* Palo Alto, CA: Consulting Psychologists Press.

Graham, J. R. (1990). *MMPI-2: Assessing personality and psychotherapy.* New York: Oxford University Press.

Graham, J. R., & Strenger, V. E. (1988). MMPI characteristics of alcoholics: A review. *Journal of Consulting & Clinical Psychology, 56,* 197–205.

Greene, R. L. (1987). Ethnicity and MMPI performance: A review. *Journal of Consulting and Clinical Psychology, 35,* 497–512.

Greene, R. L. (1989). *The MMPI: An interpretive manual* (2nd ed.). New York: Grune & Stratton.

Greist, J. H., Jefferson, J. W., & Spitzer, R. L. (Eds.). (1982). *Treatment of mental disorders.* New York: Oxford University Press.

Gross, M. L. (1962). *The brain watchers.* New York: New American Library.

Groth-Marnat, G. (1984). *Handbook of psychological assessment.* New York: Van Nostrand Reinhold.

Guilford, J. P. (1959). *Personality.* New York: McGraw-Hill.

Guilford, J. S., Guilford, J. P., & Zimmerman, W. S. (1976). *Interpretation system for the Guilford-Zimmerman Temperament Survey.* Orange, CA: Sheridan Psychological Services.

Guilford, J. S., Guilford, J. P., & Zimmerman, W. S. (1978). *The Guilford-Zimmerman Temperament Survey: Directions for administering, scoring, and interpreting.* Orange, CA: Sheridan Psychological Services.

Hammen, C. L. (1980). Depression in college students: Beyond the Beck Depression Inventory. *Journal of Consulting and Clinical Psychology, 45,* 126–128.

Haney, W. (1981). Validity, vaudeville, and values: A short history of social concerns over standardized testing. *American Psychologist, 36,* 1021–1034.

Hansen, J. C., & Campbell, D. P. (1985). *Manual for the SVIB-SCII* (4th ed.). Stanford, CA: Stanford University Press.

Hanson, G. R., Noeth, R. J., & Prediger, D. J. (1977). Validity of diverse procedures for reporting interest scores: An analysis of longitudinal data. *Journal of Counseling Psychology, 24,* 487–493.

Hanson, G. R., Prediger, D. S., & Schussel, R. H. (1977). *Development and validation of sex-balanced interest inventory scales.* ACT Research Report #78. Iowa City, IA: American College Testing Program.

Harmon, L. W. (1985). Review of Career Decision Scale. In J. V. Mitchell, Jr. (Ed.), *The ninth mental measurements yearbook* (p. 270). Lincoln, NE: Buros Institute of Mental Measurements.

Harmon, L. W. (1988). Review of Values Scale. In J. T. Kapes & M. M. Mastie (Eds.), *A counselor's guide to career assessment instruments* (2nd ed.) (pp. 155–158). Alexandria, VA: National Career Development Association.

Harren, V. A. (1979). A model of career decision making for college students. *Journal of Vocational Behavior, 14,* 119–133.

Harrington, T. F., & O'Shea, A. J. (Eds.). (1984). *Guide for occupational exploration* (2nd ed.). Circle Pines, MN: American Guidance Service.

Harrington, T. F., & O'Shea, A. J. (1988). *Career Decision-Making System*. Circle Pines, MN: American Guidance Service.

Harris, R., & Lingoes, J. (1968). *Subscales for the Minnesota Multiphasic Personality Inventory*. Mimeographed materials, The Langley Porter Clinic, 401 Parnassus Ave., San Francisco, CA 94143.

Hay, R. G. (1988). Screening counseling center clients for drinking problems. *Journal of College Student Development, 29,* 79–81.

Hayden, D., & Furlong, M. (1988). *DSM-III-R tutorial*. Santa Barbara, CA: Psychoeducational Software Systems.

Healy, C. C. (1990). Reforming career appraisals to meet the needs of clients in the 1990s. *The Counseling Psychologist, 18,* 214–226.

Hendel, D. D., & Weiss, D. J. (1970). Individual inconsistency and reliability of measurement. *Educational and Psychological Measurement, 30,* 579–593.

Heppner, P. P., & Krauskopf, C. J. (1987). An information-processing approach to personal problem solving. *The Counseling Psychologist, 15,* 371–447.

Herman, D. O. (1985). Review of Career Decision Scale. In J. V. Mitchell, Jr. (Ed.), *The ninth mental measurements yearbook* (pp. 270–271). Lincoln, NE: Buros Institute of Mental Measurements.

Herr, E. L., & Niles, S. G. (1988). Review of Adult Career Concerns Inventory. In J. T. Kapes & M. M. Mastie (Eds.), *A counselor's guide to career assessment instruments* (2nd ed.) (pp. 160–164). Alexandria, VA: National Career Development Association.

Hersh, J. B., Nazario, N. S., & Backus, B. A. (1983). DSM-III and the college mental health setting: the University of Massachusetts experience. *Journal of American College Health, 31,* 247–252.

Hieronymus, A. N., & Hoover, H. D. (1986). *Iowa Tests of Basic Skills, Manual for school administrators*. Chicago, IL: Riverside.

Hoffman, J. A., & Weiss, B. (1986). A new system for conceptualizing college students' problems: Types of crises and the Inventory of Common Problems. *Journal of American College Health, 34,* 259–266.

Holland, J. L. (1985a). *Making vocational choices: A theory of vocational personalities and work environments* (2nd ed.). Englewood Cliffs, NJ: Prentice-Hall.

Holland, J. L. (1985b). *Professional manual for the Self-Directed Search*. Odessa, FL: Psychological Assessment Resources.

Holland, J. L. (1987). *Manual supplement for the Self-Directed Search*. Odessa, FL: Psychological Assessment Resources.

Holland, J. L., Birk, J. M., Cooper, J. F., Dewey, C. R., Dolliver, R. H., Takai, R., & Tyler, L. E. (1980). *Counselor's guide to the Vocational Exploration and Insight Kit (VEIK)*. Palo Alto, CA: Consulting Psychologists Press.

Holland, J. L., Daiger, D. C., & Power, P. G. (1980). *My Vocational Situation*. Palo Alto, CA: Consulting Psychologists Press.

Holmberg, K., Rosen, D., & Holland, J. L. (1990). *The leisure activities finder*. Odessa, FL: Psychological Assessment Resources.

Hood, A. B. (1968). *What type of college for what type of student?* Minneapolis: University of Minnesota Press.

Hood, A. B. (1986). *The Iowa Student Development Inventories*. Iowa City, IA: Hitech Press.

Horan, J. J. (1979). *Counseling for effective decision-making: A cognitive-behavioral perspective*. North Scituate, MA: Duxbury Press.

Horn, J. L., Wanberg, K. W., & Foster, F. M. (1986). *Alcohol Use Inventory*. Minneapolis, MN: National Computer System.

Hoyt, D. P. (1960). Measurement and prediction of the permanence of interests.

In W. L. Layton (Ed.), *The Strong Vocational Interest Blank: Research and uses* (pp. 93–103). Minneapolis: University of Minnesota Press.

Jackson, D. N. (1976). *Jackson Personality Inventory Manual*. Port Huron, MI: Research Psychologists Press.

Jackson, D. N. (1984a). *Multidimensional Aptitude Battery Manual*. Port Huron, MI: Research Psychologists Press.

Jackson, D. N. (1984b). *Personality Research Form Manual*. Port Huron, MI: Research Psychologists Press.

Jensen, A. R. (1988). Review of the Armed Services Vocational Aptitude Battery (ASVAB). In J. T. Kapes & M. M. Mastie (Eds.), *A counselor's guide to career assessment instruments* (2nd ed.) (pp. 58–62). Alexandria, VA: National Career Development Association.

Jepsen, D. A. (1988). Review of Kuder General Interest Survey-Form DD. In J. T. Kapes and M. M. Mastie (Eds.), *A counselor's guide to career assessment instruments* (2nd ed.) (pp. 105–109). Alexandria, VA: National Career Development Association.

Johansson, C. B. (1986). *Manual for career assessment inventory: The enhanced version*. Minneapolis: National Computer Systems.

Johansson, C. B., & Campbell, D. P. (1971). Stability of the Strong Vocational Interest Blank for Men. *Journal of Applied Psychology, 55,* 34–36.

Johnson, R. W. (1977). Relationships between female and male interest scales for the same occupations. *Journal of Vocational Behavior, 11,* 239–252.

Johnson, R. W. (1987). Review of Assessment of Career Decision Making. *Journal of Counseling and Development, 65,* 567–569.

Johnson, R. W., Ellison, R. A., & Heikkinen, C. A. (1989). Psychological symptoms of counseling center clients. *Journal of Counseling Psychology, 36,* 110–114.

Johnson, R. W., Heikkinen, C. A., & Ellison, R. A. (1988). [Frequency of symptoms indicating depression among counseling service clients]. Unpublished raw data.

Johnson, R. W., & Johansson, C. B. (1972). Moderating effect of basic interests on predictive validity of SVIB Occupational scales. *Proceedings of the 80th Annual Convention of the American Psychological Association, 7,* 589–590.

Jordan, R. P., & Jepsen, D. A. (1988). Sources of information about tests and testing. In J. T. Kapes & M. M. Mastie (Eds.), *A counselor's guide to career assessment instruments* (pp. 313–324). Alexandria, VA: National Career Development Association.

Kane, S. T. (1989). A review of the COPS Interest Inventory. *Journal of Counseling and Development, 67,* 361–363.

Kapes, J. T., Borman, C. A., & Frazier, N. (1989). An evaluation of the SIGI and DISCOVER microcomputer-based career guidance systems. *Measurement and Evaluation in Counseling and Development, 22,* 126–136.

Kapes, J. T., & Mastie, M. M. (Eds.). (1988). *A counselor's guide to career assessment instruments* (2nd ed.). Alexandria, VA: National Career Development Association.

Katkin, E. S. (1978). Review of State-Trait Anxiety Inventory. In O. K. Buros (Ed.), *The eighth mental measurements yearbook* (pp. 683–684). Highland Park, NJ: Gryphon Press.

Keesling, J. W., & Healy, C. C. (1988). Review of the USES General Aptitude Test Battery (GATB). In J. T. Kapes & M. M. Mastie (Eds.), *A counselor's guide to career assessment instruments* (2nd ed.) (pp. 69–74). Alexandria, VA: National Career Development Association.

Kenrick, D. T., & Funder, D. C. (1988). Profiting from controversy: Lessons from the person-situation debate. *American Psychologist, 43*, 23–34.

Keyser, D. J., & Sweetland, R. C. (Eds.). (1984–1990). *Test critiques: Volumes I–VIII.* Kansas City, MO: Test Corporation of America.

Kiersey, D., & Bates, M. (1978). *Please understand me.* Del Mar, CA: Prometheus Nemesis Books.

Kinnier, R. T., & Krumboltz, J. D. (1984). Procedures for successful career counseling. In N. C. Gysbers (Ed.), *Designing careers* (pp. 307–335). San Francisco: Jossey-Bass.

Kiresuk, T. J., & Sherman, R. (1968). Goal attainment scaling: A general method for evaluating comprehensive mental health programs. *Community Mental Health Journal, 4*, 443–453.

Kitano, H. H. L., & Matsushima, N. (1981). Counseling Asian-Americans. In P. P. Pedersen, J. G. Draguns, W. J. Lonner, & J. E. Trimble (Eds.), *Counseling across cultures* (pp. 163–180). Honolulu: University Press of Hawaii.

Kitchener, K. S., & King, C. M. (1981). Reflective judgment: Concepts of justification and their relationship to age and education. *Journal of Applied Developmental Psychology, 2*, 89–116.

Knapp, R. R., & Knapp, L. (1986). *Career Occupational Preference System (COP-System) examiner's guide.* San Diego, CA: Educational and Industrial Testing Service.

Kohlberg, L. (1969). Stage and sequence: The cognitive developmental approach to socialization. In D. Goslin (Ed.), *Handbook of socialization theory and research* (pp. 347–480). Chicago: Rand McNally.

Kohlberg, L. (1971). Stages of moral development. In C. M. Beck, V. S. Crittenden, & E. B. Sullivan (Eds.), *Moral education.* Toronto: University of Toronto Press.

Kroeger, O., & Thuesen, S. M. (1988). *Type talk.* New York: Delacorte.

Kuder, F., & Diamond, E. E. (1979). *Occupational Interest Survey, general·manual.* Chicago: Science Research Associates.

Kuder, G. F. (1988). *General manual for Kuder General Interest Survey, Form E.* Chicago: Science Research Associates.

Lachar, D., & Wrobel, T. A. (1979). Validating clinicians' hunches: Construction of a new MMPI critical item set. *Journal of Consulting and Clinical Psychology, 47*, 277–284.

Laing, J., & Farmer, M. (1984). *Use of the ACT assessment by examinees with disabilities. Research Report #84.* Iowa City, IA: American College Testing Program.

Lamb, R. R. (1974). *Concurrent validity of the American College Testing Interest Inventory for minority group members.* Unpublished doctoral dissertation, University of Iowa.

Lambe, T. A., Nelson, M. J., & French, J. L. (1973). *Manual for the Henman-Nelson Test of Mental Ability.* Chicago: Riverside.

Lampe, R. E. (1985). Self-scoring accuracy of the Kuder General Interest Survey. *The School Counselor, 32*, 319–324.

Lanyon, R. I. (1978). *Manual for Psychological Screening Inventory.* Port Huron, MI: Research Psychologists Press.

Law Schools Admissions Services. (1988). *Law School Admission Test general information booklet.* Washington, DC: Law School Admission Council.

Lawrence, G. D. (1982). *People types and tiger stripes.* Gainesville, FL: Center for Applications of Psychological Type.

Layton, W. L. (1985). Review of the Strong-Campbell Interest Inventory. In J.

V. Mitchell, Jr. (Ed.), *The ninth mental measurements yearbook* (pp. 1480–1481). Lincoln, NE: Buros Institute of Mental Measurements.

LeBold, W. K., & Shell, K. D. (1986). *Purdue Interest Questionnaire: A brief interpretive guide for the revision.* West Lafayette, IN: Purdue University, Department of Freshman Engineering.

Levine, P. R., & Wallen, R. (1954). Adolescent vocational interests and later occupation. *Journal of Applied Psychology, 38,* 428–431.

Lewin, K. (1935). *A dynamic theory of personality: Selected papers.* New York: McGraw-Hill.

Lipsett, L., & Wilson, J. W. (1954). Do suitable interests and mental ability lead to job satisfaction? *Educational and Psychological Measurement, 14,* 373–380.

Locke, D. C. (1988). Review of the Career Development Inventory. In J. T. Kapes & M. M. Mastie (Eds.), *A counselor's guide to career assessment instruments* (2nd ed.) (pp. 175–179). Alexandria, VA: National Career Development Association.

Lofquist, L. H., & Dawis, R. B. (1969). *Adjustment to work: A psychological view of man's problems in a work-oriented society.* New York: Appleton-Century-Crofts.

Lonner, W. J., & Sundberg, N. D. (1987). Assessment in cross-cultural counseling and therapy. In P. Pederson, *Handbook of cross-cultural counseling and therapy* (pp. 199–205). New York: Praeger.

Lubin, B., Larsen, R. M., & Matarazzo, J. D. (1984). Patterns of psychological test usage in the United States: 1935–1982. *American Psychologist, 39,* 451–454.

Lustman, P. J., Sowa, C. J., & O'Hara, D. J. (1984). Factors influencing college student health: Development of the Psychological Distress Inventory. *Journal of Counseling Psychology, 31,* 28–35.

Maloney, M. P., & Ward, M. P. (1976). *Psychological assessment: A conceptual approach.* New York: Oxford University Press.

Marks, I. M., & Mathews, A. M. (1978). Brief standard self-rating for phobic patients. *Behavior Research and Therapy, 17,* 263–267.

Marlatt, G. A., & Miller, W. R. (1984). *Comprehensive Drinking Profile.* Odessa, FL: Psychological Assessment Resources.

McAllister, L. W. (1988). *A practical guide to CPI interpretation* (2nd ed.). Palo Alto, CA: Consulting Psychologists Press.

McArthur, C. (1954). Long-term validity of the Strong Interest Test in two subcultures. *Journal of Applied Psychology, 38,* 346–354.

McArthur, C., & Stevens, L. B. (1955). The validation of expressed interests as compared with inventoried interests: A fourteen year follow-up. *Journal of Applied Psychology, 39,* 184–189.

McCrae, R. R., & Costa, P. T. (1986). Clinical assessment can benefit from recent advances in personality psychology. *American Psychologist, 41,* 1001–1003.

McGoldrick, M., & Gerson, R. (1985). *Genograms in family assessment.* New York: Norton.

McKinney, M. W. (1984). *Final report: Validity generalization study.* Raleigh, NC: Employment Security Commission of North Carolina, Southern Test Development Field Center.

McRae, G. G. (1959). *The relationships of job satisfaction and earlier measured interests.* Unpublished doctoral dissertation, University of Florida.

Megargee, E. (1972). *The California Psychological Inventory handbook.* Palo Alto, CA: Consulting Psychologists Press.

Mehrens, W. A. (1988). Review of Vocational Interest, Experience, and Skill

Assessment (VIESA). In J. T. Kapes, & M. M. Mastie (Eds.), *A counselor's guide to career assessment instruments* (pp. 132–136). Alexandria, VA: National Career Development Association.

Mendelsohn, G. A., & Kirk, B. A. (1962). Personality differences not used. *Journal of Counseling Psychology, 9*, 341–346.

Messick, S. (1980). Test validity and the ethics of assessment. *American Psychologist, 35*, 1012–1027.

Messick, S. (1981). The controversy over coaching: Issues of effectiveness and equity. In B. F. Green (Ed.), *Issues in testing: Coaching, disclosure, and ethnic bias* (pp. 21–53). San Francisco: Jossey-Bass.

Miles, C. P. (1977). Conditions predisposing to suicide: A review. *Journal of Nervous and Mental Disease, 164*, 231–246.

Miller, W. R. (1976). Alcoholism scales and objective assessment methods: A review. *Psychological Bulletin, 83*, 649–674.

Miller, W. R., & Munoz, R. F. (1982). *How to control your drinking: A practical guide to responsible drinking* (rev. ed.). Albuquerque, NM: University of New Mexico Press.

Millon, T. (1969). *Modern psychopathology*. Philadelphia: Saunders.

Millon, T. (1981). *Disorders of personality: DSM-III, Axis II*. New York: Wiley.

Millon, T. (1987). *Manual for the MCMI-II* (2nd ed.). Minneapolis: National Computer Systems.

Mintz, L. B., & Betz, N. E. (1988). Prevalence and correlates of eating disordered behaviors among undergraduate women. *Journal of Counseling Psychology, 35*, 463–471.

Mitchell, J. V., Jr. (Ed.). (1985). *The ninth mental measurements yearbook*. Lincoln, NE: Buros Institute of Mental Measurements.

Mitchell, L. K., & Krumboltz, J. D. (1987). The effects of cognitive restructuring and decision-making training on career indecision. *Journal of Counseling and Development, 66*, 171–174.

Mooney, R. L., & Gordon, L. V. (1950). *The Mooney Problem Checklists*. New York: Psychological Corporation.

Moore, W. S. (1988). *The Measure of Intellectual Development: An instrument manual*. Farmville, VA: Center for the Study of Intellectual Development.

Moos, R. H. (1974). *The social climate scales: An overview*. Palo Alto, CA: Consulting Psychologists Press.

Moos, R. H. (1976a). *Family Environment Scale manual*. Palo Alto, CA: Consulting Psychologists Press.

Moos, R. H. (1976b). *The human context: Environmental determinants of behavior*. New York: Wiley.

Moreland, K. L. (1985). Validation of computer-based test interpretations: Problems and prospects. *Journal of Consulting and Clinical Psychology, 53*, 816–825.

Murray, H. A. (1938). *Explorations in personality*. New York: Oxford University Press.

Murray, H. A. (1943). *Thematic Apperception Test manual*. Cambridge, MA: Harvard University Press.

Myers, I. B. (1980a). *Introduction to type*. Palo Alto, CA: Consulting Psychologists Press.

Myers, I. B., & Myers, P. B. (1980b). *Gifts differing*. Palo Alto, CA: Consulting Psychologists Press.

Myers, I. B., & McCaulley, M. H. (1985). *Manual: A guide to the development and use of the Myers-Briggs Type Indicator*. Palo Alto, CA: Consulting Psychologists Press.

Myers, R. A., Thompson, A. S., Lindeman, R. H., Super, D. E., Patrick, T. A., & Friel, T. W. (1972). *The Educational and Career Exploration System: A two-year field trial*. New York: Teachers College, Columbia University.

National Computer System. (1984). *Vocational Interest Profile sample report*. Minneapolis, MN: Author.

Neimeyer, G. J. (1989). Applications of repertory grid technique to vocational assessment. *Journal of Counseling and Development, 67*, 585–589.

Nevill, D. D., & Super, D. E. (1986a). *Manual for the Salience Inventory*. Palo Alto, CA: Consulting Psychologists Press.

Nevill, D. D., & Super, D. E. (1986b). *Manual for the Values Scale*. Palo Alto, CA: Consulting Psychologists Press.

Nguyen, T. D., Attkisson, C. C., & Stegner, B. L. (1983). Assessment of patient satisfaction: Development and refinement of a service evaluation questionnaire. *Evaluation and Program Planning, 6*, 299–314.

Norris, L., & Cochran, D. J. (1977). The SIGI prediction system: Predicting college grades with and without tests. *Measurement and Evaluation in Guidance, 10*, 134–140.

Osgood, C. E., Suci, G. J., & Tannenbaum, P. H. (1957). *The measurement of meaning*. Urbana, IL: University of Illinois Press.

Osipow, S. H., Carney, C. G., & Barak, A. (1976). A scale of educational-vocational undecidedness: A typological approach. *Journal of Vocational Behavior, 9*, 233–243.

Othmer, E., & Othmer, S. C. (1989). *The clinical interview: Using DSM-III-R*. Washington, DC: American Psychiatric Press.

Otis, A. S., & Lennon, R. T. (1982). *Manual for the Otis-Lennon School Ability Test*. San Antonio, TX: Psychological Corportation.

Otis, A. S., & Lennon, R. T. (1989). *Otis-Lennon School Ability Test, sixth edition, preliminary technical manual*. San Antonio, TX: Psychological Corporation.

Owens, W. A. (1983). Background data. In M. D. Dunnette (Ed.), *Handbook of industrial and organizational psychology* (pp. 609–644). New York: Wiley.

Pace, C. R. (1969). *College and university environment scales (CUES)*. Princeton, NJ: Educational Testing Service.

Pace, C. R., & Stern, G. G. (1958). An approach to the measurement of psychological characteristics of college environments. *Journal of Educational Psychology, 49*, 269–277.

Paritzky, R. S., & Magoon, T. M. (1982). Goal attainment scaling models for assessing group counseling. *Personnel and Guidance Journal, 60*, 381–384.

Parker, J., & Hood, A. B. (1986). The Parker Cognitive Development Inventory. In A. B. Hood, (Ed.), *The Iowa Student Development Inventories* (pp. 1–26). Iowa City, IA: Hitech Press.

Parks, C. W., Jr., & Hollon, S. D. (1988). Cognitive assessment. In A. S. Bellack & M. Hersen (Eds.), *Behavioral assessment: A practical handbook* (pp. 161–212). New York: Pergamon.

Patel, N. S. (1974). Attempted and completed suicide. *Medical Science Law, 14*, 273–279.

Patterson, W. M., Dohn, H. H., Bird, J., & Patterson, G. A. (1983). Evaluation of suicidal patients: The SAD PERSONS Scale. *Psychosomatics, 24*, 343–349.

Pekarik, G. (1988). Relation of counselor identification of client problem description to continuance in a behavioral weight loss program. *Journal of Counseling Psychology, 35*, 66–70.

Pennock-Roman, M. (1988). Review of the Differential Aptitude Tests. In J. T. Kapes & M. M. Mastie (Eds.), *A counselor's guide to career assessment instruments* (2nd ed.) (pp. 63–68). Alexandria, VA: National Career Development Association.

Perry, W. (1970). *Forms of intellectual and ethical development in college years: A scheme*. New York: Holt, Rinehart & Winston.

Peterson, C., & Austin, J. T. (1985). Review of Coopersmith Self-Esteem Inventories. In J. V. Mitchell, Jr. (Ed.), *The ninth mental measurements yearbook* (pp. 396–397). Lincoln, NE: Buros Institute of Mental Measurements.

Physicians' Desk Reference. (1989). Oradell, NJ: Medical Economics Co.

Piaget, J. (1965). *The moral judgment of the child.* New York: Free Press.

Piers, E. B. (1984). *Piers-Harris Children's Self-Concept Scale, Revised manual.* Los Angeles, CA: Western Psychological Services.

Plake, B. S., & Parker, C. S. (1982). The development and validation of a revised version of the Mathematics Anxiety Rating Scale. *Educational and Psychological Measurement, 42,* 551–557.

Ponterotto, J. G., Pace, T. M., & Kavan, M. G. (1989). A counselor's guide to the assessment of depression. *Journal of Counseling and Development, 67,* 301–309.

Porteus, M. A. (1985). *Porteus Problem Checklist.* Windsor, England: NFER-Nelson Publishing.

Prediger, D. (Ed.). (1972). Symposium: Tests and counseling—The marriage that failed? *Measurement and Evaluation in Guidance, 5,* 395–429.

Prediger, D. J. (1987). *Career counseling validity of the ASVAB Job Cluster scales used in DISCOVER.* (ACT Research Report Series No. 87–2). Iowa City, IA: American College Testing Program.

Prediger, D. J. (1988). Review of Assessment of Career Decision Making. In J. T. Kapes & M. M. Mastie (Eds.), *A counselor's guide to career assessment instruments* (2nd ed.) (pp. 165–169). Alexandria, VA: National Career Development Association.

Prediger, D. J., & Johnson, R. W. (1979). *Alternatives to sex-restrictive vocational interest assessment.* (ACT Research Report No. 79). Iowa City, IA: American College Testing Program.

Prescott, G. A., Balow, I. H., Hogan, T. P., & Farr, R. C. (1987). *Metropolitan Achievement Tests, sixth edition: Administrator's guide.* San Antonio, TX: Psychological Corporation.

Provost, J. A., & Anchors, S. (1987). *Applications of the Myers-Briggs Type Indicator in higher education.* Palo Alto, CA: Consulting Psychologists Press.

Psychological Corporation. (1987a). *Miller Analogies Test manual.* San Antonio, TX: Psychological Corporation.

Psychological Corporation. (1987b). *1987 catalog of tests, products, and services for education.* San Antonio, TX: Author.

Psychological Corporation. (1990). *1990 catalog of tests, products, and services for education.* San Antonio, TX: Author.

Pyle, K. R. (1984). Career counseling and computers: Where is the creativity? *Journal of Counseling and Development, 63,* 141–144.

Raven, J. C., Court, J. H., & Raven, J. (1978). *Manual for Raven's Progressive Matrices and Vocabulary Scales.* San Antonio, TX: Psychological Corporation.

Rayman, J. R. (1976). Sex and the Single Interest Inventory: The empirical validation of sex-balanced interest inventory items. *Journal of Counseling Psychology, 23,* 239–246.

Regier, D. A., Boyd, J. H., Burke, J. D., Rae, D. S., Myers, J. K., Kramer, M., Robins, L. N., George, L. K., Karno, M., & Locke, B. Z. (1988). One-month prevalence of mental disorders in the United States. *Archives of General Psychiatry, 45,* 977–986.

Rest, J. (1979). *Development in judging moral issues.* Minneapolis: University of Minnesota Press.

Rest, J. R. (1974). *Manual for the Defining Issues Test.* (Available from J. R. Rest, 330 Burton Hall, University of Minnesota, Minneapolis, MN 55455).

Robins, L. N., Helzer, J. E., Weissman, M. M., Orvaschel, H., Gruenberg, E.,

Burke, J. D., & Regier, D. A. (1984). Lifetime prevalence of specific psychiatric disorders in three sites. *Archives of General Psychiatry, 41*, 949–958.

Roid, G. H., & Fitts, W. H. (1988). *Tennessee Self-Concept Scale, Revised manual.* Los Angeles, CA: Western Psychological Services.

Roselle, B. E., & Hummel, T. J. (1988). Intellectual development and interaction effectiveness with DISCOVER. *Career Development Quarterly, 36*, 241–250.

Rosen, D., Holmberg, K., & Holland, J. L. (1987). *The college majors finder.* Odessa, FL: Psychological Assessment Resources.

Rosen, J. C., Silberg, N. T., & Gross, J. (1988). Eating Attitudes Test and Eating Disorders Inventory: Norms for adolescent girls and boys. *Journal of Consulting & Clinical Psychology, 56*, 305–308.

Rosen, S. D., Weiss, D. J., Hendel, D. D., Dawis, R. V., & Lofquist, L. H. (1972). *Occupational Reinforcer Patterns: II (Minnesota Studies in Vocational Rehabilitation: XXIX).* Minneapolis: University of Minnesota, Industrial Relations Center.

Rosenthal, R. (1990). How are we doing in soft psychology? *American Psychologist, 45*, 775–776.

Rosnow, R. L., & Rosenthal, R. (1988). Focused tests of significance and effect size estimation in counseling psychology. *Journal of Counseling Psychology, 35*, 203–208.

Rotter, J. B., & Rafferty, J. E. (1950). *Manual for the Rotter Incomplete Sentence Blank, College Form.* San Antonio, TX: Psychological Corporation.

Rounds, J. B., Jr., Henly, G. A., Dawis, R. V., Lofquist, L. H., & Weiss, D. J. (1981). *Manual for the Minnesota Importance Questionnaire: A measure of vocational needs and values.* Minneapolis: University of Minnesota, Department of Psychology.

Sabourin, S., Laferriere, N., Sicuro, F., Coallier, J., Cournoyer, L., & Gendreau, P. (1989). Social desirability, psychological distress, and consumer satisfaction with mental health treatment. *Journal of Counseling Psychology, 36*, 352–356.

Sampson, J. P. (1990). Computer-assisted testing and the goals of counseling psychology. *The Counseling Psychologist, 18*, 227–239.

Samuda, R. J. (1975). Compendium of tests for minority adolescents and adults. In R. J. Samuda (Ed.), *Psychological testing of American minorities* (pp. 177–204). New York: Dodd, Mead.

Sanford, N. (1962). Developmental status of the entering freshman. In N. Sanford (Ed.), *The American college* (pp. 253–282). New York: Wiley.

Sarason, I. G. (Ed.). (1980). *Test anxiety: Theory, research, and applications.* Hillsdale, NJ: Erlbaum.

Sarason, I. G., Johnson, J. H., & Siegel, J. M. (1978). Assessing the impact of life changes: Development of the Life Experiences Survey. *Journal of Consulting and Clinical Psychology, 46*, 932–946.

Savickas, M. L., Brizzi, J. S., Brisbin, L. A., & Pethtel, L. L. (1988). Predictive validity of two medical specialty preference inventories. *Measurement and Evaluation in Counseling and Development, 21*, 106–112.

Schinka, J. A. (1984). *Personal Problems Checklist-Adult.* Odessa, FL: Psychological Assessment Resources.

Schinka, J. A. (1985). *Personal Problems Checklist-Adolescent.* Odessa, FL: Psychological Assessment Resources.

Scholastic Testing Service. (1982). *Technical report, Kuhlmann-Anderson tests.* Bensenville, IL: Scholastic Testing Service.

Seligman, L. (1990). *Selecting effective treatments: A comprehensive, systematic guide to treating adult mental disorders.* San Francisco: Jossey-Bass.

Sell, J. M., & Torres-Henry, R. (1979). Testing practices in university and college counseling centers in the United States. *Professional Psychology, 10,* 774–779.

Selzer, M. L. (1971). The Michigan Alcoholism Screening Test: The quest for a new diagnostic instrument. *American Journal of Psychiatry, 127,* 1653–1658.

Sewell, T. E. (1985). Review of Coopersmith Self-Esteem Inventories. In J. V. Mitchell, Jr. (Ed.), *The ninth mental measurements yearbook* (pp. 397–398). Lincoln, NE: Buros Institute of Mental Measurements.

Shrauger, J. S., & Osberg, R. M. (1981). The relative accuracy of self-predictions and judgments by others in psychological assessment. *Psychological Bulletin, 90,* 322–351.

Simon, S. B., Howe, L. W., & Kirschenbaum, H. (1978). *Values clarification: A handbook of practical strategies for teachers and students.* New York: Dodd, Mead.

Slaney, R. B. (1988). Review of the Career Decision Scale. In J. T. Kapes & M. M. Mastie (Eds.), *A counselor's guide to career assessment instruments* (2nd ed.) (pp. 170–174). Alexandria, VA: National Career Development Association.

Smith, D. L. (1976). Goal attainment scaling as an adjunct to counseling. *Journal of Counseling Psychology, 23,* 22–27.

Snyder, D. K. (1981). *Marriage Satisfaction Inventory manual.* Los Angeles, CA: Western Psychological Services.

Sobell, M. B., Maisto, S. A., Sobell, L. C., Cooper, A. M., Cooper, T. C., & Sanders, B. (1980). Developing a prototype for evaluating alcohol treatment effectiveness. In L. C. Sobell, M. B. Sobell, & E. Ward (Eds.), *Evaluating alcohol and drug abuse treatment effectiveness: Recent advances* (pp. 129–150). New York: Pergamon.

Spielberger, C. D., Gorsuch, R. L., Lushene, R., Vagg, P. R., & Jacobs, G. A. (1983). *Manual for State-Trait Anxiety Inventory.* Palo Alto, CA: Consulting Psychologists Press.

Stern, G. G. (1962). *Stern Activities Index.* Syracuse, NY: Evaluation Research Associates.

Strong, E. K., Jr. (1955). *Vocational interests 18 years after college.* Minneapolis: University of Minnesota Press.

Stuart, R. B., & Stuart, F. (1975). *Premarital Counseling Inventory manual.* Ann Arbor, MI: Compuscore.

Sturgis, E. T., & Gramling, S. (1988). Psychophysiological assessment. In A. S. Bellack & M. Hersen (Eds.), *Behavioral assessment: A practical handbook* (pp. 213–251). New York: Pergamon.

Sue, S., & Sue, D. W. (1974). MMPI comparisons between Asian-American and non-Asian students utilizing a student health psychiatric clinic. *Journal of Counseling Psychology, 21,* 423–427.

Super, D. E. (1957). *The psychology of careers: An introduction to vocational development.* New York: Harper.

Super, D. E. (1970). *Manual for the Work Values Inventory.* Boston: Houghton Mifflin.

Super, D. E. (1980). A life-span, life-space approach to career development. *Journal of Vocational Behavior, 16,* 282–298.

Super, D. E. (1981). *Counselor's manual for DAT Career Planning Program.* New York: Psychological Corporation.

Super, D. E. (1984). Career and life development. In D. Brown & L. Brooks (Eds.), *Career choice and development* (pp. 192–234). San Francisco: Jossey-Bass.

Super, D. E., & Thompson, A. S. (1979). A six-scale, two-factor measure of adolescent career or vocational maturity. *Vocational Guidance Quarterly, 28,* 6–15.

Super, D. E., Thompson, A. S., & Lindeman, R. H. (1988). *Adult Career Concerns Inventory: Manual for research and exploratory use in counseling.* Palo Alto, CA: Consulting Psychologists Press.

Sweetland, R. C., & Keyser, D. J. (Eds.). (1990). *Tests: A comprehensive reference for assessments in psychology, education, and business* (3rd ed.). Kansas City, MO: Test Corporation of America.

Taylor, R. M., Morrison, W. L., & Nash, L. (1985). *Taylor-Johnson Temperament Analysis handbook.* Los Angeles, CA: Western Psychological Services.

Technical Education Research Centers, Incorporated. (1977). *Guidance, counseling, and support services for high school students with physical disabilities.* Cambridge, MA: Author.

Tennen, H., Affleck, G., & Herzberger, S. (1985). SCL-90-R. In D. J. Keyser & R. C. Sweetland (Eds.), *Test critiques* (vol. III) (pp. 583–594). Kansas City, MO: Test Corporation of America.

Thompson, A. S., Lindeman, R. H., Super, D. E., Jordaan, J. P., & Myers, R. A. (1981). *Career Development Inventory (vol. I: User's manual).* Palo Alto, CA: Consulting Psychologists Press.

Thompson, A. S., Lindeman, R. H., Super, D. E., Jordaan, J. P., & Myers, R. A. (1982). *Career Development Inventory: College and University Form. Supplement to user's manual.* Palo Alto, CA: Consulting Psychologists Press.

Thorndike, R. L., & Hagen, E. P. (1978). *The Cognitive Abilities Test.* Chicago: Riverside.

Thorndike, R. L., Hagen, E. P., & Sattler, J. M. (1986a). *The Stanford-Binet Intelligence Scale: Fourth edition, Guide for administering and scoring.* Chicago: Riverside.

Thorndike, R. L., Hagen, E. P., & Sattler, J. M. (1986b). *The Stanford-Binet Intelligence Scale: Fourth edition, Technical manual.* Chicago: Riverside.

Trimble, J. T. (1966). A ten-year longitudinal follow-up of inventoried interests of selected high school students (Doctoral dissertation, University of Missouri, 1965). *Dissertation Abstracts International, 24,* 5252–5253.

Tyler, L. E. (1961). Research explorations in the realm of choice. *Journal of Counseling Psychology, 8,* 195–210.

U. S. Department of Labor. (1977). *Dictionary of occupational titles* (4th ed.). Washington, DC: U.S. Government Printing Office.

U. S. Department of Labor. (1979). *USES Interest Check List.* Washington, DC: U.S. Government Printing Office.

U. S. Department of Labor. (1981). *USES Interest Inventory.* Washington, DC: U.S. Government Printing Office.

U. S. Department of Labor. (1982). *Manual for General Aptitude Test Battery, Section I: Administration and scoring, Forms A and B.* Washington, DC: U.S. Government Printing Office.

U. S. Military Entrance Processing Command. (1985). *ASVAB technical supplement to the counselor's manual.* North Chicago, IL: Author.

Vilas, R. C. (1988). *Counseling outcome as related to MBTI client type, counselor type and counselor-client type similarity.* Unpublished doctoral dissertation, The University of Iowa, Iowa City.

Vocational Studies Center. (1989). *Career skills workbook.* Madison, WI: University of Wisconsin, Vocational Studies Center.

Vuchinich, R. E., Tucker, J. A., & Harllee, L. N. (1988). Behavioral assessment. In D. M. Dononvan & G. A. Marlatt (Eds.), *Assessment of addictive behaviors* (pp. 51–83). New York: Guilford.

Wagner, E. E. (1987). A review of the 1985 Standards for Educational and Psychological Testing: User responsibility and social justice. *Journal of Counseling and Development, 66,* 202–203.

Waldinger, R. J. (1986). *Fundamentals of psychiatry.* Washington: American Psychiatric Press.

Walsh, W. B., & Betz, N. E. (1990). *Tests and assessment* (2nd ed.). Englewood Cliffs, NJ: Prentice-Hall.

Watkins, C. E., Jr., Campbell, V. L., & McGregor, P. (1988). Counseling psychologists' uses of and opinions about psychological tests: A contemporary perspective. *Counseling Psychologist, 16,* 476–486.

Wechsler, D. (1974). *Manual for the Wechsler Intelligence Scale for Children–Revised Manual.* San Antonio, TX: Psychological Corporation.

Wechsler, D. (1981). *WAIS-R Manual Wechsler Adult Intelligence Scale–Revised.* San Antonio, TX: Psychological Corporation.

Wechsler, D. (1989). *Manual: Wechsler Preschool and Primary Scale of Intelligence.* San Antonio, TX: Psychological Corporation.

Weiss, D. J. (1978). Review of the Armed Services Vocational Aptitude Battery. In J. V. Mitchell, Jr., (Ed.), *The eighth mental measurements yearbook* (pp. 645–650). Lincoln, NE: Buros Institute of Mental Measurements.

Werts, C. E., & Watley, D. J. (1969). A student's dilemma: Big fish—little pond or little fish—big pond. *Journal of Counseling Psychology, 16,* 14–19.

Westbrook, B. W. (1985). Review of the Strong-Campbell Interest Inventory. In J. V. Mitchell, Jr., (Ed.), *The ninth mental measurements yearbook* (pp. 1481–1483). Lincoln, NE: Buros Institute of Mental Measurements.

Wetzel, R. D. (1976). Hopelessness, depression, and suicide intent. *Archives of General Psychiatry, 33,* 1069–1073.

White, R. W. (1966). *Lives in progress* (2nd ed.). New York: Holt, Rinehart & Winston.

Wiggins, J. D. (1985). Review of Career Skills Assessment Program. In J. V. Mitchell, Jr., (Ed.), *The ninth mental measurements yearbook* (pp. 202–203). Lincoln, NE: Buros Institute of Mental Measurements.

Williams, C. L. (1989). Use of the MMPI-2 with adolescents. In J. N. Butcher & J. R. Graham (Eds.), *Topics in MMPI-2 interpretation* (pp. 58–62). Minneapolis: University of Minnesota, Department of Psychology.

Williams, R. L. (1972). *Black Intelligence Test of Cultural Homogeneity (BITCH) manual.* St. Louis, MO: Robert L. Williams & Associates.

Winston, R. B., & Miller, T. K. (1987). *Student developmental task and lifestyle inventory.* Athens, GA: Student Development Associates.

Wisconsin Clearinghouse. (1987). *Alcohol and Other Drugs: A Self Test.* Madison, WI: Author.

Wise, S. L., & Plake, B. S. (1990). Computer-based testing in higher education. *Measurement and Evaluation in Counseling and Development, 23,* 3–10.

Wonderlic, E. F. (1983). *Wonderlic Personnel Test manual.* Northfield, IL: E. F. Wonderlic Personnel Test Incorporated.

Wrenn, C. G. (1941). *Wrenn Study Habits Inventory manual.* Palo Alto, CA: Consulting Psychologists Press.

Ziemelis, A. (1988). *Report of University of Wisconsin-La Crosse Alcohol and Drug Issues Survey.* La Crosse, WI: Counseling and Testing Center, University of Wisconsin.

Zimny, G. H., & Senturia, A. G. (1976). *Medical Specialty Preference Inventory.* St. Louis, MO: St. Louis University Medical Center, Department of Psychiatry.

Zytowski, D. G. (1972). A concurrent test of accuracy-of-classification for the

Strong Vocational Interest Blank and the Kuder Occupational Interest Survey. *Journal of Vocational Behavior, 2,* 245–250.

Zytowski, D. G. (1974). Predictive validity of the Kuder Preference Record, Form B, over a 25-year span. *Measurement and Evaluation in Guidance, 7,* 122–129.

Zytowski, D. G. (1976a). Predictive validity of the Kuder Occupational Interest Survey: A 12- to 19-year follow-up. *Journal of Counseling Psychology, 23,* 221–233.

Zytowski, D. G. (1976b). Long-term profile stability of the Kuder Occupational Interest Survey. *Educational and Psychological Measurement, 36,* 689–692.

Zytowski, D. G. (1977). The effects of being interest-inventoried. *Journal of Vocational Behavior, 11,* 153–157.

Zytowski, D. G. (1978). Review of Career Maturity Inventory. In O. K. Buros (Ed.), *The eighth mental measurements yearbook* (pp. 1565–1567). Highland Park, NJ: Gryphon Press.

Zytowski, D. G. (1985). *Kuder DD Occupational Interest Survey, manual supplement.* Chicago: Science Research Associates.

Zytowski, D. G. (1988). Review of the Salience Inventory. In J. T. Kapes & M. M. Mastie (Eds.), *A counselor's guide to career assessment instruments* (2nd ed.) (pp. 150–154). Alexandria, VA: National Career Development Association.

Zytowski, D. G., & Laing, J. (1978). Validity of other-gender-normed scales on the Kuder Occupational Interest Survey. *Journal of Counseling Psychology, 25,* 205–209.

Zytowski, D., & Warman, R. E. (1982). The changing use of tests in counseling. *Measurement and Evaluation in Guidance, 15,* 147–152.

Index